Schools for Thought

Schools for Thought

A Science of Learning in the Classroom

John T. Bruer

A Bradford Book

The MIT Press
Cambridge, Massachusetts
London, England

Set in Bembo by DEKR Corporation.

Printed and bound in the United States of America.

Library of Congress Cataloging-in-Publication Data

Bruer, John T., 1949–
Schools for thought : a science of learning in the classroom /
John T. Bruer.
    p. cm.
"A Bradford book."
Includes bibliographical references and index.
ISBN 0-262-02352-0
1. Learning, Psychology of. 2. Cognitive science. 3. Cognition in children. 4. Teaching. 5. Education—United States—Aims and objectives. I. Title.
LB1060.B78   1993
370.15'23—dc20   92-29484
                                                   CIP

To my parents, John and Eileen, who taught me to value education.

Contents

Acknowledgements

One of the perquisites of being a program officer in foundations that fund research is that it offers opportunities for continuing adult education. I started learning about cognitive science in 1981 when I was at the Josiah Macy, Jr. Foundation. Shortly after joining Macy, I met Jill Larkin of Carnegie Mellon University at a conference on medical education organized by the University of North Carolina at Chapel Hill. At that meeting, Dr. Larkin spoke about the implications of cognitive research for medical education. Her talk eventually led to a Macy Foundation program on cognitive science and medical education. In 1986, when I became president of the James S. McDonnell Foundation, with the help of Larkin and Robert Glaser, co-director of the Learning Research and Development Center at the University of Pittsburgh, I established a program, Cognitive Studies for Educational Practice, that supports collaborations between researchers and teachers to bring cognitive science into the classroom.

It takes a long time to move from basic cognitive research to classroom applications. I would like to acknowledge the vital role of all the federal agencies and foundations in addition to my own which over the last two decades helped fund the research described here. The National Science Foundation is a major source of support for research on mathematics and science education. For a number of years, the National Institute of Education helped attract cognitive scientists to educational problems, an effort that made a science of learning possible. A much smaller research effort continues under the Office of Educational Research and Improvement. The National Institute of Mental Health and the National Institute of Child Health and Human Development both support research on cognitive development that contributes to our understanding of how children learn.

Among private foundations, the Sloan Foundation helped establish cognitive science as a research field. Because of the military's substantial interest in training, the Office of Naval Research, the Army Research Institute, and other Department of Defense agencies have played an important role in developing cognitive research on learning and instruction. The Spencer, MacArthur, and Mellon Foundations, the Carnegie Corporation, and the Exxon Education Fund are active in the support of educational research.

Many people helped me learn about cognitive science and helped me write this book. Bob Siegler read an early draft of chapter 2. John Bransford, Robbie Case, Ken Koedinger, and Janet Schofield commented on chapter 4. On science education, early drafts benefited from review by Earl Hunt, Jill Larkin, Jim Minstrell, Fred Reif, and Barbara White. Isabel Beck, George A. Miller, Annemarie Palincsar, and Kathryn Ransom provided extensive comments on chapter 6. Conversations and critiques from Carl Bereiter, Linda Flower, Glynda Hull, Mike Rose, and Marlene Scardamalia contributed to the chapter on writing. Lee Shulman read an earlier draft of chapter 8. Henry and Liz Romney offered helpful suggestions on chapters 1–5. Bill Hirst reviewed drafts of several chapters and responded (succinctly) to numerous telephone inquiries. Susan Chipman read the penultimate draft of the entire manuscript and provided invaluable advice as a constant e-mail teacher and coach. Howard Gardner also read and commented on that draft.

A special thanks to Harry and Betty Stanton and their colleagues at The MIT Press for their help and support.

My wife, Lili, persuaded me to start this project, encouraged me throughout the process, and patiently tolerated, for two years, the stress and inconveniences that writing a book brings to family life. I couldn't have a more sensitive critic and loving companion. I can't thank her enough.

Schools for Thought

1

Applying What We Know in Our Schools: A New Theory of Learning

If we want to improve America's schools, we will have to apply in the classroom what we know about humans as intelligent, learning, thinking creatures. The publication of *A Nation at Risk* in 1983 focused attention on the state of American public education. As a nation, the report said, we were committing "an act of unthinking, unilateral educational disarmament" (National Commission on Excellence in Education 1983, p. 5). That report made education a political issue to such an extent that candidates vied to be "education governors" or "the education president." The business community became an advocate of educational reform.

In the ensuing decade there has been a steady stream of reports, recommendations, articles, and books on the deficiencies of American education. The reports tell us that to improve schools we must change curricular content, raise school standards, embrace site-based management, increase school and teacher accountability, lengthen the school year, and allow parents to choose which school their child attends. These suggestions are surely part of the reform agenda, but they do not go deep enough. None of these reform themes addresses the fundamental need to change how teachers teach and how children learn in the classroom. To improve teaching and learning in our schools, we will have to apply what we have learned from three decades of research on how the human mind works.

In 1956, a group of psychologists, linguists, and computer scientists met at the Massachusetts Institute of Technology for a symposium on information science (Gardner 1985). This three-day meeting was the beginning of the cognitive revolution in psychology. In essence, the revolutionaries claimed that human minds and computers are sufficiently similar that a single theory—the theory of computation—could guide research in both psychology and computer science. "The basic point of view inhabiting our work," wrote two of the participants, "has been that the programmed computer and human problem solver are both species belonging to the genus IPS" (Newell and Simon 1972, p. 870). Both are species of the genus *information-processing system;* both are devices that process symbols.

That scientific revolution became a movement, and eventually a discipline, called cognitive science. Cognitive scientists study how our minds work—how we think, remember, and learn. Their studies have profound implications for restructuring schools and improving learning environments. Cognitive science—the science of mind—can give us an applied science of learning and instruction. Teaching methods based on this research—methods that result in some sixth-graders' having a better understanding of Newtonian physics than most high school students, or that help remedial students raise their reading comprehension scores four grade levels after 20 days of instruction—are the educational equivalents of polio vaccine and penicillin. Yet few outside the educational research community are aware of these breakthroughs or understand the research that makes them possible.

Certainly cognitive science, or even educational research in general, isn't the sole answer to all our educational problems. Yet it has to be part of any attempt to improve educational practice and to restructure our schools. The science of mind can guide educational practice in much the same way that biology guides medical practice. There is more to medicine than biology, but basic medical science drives progress and helps doctors make decisions that promote their patients' physical well-being. Similarly, there is more to education than cognition, but cognitive science can drive progress and help teachers make decisions that promote their students' educational well-being.

What Most Students Can Do Is No Longer Enough

A Nation at Risk vividly describes the serious mismatch between what most students can do and what society now expects. Scores on standardized tests, poor showings in international comparisons, and ongoing national assessments provide "indicators of the risk," as the report says. We know in some detail what students in our schools can and cannot do.

Among the most useful indicators of student accomplishment are the results of the US Department of Education's National Assessment of Educational Progress (NAEP). Every four years, NAEP tests the performance of a representative sample of school children in mathematics, science, reading, and writing. The statistical methods used to construct the samples allow reliable statistical generalizations from the sample to the entire population of American students. There have been math, science, and reading assessments since 1969–70. In these subject areas, the NAEP assesses the performance of 9-, 13-, and 17-year-olds. Assessment of the writing performance of fourth-, eighth-, and eleventh-graders began in 1984. The Department of Education publishes the results of the assessments in a series called *The Nation's Report Card.*

One reason the NAEP tests are important indicators of educational problems is that their design makes it possible to compare students' performance over time and to identify trends. The tests let us make legitimate comparisons between today's 17-year-olds and those of 20 years ago. When we make such comparisons and observe trends in the scores over the years, it becomes evident why many claim that our nation is educationally at risk. Although today's students do better than students did in the 1980s, they perform at the same level as the students of the 1970s.

A headline on page 1 of the October 1, 1991 *New York Times* summarizes the problem: "Pupils in America Reverse Declines to Regain '70 Level." Diane Ravitch, Assistant Secretary of Education for Educational Research and Improvement, is quoted in the *Times* article as having said: "The achievement trend lines are essentially flat over the past 20 years. What was good enough 20 years ago is not good enough anymore." Consistently, the assessments show that the educational crisis is not one of decline; it is one of stagnation. Schools have not kept pace with society's expectations.

Much of the popular discussion of school reform, fueled by a steady stream of reports and recommendations, has concentrated on articulating society's new educational expectations. Too little attention has been paid to what teachers and schools might need to meet those expectations: new pedagogical tools and methods, new and better ways of interacting with students in the classroom. This becomes evident when we look beneath the NAEP trend lines and examine how students perform within the subject areas tested.

Level 150   Simple Arithmetic Facts
  - know some basic addition and subtraction facts
  - add two digit numbers without regrouping
  - developing basic classification skills

Level 200   Beginning Skills and Understanding
  - understanding two-digit numbers
  - add two-digit numbers, learning to regroup in subtraction
  - know some multiplication and division facts
  - can read information from charts and graphs

Level 250   Basic Operations and Beginning Problem Solving
  - understand the four basic arithmetic operations
  - can solve one-step word problems
  - can find product of two-digit and one-digit number
  - can compare information from charts and graphs

Level 300   Moderately Complex Procedures and Reasoning
  - beginning to understand number systems
  - compute with decimals, simple fractions, and percents
  - develop some basic geometric understanding
  - interpret inequalities, evaluate formulas, find averages

Level 350   Multi-step Problem Solving and Algebra
  - apply reasoning skills to solve multi-step problems
  - can work with exponents and square roots
  - can solve two-step problems using variables
  - developing understanding of functions and coordinates

Figure 1.1
Summary of the five proficiency levels defined for the National Assessment of Educational Progress mathematics test. (From Dossey et al. 1988, p. 31.)

Using advice from experts and sophisticated statistical techniques, the NAEP tests define five levels of proficiency within a subject. As an example, figure 1.1 summarizes the five proficiency levels on the mathematics assessment and gives the associated numerical scores. Analysis of the NAEP data shows that, in all subjects tested, almost all students achieve the lower proficiency levels but distressingly few students perform at the highest levels.

On the 1986 mathematics assessment, 73 percent of 13-year-olds and 96 percent of 17-year-olds achieved the third proficiency level, but only 0.4 percent of 13-year-olds and 6.4 percent of 17-year-olds reached the fifth and highest NAEP proficiency level. This means that only 4 out of 1000 junior high school students and 64 out of 1000 senior high school students could solve multi-step math problems and understand algebra (Dossey et al. 1988).

Results from the science assessment were similarly poor. Only 9.4 percent of 13-year-olds and 41.4 percent of 17-year-olds performed at the fourth proficiency level, scoring 300 or better. This means that nearly 60 percent of high school students can't analyze scientific procedures, explain how data support a theory, or understand the design of a scientific experiment. Only 7.5 percent of high school students can draw correct conclusions using detailed scientific knowledge (Mullis and Jenkins 1988).

The assessment of reading—the fundamental learning skill—showed that only 41.8 percent of high school students could comprehend moderately difficult texts and then summarize and elaborate on what they had read. Fewer than 5 percent of 17-year-olds were expert readers with the ability to integrate information, comprehend specialized content, and state their own views and ideas about what they had read (Mullis and Jenkins 1990).

Results from the writing assessment are equally troubling. Among high school students, 68.5 percent could write narratives based on their personal experience at the fourth proficiency level and 53.3 percent could write factual reports at this level. However, only 27 percent of the eleventh-graders could write an adequate persuasive essay, and only 1 percent qualified as expert persuasive writers (Applebee et al. 1990).

The NAEP results show that most students have command of lower-level, rote skills, such as computation in math, recalling facts in science, decoding words in reading, and spelling, grammar, and punctuation in writing. Most students can remember facts, solve routine textbook problems, and apply formulas. Many fewer students can use what knowledge they have to solve more complex problems—problems that might take several steps and have no obvious, immediate answer. Many if not most students have difficulty using what they know to interpret an experiment, comprehend a text, or persuade an audience. They can't rise above the rote, factual level to think critically or creatively. They can't apply what they know flexibly and spontaneously to solve ill-structured, ambiguous problems that require interpretation.

In short, the NAEP results indicate that current curricula and teaching methods successfully impart facts and rote skills to most students but fail to impart high-order reasoning and learning skills. As Gordon Anrig, president of the Educational Testing Service, has noted, 20 years of NAEP testing "has documented a critical shortage of effective reasoning skills among our young people" (Dossey et al. 1988, p. 7). If we want more students to have these skills, we need new teaching methods and new approaches to education.

New Expectations

Unlike 20 years ago, we now expect all young people to leave school with the ability to perform at the highest NAEP proficiency levels and with the ability to use high-order thinking skills. Employers want entry-level workers to have these skills, and college educators expect entering students to have them.

Although much of the evidence is anecdotal, employers claim that too many job applicants lack the comprehension, communication, and reasoning skills needed in the modern workplace. The Business Roundtable's Ad Hoc Committee on Education reported that 60 percent of high school graduates were not ready for entry-level jobs (Doyle 1989). Even a casual glance at newspapers, magazines, and business publications reveals that many businesses want employees who are critical, analytic thinkers, who can innovate and solve problems, who have superior speaking and writing skills, and who can learn on the job. They want people who know how to learn. Business wants employees who have and use high-order skills.

Anecdotes and some research suggest a similar lack of entry-level skills among those going to college. Instructors claim that many freshmen arrive on campus unprepared for college-level work. Students write poorly, they lack a reasonable understanding of history and culture, and they cannot adapt to college-level demands in math and science. Many entering freshman are incapable of abstract thinking and lack adequate formal reasoning skills (Nickerson et al. 1985, p. 5).

Furthermore, over the last decade the entry-level skills for post-secondary education have become the entry-level skills for post-secondary employment. According to Lauren Resnick, co-director of Pittsburgh University's Learning Research and Development Center, the skills and abilities employers demand today are at least the skills and abilities required for college entrance as recently as 1983 (Resnick 1986, p. 9). In the future, she projects, we can expect that entry-level jobs will require skills equivalent to those of today's college sophomore. If we expect every high school graduate to either enter college or find employment, then we expect all students to have high-order skills—skills that a generation ago we looked for only in those attending the best colleges.

These rising expectations represent an unprecedented challenge to public education. No educational system has ever tried to educate all its students to be high-order thinkers. Improving our schools to educate everyone to this level, not just the select few, may not be possible if all we do is reaffirm past standards, raise graduation requirements, and apply existing methods and practices more rigorously. Twenty years' NAEP data tell us that current educational practices successfully impart high-order skills to few students.

Robert Glaser, the Learning Research and Development Center's other co-director and a pioneer in the field of instructional psychology, fears that the prevailing theories of instruction and schooling practices fail to meet current demands. "We need," he suggests, "a stronger theoretical base if we are to teach a far broader range of students and take them farther than ever before as modern society demands." (Glaser 1988, p. 21)

We have to change the way teachers interact with students in the classroom—and the changes must be grounded in an understanding of how children learn.

Arthur Wise, president of the National Council for Accreditation of Teacher Education, maintains that any attempts at systematic school reform will quickly run up against the fact that established knowledge and proven innovations are scarce. He notes that "many of the proposed 'solutions' to current problems have little theoretical or empirical grounding" (Wise 1989, p. 36). These proposed solutions include school-based management, market incentives, more testing, and greater school accountability. Without some attention to Glaser's theoretical base and a national commitment to evaluate instructional alternatives, we run the risk of changing our schools without improving them. Wise worries that we will "waste resources in poorly grounded efforts simply to do things differently."

A Science of Mind: The MIT Meeting

If we want to do things better and not just differently, we need, as Glaser claims, a better theory of instruction. We need an applied science of learning. The 1956 MIT symposium and the subsequent cognitive revolution in psychology were the first steps toward this applied educational science.

In the mid 1950s, behaviorism was the prevailing orthodoxy in American psychological science. B. F. Skinner and other behaviorists believed that a scientific psychology had to be based solely on observed behavior. For the behaviorists, acceptable psychological explanations could appeal only to observable environmental stimuli and to the observable responses the stimuli evoked from organisms. Appeals to mysterious, unobservable mental processes were scientifically inadmissible.

There could be no *science* of the *mind*—such a notion was scientifically self-contradictory, behaviorists claimed. On their theory, to teach an animal a new behavior you expose it to appropriate environmental stimuli and reward it when it makes the proper response. In education, behaviorist learning theory emphasized arranging the student's environment so that stimuli occurred in a way that would instill the desired stimulus–response chains. Teachers would present lessons in small, manageable pieces (stimuli), ask students to give answers (responses), and then dispense reinforcement (preferably positive rather than negative) until their students became conditioned to give the right answers. Behaviorism is a simple, elegant scientific theory that has both methodological and intuitive appeal. But humans are more complicated than behaviorism allows.

Why and how we are more complicated was becoming evident around the time of the 1956 MIT symposium. The participants realized that a number of previously independent research programs were merging and pointing to a new research paradigm in psychology. Presentations by Noam Chomsky, George Miller, Herbert Simon, and Allen Newell implied that a science of the mind was not only possible but necessary. There had to be a science of how we perceive, remember, learn, plan, and reason. Participants left the meeting convinced that behaviorism was too narrow a theoretical basis for psychology.

Language has a central place in psychology, because any adequate theory of behavior must be able to explain this uniquely human ability. Linguists call a formal theory of a language a *grammar*. A grammar for English should contain rules that can generate all correct (that is, grammatical) English sentences, but only those sentences. In his paper for the MIT symposium the theoretical linguist Noam Chomsky began by showing that a grammar built strictly on behaviorist principles couldn't do this (Chomsky 1956). A behaviorist grammar couldn't account for our ability to generate and understand a potentially infinite number of sentences, most of which we have never heard before and some of which could be indefinitely long. How, Chomsky asked, could exposure to a finite set of environmental stimuli lead to such infinitely varied responses?

Then Chomsky presented his alternative: a theory of *transformational grammar*. Transformational grammar explains our language behavior by assuming that we mentally store our linguistic knowledge as a small set of simple sentences. Chomsky called these simple sentences *deep structures*. A set of mental transformations, or rules, operate on the deep structures to generate the sentences, or *surface structures,* that we speak, write, and understand. His idea was that a small set of basic symbol structures plus a small but powerful set of mental rules or operators could generate an infinite number of sentences. In some ways, language is a symbol system like the number system. By using ten number symbols (0, . . . , 9) and a few rules, we can make an infinity of new number symbols. Chomsky argued that our ability to speak and understand language results from the processing of unobservable, mental, symbol structures. If psychology has to explain language, then psychology has to be a science of the mind.

George Miller, a psychologist, presented a version of his paper "The Magical Number Seven, Plus or Minus Two" (Miller 1956). Miller observed that the number seven appears widely in the psychological literature as a limit on the capacity of the human nervous system. Psychologists had shown that our short-term memory—the memory capacity we use to remember a phone number long enough to dial it—has seven plus or minus two "slots." We know from everyday experience that we can remember one unfamiliar phone number long enough to dial it, but not two. Miller's paper pointed out something interesting about the slots.

The topic of the MIT symposium was information science, and one thing information scientists do is measure how much information a communication channel can transmit. They use the *bi*nary dig*it,* or *bit,* as their unit of measurement. Binary digits are strings of zeros and ones. Bits can encode any piece of information. This binary code is the code computers use.

Miller argued that the capacity of short-term memory cannot be measured in bits. Most of us can hold a string of about seven zeros and ones (for example, 1,0,0,1,1,0,1) in short-term memory, but have trouble if the string gets much longer. By definition, this string contains seven bits of information. We also can easily remember a seven-decimal-digit telephone number, like 822-7128. Written in bits, the seven digits of this telephone number would be 01000, 00010, 00010, 00111, 00001, 00010, and 01000. The telephone number contains 35 bits of information, but its decimal encoding takes only seven symbols. In each case we can remember seven symbols, but in the first case the symbols encode seven bits and in the second 35! The limit on the capacity of short-term memory is the number of *symbols* it can hold—one per slot—and not the amount of information each symbol encodes.

Miller concluded that short-term memory capacity must be measured in *chunks*, a term that was to gain wide currency in psychology. Chunks are psychologically important because they give us a way to overcome our limited short-term memory capacity: we can recode information that we can't remember (such as the 35-bit phone number) into its decimal equivalent, which we can remember. If we construct the chunks cleverly—if we recode information into fewer, larger chunks, each containing more information—we can increase our short-term memory capacity. One experimental subject increased his short-term memory span for decimal digits to over 80 by remembering them as three- and four-digit chunks that he associated with winning times in track events (Chase and Ericsson 1981). Miller suggested that learning may involve constantly recoding knowledge into different symbol structures in an attempt to discover the most efficient chunks. His presentation implied that we are not passive communication channels linking stimuli and responses, but active information processors engaged in recoding and managing internal symbol structures. Miller's paper suggested that we actively work to make the most of our limited cognitive capacity. If so, a scientific psychology has to be a science of mental symbol processing, not just a science of observable behavior.

Newell and Simon's paper (1956) did not deal with humans at all. Rather, it described a computer program called the Logic Theorist (LT)—the first working artificial intelligence program. LT could prove logical theorems using methods a human expert might use. It could prove all the theorems in chapter 2 of Alfred North Whitehead and Bertrand Russell's *Principia Mathematica,* and with some refinements it could prove most of the theorems in chapter 3. The *Principia* was one of the first and greatest achievements of mathematical logic.

LT replicated this monumental cognitive achievement by using a set of rules to manipulate symbol structures.

LT provided the theoretical link between psychology and computation. Computers and minds might differ in a variety of ways; however, as the symposium papers showed, both computers and minds process symbols. Maybe, the symposiasts realized, a common underlying theory—the theory of symbol processing or computation—could be used to understand symbol-processing devices of both kinds. If so, the theory of computation would give psychologists an exact language with which to formulate and test hypotheses about human mental processes. Maybe humans, like computers, have built-in resources—symbols, operators, and memories—for constructing and running programs. If we can discover what these mental resources are and how they work, we should be able to write programs, like LT, that solve other problems. The programs would be detailed descriptions—as detailed as the code in a computer program—of the way our mental processes guide our behavior; the programs would tell us what knowledge we need and how we use it to solve problems. The programs would be psychological theories—cognitive theories—about how we prove theorems, use language, or play chess.

Chomsky and Miller argued that a scientific psychology had to include mental symbol structures and operations. Newell and Simon showed that the theory of computation provides an appropriate theoretical framework within which to study mental processes. The programmed computer and the human problem solver were both information-processing devices.

The cognitive revolution in psychology had started.

The Revolution Becomes a Discipline

Over the next 16 years, the cognitive revolution spread and developed into a scientific discipline. Cognitive scientists, as the revolutionaries eventually called themselves, worked to exploit the similarities between thinking and information processing. Besides logic, Newell and Simon studied problem solving in other areas, ranging from tic-tac-toe to arithmetic puzzles to chess. Problem solving in each of these areas depends on learning facts, skills, and strategies that are unique to the area. As cognitive scientists say, expertise in each area requires mastery of a distinct knowledge *domain*. Cognitive research began to have relevance for education as scientists gradually started to study knowledge domains that are included in school instruction—math, science, reading, and writing. In their 1972 book *Human Problem Solving,* Newell and Simon summarized the results of this early research program and established a theoretical outlook and research methods that would guide much of the work that now has educational significance. Newell and Simon argued that if we want to understand learning in a domain, we have to start with a detailed analysis of how people solve problems in that domain. The first step is to try to discover the mental processes, or programs, that individuals use to solve a problem. To do this, cognitive scientists give a person a problem and observe everything the subject does and says while attempting a solution. Newell and Simon prompted their subjects to "think aloud"—to say everything that passed through their minds as they worked on the problems. Analysis of such data allows cognitive scientists to form hypotheses about what program an individual uses to solve a problem. Cognitive scientists can test their hypotheses by writing computer programs based on their hypotheses to simulate the subject's problem-solving performance. If the scientists' analysis is correct, the computer simulation should perform the same way the human did on the problem. If the simulation fails, the scientists revise their hypotheses accordingly and try again. After studying and simulating performances from a variety of subjects, Newell and Simon could trace individual differences in problem-solving performance to specific differences in the mental programs the subjects used.

To be sure they could find clear-cut differences among individual programs, Newell and Simon initially compared the problem-solving performances of experts and novices—which were almost certain to be different—in a variety of domains. In such studies (now a mainstay of the discipline), cognitive scientists consider any individual who is highly skilled or knowledgeable in a given domain to be an "expert" in that domain. The domains can be ordinary and commonplace; they don't have to be arcane and esoteric. In the cognitive scientists' sense of the word, there are experts at tic-tac-toe, third-grade arithmetic, and high school physics. Comparing experts with novices makes it possible to specify how experts and novices differ in understanding, storing, recalling, and manipulating knowledge during problem solving.

Of course Newell and Simon knew that experts in a domain would be better at solving problems in that domain than novices, but it was not always obvious how experts and novices actually differed in their problem-solving behavior. In one early expert-novice study, Simon and Chase (1973) looked at chess players. One thing we do when playing chess is to choose our next move by trying to anticipate what our opponent's countermove might be, how we might respond to that move, how the opponent might counter, and so on. That is, we try to plan several moves ahead. One might think that experts and novices differ in how far ahead they plan: a novice might look ahead two or three moves, an expert ten or twelve. Surprisingly, Simon and Chase found that experts and novices both look ahead only two or three moves. The difference is that experts consider and choose from among vastly superior moves. Chunking, rather than planning farther ahead, accounts for the experts' superiority. When expert chess players look at a board, they see configurations and familiar patterns of pieces. Novices, in contrast, see individual pieces. The experts' more effective, more information-rich chunks allow them to see superior possible moves and choose the best of these. Experts process more and better information about the next few moves than novices.

Newell and Simon's emphasis on problem-solving performance and expert-novice differences was a first step toward a new understanding of learning. In short, learning is the process by which novices become experts. As one learns chess, math, or physics, one's problem-solving performance in the domain improves as the programs one uses to solve problems improve. If we know what programs a person first uses to solve problems in a domain, and if we can compare them with the programs the person eventually constructs, we have a measure and a description of what the person learned. We can study learning by tracing changes in the mental processes students use as they progress from novice to higher levels of proficiency. If we have detailed knowledge of these processes, such as the computer simulations give us, we can know not only that learning has occurred but also *how* it has occurred.

Other investigators joined in the program that Newell and Simon had outlined, and the research developed and expanded along two dimensions.

First, the kinds of problems and tasks the scientists studied became more complex. To play games and solve puzzles, even in logic and chess, one has to know a few rules, but one doesn't need much factual knowledge about the world. As cognitive scientists honed their methods on puzzle problems and accumulated insights into how people solve them, they became more ambitious and began applying their methods to more knowledge-rich domains. They started to study problem solving in physics, mathematics, and medical diagnosis. They began to study language skills, such as reading and writing, and how students use these skills to acquire more knowledge. Extending their research into these domains made it applicable to understanding expert and novice performance in school subjects.

Second, the research evolved from merely comparing novices against experts to studying the process by which novices *become* experts. Psychologists began to develop intermediate models of problem-solving performance in a variety of domains. The intermediate models describe how domain expertise *develops* over time and with experience. The intermediate models describe the stages through which students progress in school. If learning is the process by which novices become experts, a sequence of intermediate models in a domain traces the learning process in that domain.

By the mid 1970s, cognitive scientists were studying school tasks over a range of competencies—from novice to expert, from preschool through college. By the early 1980s, the revolution that started in 1956 had given us a new theory of learning. As Glaser (1986, p. 331) describes it, learning theory "is taking on the characteristics of a developmental psychology of performance changes—the study of changes that occur as knowledge and complex cognitive strategies are acquired."

This modern learning theory is the basis for an applied science of learning—the stronger theoretical base we need to improve school instruction. In many subject areas, our knowledge of students' cognitive processes is sufficiently detailed that we can begin to describe their performance at every level of competence, from novice to expert. We can describe the normal trajectory of learning in these subject areas. If we understand the mental processes that underlie expert performance in school subjects, we can ask and answer other questions that are important for education. How do students acquire these processes? Do certain instructional methods help students acquire these processes more quickly or more easily? Can we help students learn better? Answers to these questions can guide educational practice and school reform. The answers can help teachers make decisions in the classroom that promote learning and educational achievement.

Cognitive Bottlenecks and High-Order Skills

A theory of learning as a developmental psychology of changes in performance—the study of how problem-solving behavior changes as students acquire knowledge and cognitive strategies—relates directly to the deficiencies and problems which the NAEP results identify. The NAEP proficiency levels are also a developmental progression; they describe the performances we would like to see at various age levels, and the higher levels implicitly state our educational goals. The new learning theory allows us to look beneath actual or desired performances and to describe the underlying mental processes. We can then investigate how best to teach these processes. Research has already shown that some transitions on the path to expertise in school subjects are more difficult than others. There are known cognitive bottlenecks that students have to negotiate to progress from basic to intermediate to advanced proficiency.

Although there are problems unique to each subject area, the NAEP results point to a general cognitive or instructional bottleneck: too few students successfully negotiate the transition from lower-level to higher-level skills—from basic, rote skills to the high-order, flexible skills of advanced proficiency. In the following chapters we will see how researchers and teachers are applying the new learning theory to create classroom environments that help students make this transition.

We will begin by looking in greater detail at how cognitive scientists work and how their results can contribute to better instructional methods (chapter 2). Nearly three decades into the cognitive revolution, we have learned much about intelligence and expert performance. Expert performance in a subject requires specific subject-matter knowledge, but it also requires general thinking and learning skills and the ability to monitor and control one's own cognitive processes (chapter 3). The research implies that we should teach basic school subjects, such as those assessed by the NAEP, as high-order learning skills. If we do this, we can help students become experts at learning.

Cognitive research has found several cognitive bottlenecks in math learning (chapter 4). Most children come to school with considerable informal number knowledge. Children who arrive in first grade deficient in informal number knowledge have great difficulty understanding school math instruction and can quickly fall behind. With appropriate short-term instruction, these students can make up the deficiency in weeks and advance with their peers. Often, the way we teach multi-digit arithmetic, word problems, and even geometry gives students the impression that these are meaningless, artificial activities peculiar to school. As we shall see, new instructional methods that apply what we know about how children learn, remember, and use math skills can make mathematics meaningful and help more children attain the higher NAEP proficiency levels.

In science, few students can interpret how data support a theory, and few understand experimental design. Worse, after years of school science instruction, few of us, as adults, properly understand the world around us. Research on science learning shows that our naive beliefs about the world exert such a strong influence on how we interpret school instruction that the instruction is often ineffective. Curricula based on cognitive research that build from and correct our naive theories can overcome this problem (chapter 5).

Reading is a highly demanding cognitive task. A skilled reader has to process information instantaneously at many levels, from recognizing words to constructing a text's meaning. Cognitive research has described these processing skills and how they work together (chapter 6). This research has given us insights into how to teach word recognition and vocabulary knowledge. It also suggests how to design more effective reading materials and textbooks. Most important, it tells us how to teach high-order reading-comprehension skills. According to the NAEP proficiency levels for reading, from the intermediate level on students should be able to summarize, elaborate on, and make predictions from what they read. Reciprocal teaching, a technique based on cognitive research that is discussed in chapter 6, teaches "problem readers" how to summarize, elaborate, and predict with astonishing results.

Research on the cognition of writing reveals that although most children master the low-level mechanics of writing, many lack the higher-order planning and organizing skills needed for effective written communication (chapter 7). Many traditional school practices encourage students to view writing as a task wherein they recite what they know for the teacher. Students come to view all school writing tasks as routine "knowledge-telling" exercises requiring little if any high-order planning and organizing. Instructional methods that help students develop writing plans and that give them authentic, audience-directed writing tasks can help them break the knowledge-telling habit.

Cognitive research and its new theory of learning also have educational implications beyond subject-matter learning (chapter 8). First, the developmental theory of performance change presents a new theoretical basis for the testing of achievement and intelligence. Using this theory, we can design tests that diagnose learning problems—something we can't do with traditional standardized tests. Second, research at the intersection of social and cognitive psychology suggests that students' naive beliefs about what intelligence is influence their motivation and performance in school. Finally, cognitive scientists have started to study classroom teaching as a form of problem solving. We are beginning to learn what knowledge, processes, and skills distinguish more effective from less effective teaching performances. These findings are expanding the knowledge base of the teaching profession and will contribute to better teacher training.

Knowing Why

Improving our schools isn't just a matter of getting the psychology right, just as improving health care isn't just a matter of getting the biology right. Nonetheless, to improve our schools we will have to change the way in which teachers and students interact in the classroom. Research on learning and teaching can help us to design new, better teaching tools and to create better learning environments.

If we want to do things better, not just differently, we will have to acknowledge the contributions of theory, basic research, applied research, and instructional development to school reform. We are far from having all the answers, and the solutions to our educational problems aren't obvious.

The world didn't need Isaac Newton to know *that* apples fall off trees. It did need Newton to give us a general theory that explains *why* apples fall off trees. Knowing why apples fall off trees has allowed us to go to the moon and to see television images of the planets. Knowing why leads to other discoveries, new applications, and further refinements.

Educational research, and cognitive research in particular, can play an analogous role in education. Research provides "a scientific basis for the improvement of instruction" because "it will tell us not just whether an instructional program succeeds, but why" (Resnick 1984, p. 37). If we know why, and if we make a concerted effort to apply what we know, we may be able to create learning environments that would satisfy the vision expressed in the opening sentence of *A Nation at Risk:* "All, regardless of race or class or economic status, are entitled to a fair chance and to the tools for developing their individual powers of mind and spirit to the utmost."

The Science of Mind: Analyzing Tasks, Behaviors, and Representations

The claim that our minds and computers are related—that they are both species of the same genus—might seem outrageous; however, as we come to understand this claim and the research methods based on it, we will begin to appreciate the similarities between mind and machine. From these similarities cognitive scientists derive theories that help explain how children learn and, consequently, how they could be taught more effectively.

A Balance-Scale Problem

Research on how children learn to solve balance-scale problems illustrates the main ideas, methods, and instructional applications of cognitive science.

Try to solve the balance-scale problem shown in figure 2.1. Assume the scale's arm is locked so that it can't rotate around the fulcrum. If I were to unlock the arm, what would happen? Would the scale tip left, tip right, or balance?

This is a tricky problem. Figure 2.2 gives a set of rules one might use to solve it. Each rule has an IF clause that states the conditions under which the rule is applicable and a THEN clause that states what to do under those conditions. To use these rules, find the rule whose conditions fit the pattern of weights and distances in the problem. You find that P4 is the only rule whose IF clause fits the problem. Its THEN clause tells you to compute torques for each side; that is, for each side, multiply the number of weights by their distance from the fulcrum. Doing that gives $t_1 = 5 \times 3 = 15$ for the left side and $t_2 = 4 \times 4 = 16$ for the right. These new data satisfy the condition for P7; executing its THEN clause gives the correct answer, "Right side down." Some readers might remember

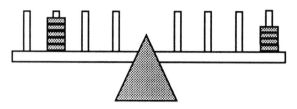

Figure 2.1
Will the scale tip left, tip right, or balance?

RULE IV

    P1   **IF** weight is the same
           THEN say "balance".

    P2   **IF** side X has more weight
           THEN say "X down".

    P3   **IF** weight is the same **AND** side X has more distance
           THEN say "X down".

    P4   **IF** side X has more weight **AND** side X has less distance
           THEN compute torques: $t_1 = w_1 \times d_1$; $t_2 = w_2 \times d_2$.

    P5   **IF** side X has more weight **AND** side X has more distance
           THEN say "X down".

    P6   **IF** the torques are equal
           THEN say "balance".

    P7   **IF** side X has more torque
           THEN say "X down".

Figure 2.2
The set of rules an expert might use to solve the balance-scale problem. (From Siegler and Klahr 1982, p. 198. Used with permission of Lawrence Erlbaum Associates.)

the THEN clause in P4 from high school physics as a version of the law of torques: Multiply weight by distance on each arm to find the torque, or rotational force; the side with the larger torque goes down. This simple law solves all balance-scale problems.

The set of rules is an English-language version of a computer program for solving balance-scale problems. It takes as input data about the weight on each side of the scale and the distance of the weight from the fulcrum. The output is the answer for a balance-scale problem: tip left, tip right, or balance. The program is a series of IF-THEN rules. Computer scientists call the IF clauses *conditions,* the THEN clauses *actions,* and the entire IF-THEN statement a *production rule.* They call computer programs written using only production rules *production systems.* Computing devices that execute production systems efficiently have a specific internal structure (or *architecture,* as computer scientists say).

Cognitive scientists claim that the human mind can be described as a computing device that builds and executes production-system programs. In fact, the rules in figure 2.2 are a production system an expert would use to solve balance-scale problems. Robert Siegler, a cognitive psychologist, showed that production systems can simulate human performance on such problems (Siegler 1976; Klahr and Siegler 1978; Siegler and Klahr 1982). He also showed that a series of increasingly complex production systems can model the way in which children gradually develop expertise on balance-scale problems from ages 5 through 17. Children learn, says Siegler, by adding better rules to their production systems. Proper instruction, he goes on to show, can help children acquire these better rules.

The Human Computer and How It Works

At the heart of the cognitive revolution was the realization that an adequate human psychology had to include the study of how the mind processes symbols. Computational theory gave psychologists a language and a framework for studying human symbol processing. Both minds and computers process symbols, use a small set of basic operations to manipulate them, and store them in memory. When we solve a balance-scale problem, we use a system of mental symbols to encode information about the problem, to manipulate that information, and to store the results of the manipulations in memory.

Symbol systems and basic operations, notions fundamental to cognitive theory, can be hard to understand. But we all understand how arithmetic works, and it provides a ready analogy for understanding symbols and operations. A symbol is an object that stands for or represents another object. In arithmetic, there are two kinds of symbols: numerals and operation signs. The content of arithmetic, what it is about, is numbers. Numerals are symbols for numbers. Each number has a unique numeral, and each numeral represents a unique number. In the Arabic system we can combine a few basic symbols (0, . . . ,9), using rules, to generate an infinity of numerals symbolizing an infinity of numbers. This ability to combine a few basic symbols systematically into more complex ones is a powerful feature of other symbol systems we use, such as the alphabet and speech sounds.

The arithmetic signs, +, −, ×, and ÷, are symbols that stand for operations on numbers. These four signs symbolize the basic processes of arithmetic. Like numerals, they can be combined to generate an infinity of other numeric operations. To find an average we combine addition and division; to figure out monthly mortgage payments we combine multiplication, addition, and division. Making more complex numerical operations out of simple ones gives arithmetic its power and its wide applicability.

Symbols and processes in computing work the same way. There are two kinds of symbols: those that stand for input or data (what the computation is about) and those that stand for operations on the data. In computing, the basic operations include recognizing when two symbols are the same, creating new symbols, storing a symbol in memory, and retrieving a symbol from memory. The basic operations are part of the computer's hardware or the primitive commands in a particular computer language. Using rules, we can combine the basic operations to form more complex operations. We call these more complex, elaborate operations *computer programs*. Depending on what the data are and how we combine the basic processes, we can make the computer into a word processor, a spreadsheet, or a flight simulator.

Cognitive scientists assume that the human mind works by applying elementary processes to symbol structures that represent the content of our thoughts. On the balance-scale problems, we use symbols to encode variables, such as sides, weights, and distances. Cognitive scientists call these symbol structures *mental representations*.

The idea of representation is fundamental to cognitive science. Representations are the symbol structures we construct to encode our experience, process it, and store it in our memories. Representations are the symbolic links between the external environment and our internal, mental world. The representations we construct in encoding our experiences have profound effects on our behavior and our learning.

In the balance-scale task, we use basic processes such as comparing two symbols (which side has more weight?), creating new symbols (finding the torques), and retrieving information from memory (what is 5 × 3?). When we combine a few basic processes in the right way, we get a production system with which to solve balance-scale problems.

The expert's production system for the balance scale is a combination of basic processes that operate on symbols representing objects in the environment. If we know the initial input to the production-system program, we can predict what the expert will say about any balance-scale problem. The program not only gives the same answer as the expert but also simulates the expert's performance by telling us exactly what the expert knows and does to arrive at that answer. The production system is a cognitive theory of expert performance on balance-scale problems.

The production system for the balance scale is an example of how a good cognitive theory of a task not only explains the task but also performs the task as a human would. The same approach and the same criterion for being a good cognitive theory apply in other domains—math, physics, reading, and even writing. What varies among the domains and among problems within the domains are the specific representations we use and the ways in which we combine our basic cognitive processes to operate on the representations. Different representations and combinations of operators allow us to play chess, solve physics problems, and write essays, just as different data programs turn a computer into a word processor or a spreadsheet. The challenge for the cognitive scientist is to identify the representations and elementary processes we use and to discover how we combine them to build the programs that guide our actions.

Processing and Storing Symbols: Human Memory Structures

Minds differ from digital computers in some obvious ways. Minds are made of neural tissue, computers from silicon and copper. Minds

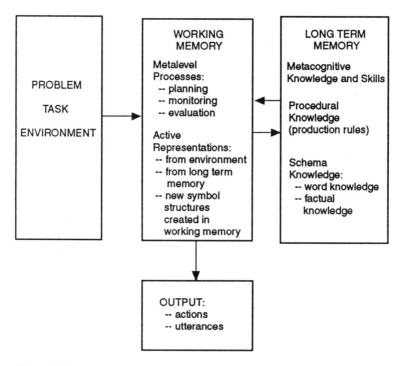

Figure 2.3
The standard picture of the human cognitive architecture.

evolved; computers are designed. Another important difference between minds and computers lies in their built-in capacities, characteristics, and memory structures—the attributes that enable them to
construct and run programs. As a computer scientist would say,
minds and computers have different *computational architectures*.

Borrowing from computing, cognitive scientists speak of our
cognitive architecture, the built-in mental features that allow our minds
to build and execute programs. Figure 2.3 gives the standard picture
of the human cognitive architecture. Information from the external
world (what cognitive psychologists sometimes call the *task environment*) comes to us through our sensory systems. Some of this information enters working memory, where we process it. We store some
of this processed information for future use in long-term memory.
Working memory is the part of our cognitive architecture where
mental computations actually take place; in this respect it is much
like a computer's central processing unit. Long-term memory is for

storage, like a computer's hard disk. Features of these two memory structures account for both the strengths and the weaknesses of human cognition.

Most of us, when we think of "memory," think of long-term memory—our permanent storehouse of knowledge and skills. Our long-term memory appears, for all practical purposes, to have unlimited capacity: no one has ever reported a case of an otherwise normal person who couldn't learn and remember new things. The most important feature of long-term memory for learning and instruction is not its capacity but its internal organization. Unlike a digital computer, you don't store a chunk of information in long-term memory by giving it an "address" in your brain, an address that you look up when you want to retrieve the information. Long-term memory has what psychologists call an *associative structure*. Symbol structures represent items or chunks of information in memory, and associative links tie the items together into networks of related information. We create associative links between chunks if we use the chunks together repeatedly, learn them together, or experience them together.

Cognitive psychologists have discovered that long-term memory is not a single entity; it comes in a variety of forms. At the most general level, they distinguish declarative from nondeclarative memory. Declarative memory contains a system for remembering specific events (what psychologists call *episodic memory*) and a system for remembering general facts and word meanings (*semantic memory*). We consciously recall items from declarative memory, and we can express or describe the items we retrieve. This is not so for the contents of nondeclarative memory. Among other things, nondeclarative memory contains our memory for motor, perceptual, and cognitive skills—our memory for procedures. The contents of nondeclarative memory are not always open to conscious recall, nor can they always be expressed or accurately described. Tennis players have a motor skill to hit backhands, but when they execute the skill they don't consciously recall the procedure; they just hit the backhand. As you read this text you are executing a complex motor, perceptual, and cognitive skill, yet you can't describe how you transform the marks on the page into meaningful prose.

To understand problem solving and high-order cognition, we can focus on semantic and procedural memory—our memories for facts and skills. Although semantic and procedural memory both have associative structures, their structures are slightly different. The expert rule system illustrated in figure 2.2 is an example of a procedural memory structure. The associations in procedural memory form rules. Individual rules represent associations between chunks of information, where the chunks are the conditions and actions in the rules. The expert has learned to associate certain actions with certain conditions. The expert also associates the seven rules together as a system because collectively the rules are useful for solving balance-scale problems. There are also implicit associations between rules. For example, the action of P4 generates the conditions for either rule P5 or rule P6. Sometimes rules used together repeatedly combine to form a single, more complex, new rule. The rules and their organization give the expert a way to move from chunk to chunk in long-term memory.

Psychologists call the associative structures in declarative memory *schemas*. Schemas are network structures that store our general knowledge about objects, events, or situations. Figure 2.4 illustrates how our general knowledge about animals might be stored as a schema in semantic memory. In this example, the central node is "animal." The "is a" links connect the major nodes in the hierarchy that organizes our biological knowledge. Both mammals and birds are animals; a canary is a bird, but a bear is not. The "has," "can," and "is" links associate the various biological types with important properties or features. When we learn something new about bears or canaries, the information isn't passively inscribed at the end of our memory tape; rather, we integrate the new item into a preexisting schema.

Our associative memory structures are like little theories we apply to negotiate and understand the world. The associative structures help us make predictions—as with the balance scale—and help us make inferences that go beyond what we literally experience. For example, if you tell me that Tweety is a canary, I can infer that he is yellow, is a bird, and has feathers. Our schemas also help us know what to expect in situations. My schema for a baseball game leads me to expect that I will spend around 3 hours at the ballpark, and that if I eat there my dinner will be hot dogs and soda, not Dover sole.

These associative structures do not simply provide a way to store information; they also influence what we notice, how we interpret it, and how we remember it. In one famous memory study,

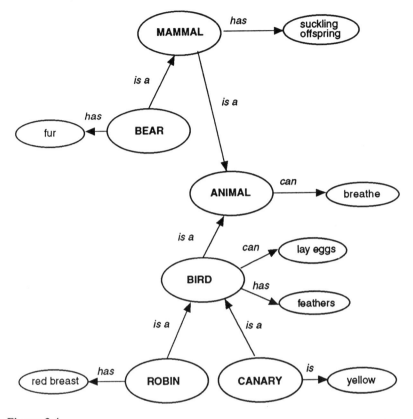

Figure 2.4
An example of a schema showing how knowledge about animals might be stored in long-term memory. The nodes represent concepts; the links represent relations among concepts. (From Just and Carpenter 1987, p. 66. Used with permission of Allyn and Bacon, Inc.)

a research assistant brought subjects, one by one, to a waiting room and told the subjects that this room was the experimenter's office (Brewer and Treyens 1981). After each subject had sat in the room for 35 seconds, the assistant took him to a seminar room and asked him to write down everything he could remember about the "office." All the subjects recalled correctly items that were in the room and were usually in most offices—a desk, a chair, etc. Yet only a third of the subjects remembered odd items, such as a skull, that were in the waiting room but not typically in an office. Conversely, a third of the subjects incorrectly reported remembering items that are usually in an office, such as books, but which were not present in the waiting room. The subjects' office schemas influenced what they noticed, what they remembered correctly, and what they "remembered" incorrectly about the waiting room.

Associative memory structures are powerful devices for organizing and deploying our skills and knowledge. Like other theories, they also actively influence what we perceive. Just as scientific theories influence what scientists see and consider important (for example, a social psychologist and an epidemiologist would notice different things about a group of coughing passengers on an airliner), our memory structures influence what we see and consider important. Prior knowledge influences what we notice and how we interpret new experiences. Thus, prior knowledge affects how we interpret school instruction and thus affects what we can learn. School instruction that ignores the influence of preexisting knowledge on learning can be highly ineffective.

If long-term memory is the storehouse, then working memory is the clearinghouse. *Working memory* is the term psychologists use to refer to the cognitive resources we use to execute mental operations and to remember the results of those operations for short periods of time (Baddeley 1992). Working memory contains all the symbol structures that are active and available for processing at any given time and keeps an internal record of the current state of mental activity. The inputs to working memory are symbols that encode information coming from the external world or symbol structures retrieved from long-term memory. When these structures are processed, the results can be new symbol structures in working memory, symbols for storage in long-term memory, or commands to the motor system to do or say something.

Working memory's most significant characteristic is its limited capacity. The capacity of short-term memory, as George Miller showed, is about seven plus or minus two chunks. In a short-term memory task, all we have to do is remember some information. Working memory is the information-processing descendant of short-term memory. Working-memory tasks combine the demand for remembering information with the demand for doing some processing on that information.

Our capacity to remember *and* process information is understandably less than our capacity to remember alone. You can convince yourself of this by some simple self-experimentation. For a short-term-memory task, cover the digits below with a piece of paper. Then uncover them one at a time, exposing one new digit every second. After 10 seconds, cover all the digits again and see how many you remember.

9 7 2 1 6 8 9 3 0 4

For a working-memory task, pick a paragraph in this book, read it aloud, and as you read try to remember the last word of every sentence. When you finish the paragraph, say aloud the words you tried to remember (Daneman and Carpenter 1980). Most people can do this for two sentences, but few people can do it for more than four. You will find that your short-term digit span is around seven plus or minus two digits, but that the capacity of your working memory, as measured by how many final words you can remember, is more like four plus or minus one.

Working memory can hold and process only a limited amount of information, and that for only short periods of time. We can quickly exceed its capacity, and when we do that any new information coming into working memory overwrites or obliterates what was previously there. Working-memory capacity is a limiting factor in our ability to process information. It is the bottleneck in our cognitive system. Skilled thinking, problem solving, and learning depend on how well we can manage this limited resource—on how efficiently we can store, process, and move information into and out of working memory.

How does the human computer work? How do these notions about symbol structures, representations, production systems, and memory structures fit together?

CYCLE	WORKING MEMORY CONTENTS	PRODUCTION
1	LEFT: w = 5, d = 3 RIGHT: w = 4, d = 4	**P4** **IF** side X has more weight and X has less distance **THEN** compute torques ...
2	LEFT: torque = 15 RIGHT: torque = 16	**P7** **IF** side X has more torques **THEN** say "Side X down."
3	SAY: "Right down."	No match, so halt.

Figure 2.5
An illustration of how an expert uses the rule in figure 2.2 to solve the balance-scale problem in figure 2.1. On each cycle the expert tries to match contents of working memory with the IF clause in a rule. When a match is found, that rule fires, changing the contents of working memory and starting a new cycle.

Using the production system illustrated in figure 2.2 to solve the balance-scale problem shown in figure 2.1 gives a simple example. Figure 2.5 sketches the process. Assume that an expert on balance-scale problems has stored the production system in long-term memory. When presented with the problem, the expert encodes relevant information about the problem into working memory. The expert forms an initial representation of the problem that includes symbols for side, weight, and distance. The first cycle starts with a search through the rules to find one whose conditions match the current contents of working memory. The contents of working memory match P4, which fires and changes the contents of working memory. Cycle 2 begins, and the only match is with P7. P7 fires, changing the contents of working memory, and cycle 3 begins. "SAY: 'Right down'" doesn't match the condition of any rule, so the program stops. Working memory sends the appropriate command to the brain's speech centers, and the expert says "Right down."

Production systems can become very complex, but the basic mode of operation remains the same. The system looks for matches between symbols active in working memory and conditions on production rules in long-term memory. When a match is found, that rule fires, modifying the contents of working memory—and the cycle begins again. When no match can be found, the program halts. That, in short, is how cognitive scientists think the human computer works.

Problems and Representations

Psychology is a science of human behavior that develops theories about how we react or respond in various situations or environments. According to cognitive science, all humans share the same basic cognitive architecture, although memory capacity and speed of processing may vary among individuals. Differences in our behavior arise from the ways in which our cognitive architectures, including individual differences in those capacities, interact with the environment. If cognitive scientists are to describe this interaction, then not only do they have to describe the computing device and its capacities carefully; they also have to describe the environment carefully.

To do the latter, cognitive scientists think of the external world in terms of *task environments.* A task environment is a problem plus the context in which a subject encounters the problem. For the balance-scale task, the environment consists of a balance scale and an experimenter who poses the problem by asking the subject for a prediction about what the scale will do.

Cognitive scientists use the word *problem* in a special way. The idea is simple, and it borrows from our everyday use of the word. As Newell and Simon wrote, "a person is confronted with a *problem* when he wants something and does not know immediately what series of actions he can perform to get it" (1972, p. 72). Cognitive psychologists elaborate and refine this general notion. They think of a problem as consisting of an *initial state* or situation and a *goal state* (i.e., what the person wants). To solve a problem, a person must figure out what to do to move from the initial state to the goal state. The things a person can do, the moves he or she can make in a problem situation, cognitive psychologists call *operators.* For example, a chess game is a problem in which the initial state is the opening position, the goal is checkmate, and the operators are legal moves. In solving a problem, then, we use operators to create a chain of working-memory states that begins with the initial state and ends with the goal state.

One way to view the development of cognitive science, especially as it relates to education, is to see how this characterization of problem solving was extended and modified as researchers applied it to increasingly complex domains. That is how this book is organized.

In the balance-scale problem, the initial state is the locked scale with weights on each arm. The goal state is the correct prediction of a unique outcome: left, right, or balance. Among the operators we could apply are the expert's production rules. As we have seen, these rules create a series of states in working memory leading from the initial state to a correct prediction.

The cognitivist's core notion of a problem applies directly to solving most school math and science problems. In a high school geometry problem, the "givens" are the initial state, "to prove" states the goal, and the operators are geometrical definitions, postulates, and theorems. There is a unique, well-defined goal, but there are various ways to move from the givens to that goal. In reading, the text is the given and the goal is to construct an interpretation of the text. However, for some kinds of texts—in contrast with solving geometry problems—there need not be a unique interpretation. That is what makes literature personally rewarding and intellectually challenging. Writing demands the solution of what cognitive scientists call *ill-defined problems.* With writing problems (for example, writing an essay), there is no unique solution and no standard, universal method of finding solutions. Often, it is only after we start solving an ill-defined problem that we have an idea of what an adequate solution might be. Teaching a classroom lesson presents an ill-defined problem that the teacher has to solve on the spot, where every student-teacher interaction can change the teacher's goals and choice of operators. Many everyday tasks (finding a job, planning a trip) and most creative tasks (writing a symphony, doing medical research) present ill-defined problems.

As was mentioned above, representations are the link between the external world and our internal processing system. A person's problem representation is what the person encodes about the problem from the task environment. It is the solver's interpretation or understanding of the problem—an interpretation based on experience and on beliefs about the major variables or factors relevant to the problem. Preexisting knowledge, stored as productions or schemas, guides the solver's interpretation.

A person's problem representation is seldom identical to the problem statement in the task environment. The famous nine-dot problem is the classic example. Draw four straight lines that pass through all nine dots without raising the pencil from the page:

.   .   .

.   .   .

.   .   .

Your initial representation dictated how hard or easy you found the problem. If you found the problem hard, most likely your representation (your interpretation of the problem statement) prohibited lines going outside the boundary defined by the dots. There was no such prohibition in the problem statement. If your representation allowed the four lines to go outside the boundary, you probably solved the problem easily. (One possible solution is shown in note 1 at the back of the book.)

What the nine-dot problem shows is that sometimes we include information in our representations that is not in the problem statement or the task environment. At other times, we might include in our representations information that is present in the task environment but that is not relevant to the problem. For example, we might encode the color of the weights in a balance-scale problem. Sometimes, too, we might fail to encode information that is present and relevant. As we will see, young children often don't encode distance information when doing balance-scale problems.

Our initial problem representations are important because they shape the course of our problem solving. The initial representation determines what we take to be the initial state and can influence what we take to be the goal and the legal operators. In this way, the initial representation constrains what cognitive psychologists call the solver's *problem space*. The problem space is the set of all possible knowledge states the solver can construct from the initial state using the legal operators. Using the operators, then, the solver can generate many possible paths, or chains of knowledge states. Some of the possible paths lead to the goal; others do not. Solving a problem consists of using the operators to find a path of knowledge states from the initial state to the goal state. A poor initial representation can make an easy problem hard or impossible. The poor initial representation of the nine-dot problem results in a choice of legal moves that can't lead to a solution. The problem space is so small that there are no paths from the initial state to the goal. A good initial representation and a suitable problem space, in contrast, can make an otherwise hard problem trivial.

Analyzing the Task

Knowing how you behaved in tackling the nine-dot problem, I could tell how you represented, or understood, the problem. I could predict something about your psychology, your internal symbol processing. How is this possible? The trick is that more information is available to me than just your performance on the problem. I have a complete understanding of the task and what it demands. I know as a matter of geometrical fact that there are only two options for drawing the straight lines: either they stay within the boundary or they go outside. I also know that there is no solution using only lines that fall inside the boundary. What I know about the task and about your problem-solving behavior allows me to figure out how you must have understood the task. I can figure out what representation you used.

In the same way, cognitive scientists can discover what representations and rules people use on more complex problems. Cognitive psychologists begin their research on problem solving with what they call a *task analysis*. They try to define what the major variables and causes are in a given type of problem. They try to figure out what knowledge and skills the problem demands, and given those demands, what ideal performance on the problem would be. Scientifically, task analysis is essential for solving the problem that cognitive scientists have set for themselves. We can think of what cognitive scientists are trying to do in terms of an equation:

Task demands + Subject's psychology = Behavior.

Most of the time, cognitive psychologists are trying to solve this equation for "Subject's psychology," the subject's unobservable mental processing. To do so they need values for the other two variables. They can observe a subject's behavior, and task analysis gives values for the "Task demands" variable. If they have possible values for the "Task demands" and "Behavior" variables, they can derive values for "Subject's psychology." Of course, we should not overinterpret this analogy. Doing cognitive research is not as simple as solving an equation. Exacting task analysis and careful observation of behavior place constraints on the subject's psychology, but may not uniquely determine it. Task analysis plus behavior allows researchers to formulate intelligent hypotheses about subjects' psychology that they can put to further experimental tests. This is what Siegler did with children who were solving balance-scale problems.

Analyzing the Balance-Scale Task

In the late 1920s, the psychologist Jean Piaget opened up a new intellectual world with his scientific studies of children's thinking, which ranged across all domains of reasoning—logical, quantitative, spatial, and causal. Piaget held that children's thinking develops from infancy through adolescence in a series of discrete stages. At each successive stage, children acquire increasingly sophisticated, abstract, logical structures that guide their reasoning across all domains (Inhelder and Piaget 1958). Modern researchers have refined, corrected, and sometimes overturned Piaget's original interpretations and some aspects of his theory, but his groundbreaking research shaped the course and agenda of research on cognitive development. One of the tasks Piaget used in his studies was the balance scale; understandably, a body of research has grown up around that task.

The beauty of the balance-scale task for developmental psychology is that it is complex enough to be interesting but simple enough for exhaustive task analysis. Two variables are relevant: the amount of weight on each arm and the distance of the weight from the fulcrum. There are three discrete outcomes: tip left, tip right, and balance. There is a simple law, the law of torques, that solves all balance-scale problems, though few of us discover this law on our own. If weight and distance are the only two relevant variables and if the scale either tips or balances, there are only six possible kinds of balance-scale problem:

· balance problems—equal weight on each side and the weights at equal distances from the fulcrum;
· weight problems—unequal weight on each side and the weights equal distance from the fulcrum;
· distance problems—equal weight on each side and the weights at unequal distances from the fulcrum;
· conflict-weight—one side has more weight, the other side has its weight at a greater distance from the fulcrum, and the side with greater weight goes down;

• conflict-distance—one side has more weight, the other side has its weight at a greater distance from the fulcrum, and the side with greater distance goes down;
• conflict-balance—one side has more weight, the other side has its weight at a greater distance from the fulcrum, and the scale balances.

Robert Siegler called the last three types "conflict" problems, because when one side has more weight but the other side has its weight farther from the fulcrum one can have conflicting intuitions about which variable dominates. (The problem illustrated in figure 2.1 is a conflict-distance problem: there is more weight on the left side, the weight is farther from the fulcrum on the right side, and the right side goes down.)

These six possibilities cover all possible cases for how weight and distance influence the action of the scale. The six cases provide a complete theory, or task analysis, of the balance scale. Notice that the six problem types place varying demands on the solver. For a balance problem or a weight problem, a solver need only consider weight. For the conflict problems, a solver has to pay attention to weight, distance, and the ways in which weight and distance interact.

Siegler formulated some psychological hypotheses about how people might solve balance-scale problems. Using the information from the task analysis, he could test his hypotheses by giving subjects problems and observing their performance. Siegler called his hypotheses "rules" and formulated them as four production-system programs. His rules I–III are given in figure 2.6; his rule IV is the expert's production system of figure 2.2 above.

The rules make different assumptions about how and when people use weight or distance information to solve the problems. Rule I considers only weight. Rule II considers distance, but only when the weights on the two sides are equal (P3). Rule III attempts to integrate weight and distance information (P4 and P5). Rule IV introduces the law of torques (P4) when one side has more weight but less distance.

Knowing the task and having hypotheses about the subjects' psychology gave Siegler values for two of the three variables in the cognitivist's equation that interrelates task, psychology, and behavior. This allowed him to generate values for the behavior variable. He could predict how subjects would perform. Siegler analyzed how the four rules worked on the six kinds of problems and determined that each rule would give a distinct pattern of right and wrong

RULE I

> **P I** **IF** wieght is the same
> **THEN** say "balance".
>
> **P2** **IF** side X has more weight
> **THEN** say "X down".

RULE II

> **P I** **IF** weight is the same
> **THEN** say "balance".
>
> **P2** **IF** side X has more weight
> **THEN** say "X down".
>
> **P3** **IF** weight is the same **AND** side X has more distance
> **THEN** say "X down".

RULE III

> **P I** **IF** weight is the same
> **THEN** say "balance".
>
> **P2** **IF** side X has more weight
> **THEN** say " X down".
>
> **P3** **IF** weight is the same **AND** side X has more distance
> **THEN** say "X down".
>
> **P4** **IF** side X has more weight **AND** side X has less distance
> **THEN** make an educated guess.
>
> **P5** **IF** side X has more weight **AND** side X has more distance
> **THEN** say "X down".

Figure 2.6
Siegler's rules I–III for the balance-scale task. (From Siegler and Klahr 1982, p. 198. Used with permission of Lawrence Erlbaum Associates.)

answers. By giving a subject a set of problems that contain several examples of each problem type, Siegler could tell which rule the subject was using.

Figure 2.7 presents the pattern of performance Siegler predicted. Notice that if there are three outcomes for a balance-scale task—tip left, tip right, and balance—then 33 percent correct is chance performance; it amounts to a guess. Guessing is clearly distinguishable from always being wrong about a problem type (getting 0 percent correct). Notice, too, that sometimes adopting a more advanced rule can result in lower rather than higher performance on some problems. Going from rule II to rule III improves overall performance, but using rule III lowers performance on conflict-weight problems from 100 percent to 33 percent correct.

Finding Out What Children Know

If children use Siegler's rules, then the pattern of a child's responses to a set of balance-scale problems that contains all six types will reveal what rule that child uses. Children's responses will tell us what they know about the balance-scale task, including how they represent the problem. Siegler tested his hypotheses and predictions by giving a battery of 30 balance-scale problems to a group of 40 children that included equal numbers of 5-year-olds, 9-year-olds, 13-year-olds, and 17-year-olds. He showed each child a balance scale that had weights placed on it and asked the child to predict what the scale would do. As soon as the child made a prediction, Siegler rearranged the weights for the next problem. He did not let the children see if their predictions were correct, because he wanted to find out what they knew initially. He wanted to avoid giving the students feedback on their performance so he could be sure they weren't learning about the task during the experiment. He wanted to look at their learning, but only after he assessed their initial understanding.

The children's performance confirmed Siegler's hypotheses. Ninety percent of them made predictions that followed the pattern associated with one of the four rules. There was also a strong developmental trend. The 5-year-olds most often used rule I. The 9-year-olds used rule II or rule III. The 13- and 17-year-olds used rule III. Only two children, a 9-year-old and a 17-year-old, used rule IV. The developmental trend matched almost exactly the pattern of predictions in figure 2.7. The developmental trend, like the pattern of

RULE

Problem Type	I	II	III	IV
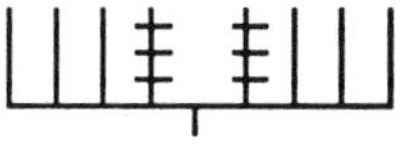 (Balance)	100	100	100	100
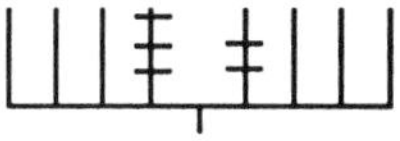 (Weight)	100	100	100	100
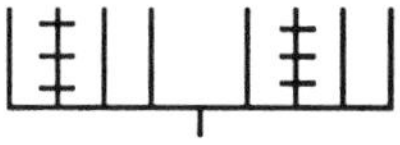 (Distance)	0	100	100	100
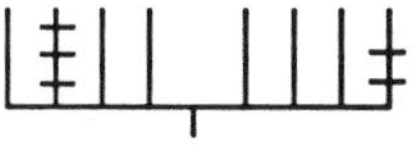 (Conflict-Weight)	100	100	33	100
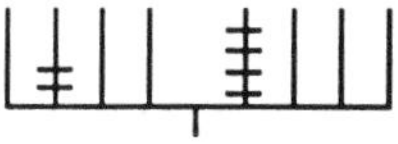 (Conflict-Distance)	0	0	33	100
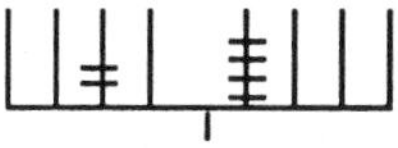 (Conflict-Balance)	0	0	33	100

Balance

Weight

Distance

Conflict-Weight

Conflict-Distance

Conflict-Balance

Figure 2.7
Siegler's predictions of the percentage of each type of balance–scale problem a subject would solve correctly using various rules. (Adapted from Siegler 1985, p. 168. Used with permission of Lawrence Erlbaum Associates.)

predictions, included a decrease in performance on conflict-weight problems as the children grew older. The 5-year-old children, the majority of whom used rule I, answered 86 percent of the conflict-weight problems correctly. The 13-year-olds and the 17-year-olds, most of whom had progressed to rule III, answered only 50 percent of the conflict-weight problems correctly.

As these results confirm, Siegler's rules qualify as a cognitive and developmental theory for the balance scale. As a cognitive theory should, his rules explain behavior in terms of symbol structures that children have stored in their long-term memories. The individual rules tell us what knowledge children use. The production system tells us how they organize their knowledge. Chunks of information which children encode from the task environment or generate in working memory are the conditions that cause the rules to fire. When written in a suitable computer language, the rules can be run as programs on computers, and they simulate human performance. As a good cognitive theory should, the theory embodied in Siegler's rules performs the task it explains and explains the task in terms of representations and mental processes.

Taken together, Siegler's four rules constitute a developmental theory that explains development in terms of changes in knowledge structures and problem representations. By age 5, most children are using rule I. By age 13, almost all are using rule III. Few children spontaneously progress to rule IV, which represents expert performance on the balance scale. Thus, the rules chart a course of normal development on the task, from novice to expert performance.

Siegler's rules also tell us what cognitive changes underlie the transition from novice to expert. On tasks like the balance scale, children progress through a series of partial understandings that gradually approach mastery. Performance improves, or learning occurs, when children add more effective production rules to the theories they have stored in long-term memory. Chunking plays a role in this process. Children chunk information about weight and distance to construct more complex condition clauses and build more sophisticated rules. The balance-scale task presents a simple example of how, as children develop or learn, the chunks or concepts they use in problem solving become larger and richer. Bigger chunks, more complex concepts, and better rules are ways in which experts differ from novices, not only on the balance-scale task, but in most subjects and problem domains.

Siegler's four rules, viewed as a developmental theory, are also a simple example of how, as Robert Glaser claimed, cognitive science can give us developmental theories of performance change. If we know what the developmental stages are and how they differ at the level of detail provided by a cognitive theory, we ought to be able to design instruction to help children advance from one stage to the next. We might be able to improve children's learning. Siegler's work on the balance-scale task, as we shall see below, is an example of this as well.

Experts and Response-Time Studies

Those familiar with physics or computer programs might question the claim that rule IV captures an expert's understanding of the balance scale. After all, we know that the law of torques is a universal rule for solving balance-scale problems. We also know that it is easy to write a computer program that computes torques: Enter the weight and distance information for each side. Multiply weight by distance for each side. If the products are the same, print "balance"; otherwise print out which side has the greater torque.

Rule IV is more complex. According to this rule an expert resorts to computing torques only in certain situations. How can a cognitive scientist claim that experts use rule IV and don't simply compute torques on all problems?

We can't decide between the two theories by looking at right and wrong answers, because both rule IV and the law of torques solve *all* problems correctly. But once we have two different expert programs that solve all the same problems, we can appeal to a different kind of data to tell which one experts really use. Some computer programs, even programs that for the same input generate the same output, can differ in how long they take to complete the computation. This can occur when one program contains more steps or takes more steps to find an answer for certain patterns of input. Rule IV and the law of torques might differ in just this way. Maybe we can look at how long it takes experts to solve certain kinds of balance-scale problems and figure out from their response times which of the two programs they use.

From the perspective of a response-time study, every balance-scale problem falls into one of two groups. We can solve balance, weight, and distance problems without computing torques, but to solve most conflict problems we have to compute torques. If experts always compute torques, then they use the same program on all problems and their response times should be the same for all problems. If experts use rule IV, then they first try to solve the problem without computing torques, and they do the numerical computation only as a last resort. This means that experts' response times on conflict problems should be longer than their response times on balance, weight, and distance problems.

Siegler tested twelve adult experts and found that they solved balance, weight, and distance problems in 1.5 to 2 seconds. To solve conflict problems, the experts took 3 to 3.5 seconds. Using response-time data, we can conclude that experts don't compute torques on all problems. Experts use rule IV.

Our ability to describe problem solving at a detailed level sometimes allows us to compare theories as we would compare computer programs. Response-time measures give us additional data that might support one cognitive theory over another. This method of response-time analysis has been particularly useful in discovering the methods children use to solve simple arithmetic problems.

Why do experts use rule IV and not the simpler law of torques? Expert behavior on the balance-scale task is just one example of how we unconsciously adopt strategies to minimize demands on working memory. To solve balance, weight, and distance problems, all we have to remember is which weight and which distance is greater. That is, we need only two items of comparative, qualitative information. To compute torques we have to remember the exact values of four numbers. Experts use the less demanding qualitative solution whenever they can and avoid committing any more cognitive capacity to a task than is necessary. The ability to manage cognitive resources efficiently and often unconsciously when solving problems in a knowledge domain is a sign of expertise in that domain.

The Balance Scale and Learning

So far, we have seen how cognitive research can generate theories about children's knowledge and how they use it to solve problems. With theories like Siegler's that describe what goes on at discrete levels of performance, we also can begin to investigate how children make transitions between levels; that is, we can study how children learn and how they might learn most effectively.

To investigate how children learn about the balance scale, Siegler conducted a training study. Working with 5-year-olds and 8-year-olds, all of whom used rule I, he had each child make predictions for 16 problems. After each prediction, Siegler released the lock on the balance scale and let the child see if his or her prediction was correct. This feedback experience gave the children an opportunity to learn about the balance scale. Two days later, the children had a retest with no feedback to see if they had learned anything from the training.

In this experiment, there were three training groups. One group of 5- and 8-year-olds served as a control group. Their training session consisted only of balance and weight problems—problems they could solve using rule I. A second group had training on distance problems, where rule II, but not rule I, would work. A third group had training on conflict problems, which require at least rule III for performance even at chance levels. With this training, would the children learn anything? Would they progress from rule I to a more advanced rule?

As expected, the children in the control group made no progress. They learned nothing from training on problems they already knew how to solve. The children in the second group, both 5- and 8-year-olds trained on distance problems, did learn something. Feedback from 16 problems was enough for these children to advance from rule I to rule II. The surprise came with the third group, the children who had training on conflict problems. The 8-year-olds in this group advanced two levels in their mastery of the balance scale, from rule I to rule III. *The 5-year-olds in this group either stayed at rule I or became so confused and erratic that it appeared they were no longer using a rule.*

From a researcher's perspective, this is a troubling result. Even if we have detailed knowledge about children's initial understanding, we can't necessarily predict how children will respond to training. There must be more involved in learning than an interaction between the children's current rule and the training they receive. Educationally, the result is even more worrisome. In most classrooms, teachers don't have the time or the tools to figure out what knowledge children have before instruction. Teachers have to give the same lessons to everyone and expect, or hope, that all students respond to instruction in approximately the same way. In view of Siegler's result, this is an unrealistic expectation.

Protocol Analysis, Encoding, and Representations

How are 8-year-olds different from 5-year-olds? Why do the older children, but not the younger children, learn from training on conflict problems? To answer this question, the cognitive scientist needs finer-grained data than are provided by task analyses, response patterns, and response times. Cognitive scientists use a method called *protocol analysis* to collect such fine-grained data.

Problem solving occurs in working memory, and we are consciously aware of at least some of the information our working memory contains. Parts of working memory are highly auditory—we can hear what's going on there. When we want to remember a phone number or the items we have to pick up at the supermarket, we often keep the information active in working memory by repeating it over and over to ourselves. More important, in solving problems, or even doing daily tasks, we often silently tell ourselves what to do as we go along. While we cook, solve crossword puzzles, or do geometry problems, we silently talk our way to a solution.

Protocol analysis exploits this "talking to ourselves" feature of working memory. To collect fine-grained, moment-by-moment data on a subject's cognitive processing, researchers have the subject "think aloud" while solving a problem. They instruct the subject to say everything he is thinking while engaged in a task. They then transcribe and analyze the verbal protocols. Often, the protocols provide data for computer simulations of problem-solving behavior.

Protocol analysis is a fundamental method of cognitive research. Alan Schoenfeld (1987, p. 1) admits that "spending 100 hours analyzing a single 1-hour videotape for a problem-solving session, and perhaps 2 or 3 years writing computer programs that 'simulate' the behavior that appeared in that 1 hour of problem solving, must appear odd to someone looking from outside the discipline." However, this often meticulous obsession with detail is what gives cognitive research its unique strengths and sets it apart from earlier attempts to understand mental functioning.

To find out why the 8-year-olds learned and the 5-year-olds didn't, Siegler and his collaborators selected several children between 5 and 10 years old for in-depth study (Klahr and Siegler 1978). Each child had a training session with the balance scale that included conflict problems. In the training session the child was asked to make a prediction for each problem and to state his or her reasons for the prediction. The experimenter then unlocked the scale's arm and the child observed the result. If the prediction was not borne out, the experimenter asked "Why do you think that happened?" The researchers videotaped the entire session with each child and transcribed all the children's verbal responses.

Lisa, a typical 5-year-old, took 30 minutes to do 16 problems. Protocols like Lisa's suggested that the younger children were not encoding or representing weight in their initial interpretations of balance-scale problems. For example, when Lisa was given a distance problem (on the left side, one weight on peg 3; on the right side, one weight on peg 1), she predicted the scale would balance—"They would both stay up," she said. Asked why she thought this, she answered "'Cause they are both the same." When she saw the left side tip down, she was genuinely puzzled: "Well, why are they both the same thing and one's up and one's down?" Lisa did not see any difference between the two sides. She was not including distance information in her initial representation of the problem. She simply did not notice and encode distance information.

An 8-year-old's protocol gave very different data. Jan was given a conflict-distance problem: on the left side, three weights on the first peg; on the right side, two weights on the third peg. She predicted incorrectly that the left side would go down. When shown what really happens (right side down) and asked for an explanation, she gave one involving both weight and distance. For her, pegs 1 and 2 on each side were "near" the fulcrum and pegs 3 and 4 were "far" from the fulcrum. She stated a rule: "If far pegs have weights, then that side will go down." She then pointed out that in this problem the far pegs on the right side had weights but the far pegs on the left had none, so the right side would go down. Jan's is not a perfect explanation, nor is her rule always true. Her protocol shows, though, that she, unlike Lisa, had noticed and encoded both weight and distance information in her representation of the problem.

On the basis of the protocols, the difference between 5-year-olds and 8-year-olds seemed to be that the younger children saw the problems in terms of weight only, whereas the older children could see the problems in terms of weight at a distance from the fulcrum. If the younger children were not encoding distance, they could not learn from training on conflict problems that differences in distance sometimes overcome differences in weight. They could not develop the concepts or build the chunks they needed for the conditions of

P4 and P5 in rule III. On the other hand, the older children, even if they were using rule I, appeared to encode distance. They could learn from training on conflict problems how to use that information to build new productions and progress to rule III.

Protocol analysis is so detailed and time consuming that researchers usually do it on only a few subjects, but these detailed analyses often suggest hypotheses that can be tested on larger groups of subjects. That is what happened here. To test possible encoding differences between 5-year-olds and 8-year-olds, Siegler presented each child with 16 problems, one at a time. The child saw the pattern of weights for 10 seconds, after which the experimenter hid the scale from sight. The experimenter then asked the child to recreate the configuration, or "make the same problem" from memory, by placing weights on the pegs of a second, identical scale. The results confirmed the hypothesis suggested by the protocol analysis. Five-year-olds were much more accurate in encoding weight than distance. They reproduced weight information correctly 51 percent of the time, but distance information correctly only 16 percent of the time. Eight-year-olds were more highly accurate on both dimensions: 73 percent correct for weight and 56 percent correct for distance information. The 5-year-old rule I users weren't encoding enough about the problem into their representations to benefit from training on conflict problems. The 8-year-old rule I users, on the other hand, were encoding information about distance that they were not using spontaneously to make predictions about the balance scale's actions. Training on conflict problems prompted the older children to see the relevance of the distance information, incorporate it into a condition, and build new and better productions.

Can 5-year-olds learn to encode both weight and distance, or is it beyond their level of cognitive development? Siegler found that giving 5-year-olds more time to study the configurations or giving them more explicit instructions ("See how the weights are on the pegs? See how many are on each side and how far they are from the center on each side?") made no difference in their ability to reproduce the configurations from memory.

Only one intervention seemed to work. *The 5-year-olds had to be told explicitly what to encode and how to encode it.* The instructor had to tell them what was important and teach them a strategy for remembering it. The instructor taught the children to count the disks on the left side, count the pegs on the left side, and then rehearse the result (i.e., say aloud "three weights on peg 4"); to repeat this process for the right side; and then to rehearse both results together ("three weights on peg 4 and two weights on peg 3"). The instructor then told the children to try to reproduce the pattern their statement described. The instructor guided each child through this strategy on seven problems. With each problem, the children took more responsibility for executing the strategy.

After this training, the 5-year-olds' performance on reconstructing distance information from memory improved. They now correctly reproduced weight information 52 percent of the time, and distance information 51 percent of the time. Although they now apparently encoded the information, they, like the 8-year-old rule I users, did not spontaneously start using it. They continued to use rule I. However, when these 5-year-olds were given training on conflict problems, they too progressed from rule I to rule III. They had to be taught explicitly what representation to use in order to learn from the training experience.

The results of this study exemplify features of learning that are common to almost all school subjects. Students learn by modifying long-term memory structures, here called production systems. They modify their structures when they encounter problems their current rules can't solve. Some children modify their structures spontaneously; that is how children normally develop through Siegler's four rules. But by giving appropriate training we can facilitate children's development. For some children, presenting anomalous problems is enough. Like the 8-year-olds confronted with conflict problems, some children can build better rules when challenged with hard problems. Other children can't. Some children have inadequate initial representations of the problem. Children have to notice the information they need and encode it if they are to build better rules.

We have seen, too, how long-term memory structures, such as schemas and production systems, can influence what we notice, recall, and remember. The existing rules and the initial representations affect one another. Effective instruction must break into and change this interaction. Breaking into and changing the interaction often requires detailed, explicit instruction on what the initial representation should be. Often this instruction also has to include teaching an effective strategy for encoding and remembering. Students who can't learn spontaneously from new experiences need direct instruction about the relevant facts *and* about the strategies to use. Teaching just facts or teaching strategies in isolation from the facts won't work. The difficulties children have in learning about the balance scale are, as we shall see, highly similar to the difficulties they encounter in learning mathematics, science, and literacy skills.

From Rule III to Rule IV

The transition from rule III to rule IV is also of educational interest. Siegler almost did not include 17-year-olds in his original study. The principal of the school where he was doing the research assured him that high school juniors and seniors had already studied the balance scale and the law of torques at least twice and "knew all there was to know about it." Siegler tested the high school students anyway. Much to everyone's surprise, only 10 percent of the high school students used rule IV spontaneously and only 20 percent discovered it after a training session. This suggests that rule IV is deceptively difficult, that high school science education is inadequate, or (most likely) both.

What kind of instruction or training sessions might help older students learn rule IV? On the basis of task analysis and how the balance scale works, Siegler conjectured that there were at least two points where students might have trouble: they might not realize that balance-scale problems have quantitative, mathematical solutions; and, even if they did, they might have trouble figuring out which algebraic equation to apply to the four variables to find and compare torques. To address the first point, training should emphasize the quantitative nature of the task. Rather than just asking on each training problem "What do you think will happen?" one should say, for example, "Three weights on the third peg versus two weights on the fourth peg; what do you think will happen?" The second point could be addressed by giving the student an external memory aid. Each time the experimenter presents a training problem, he could give the student a diagram of the problem on a piece of paper. The student could keep the diagrams and refer to them during the training session. Then, when the student developed a hypothesis about a possible equation, he or she could check the hypothesis using the data from all the previous problems as shown on the diagrams.

In an experiment, Siegler gave 13- and 17-year-olds training experiences that included hints on quantitative encoding, or the external memory aid for hypothesis checking, or both. Most 17-year-olds progressed to rule IV with the help of either the encoding hints or the external memory aid. The 13-year-olds progressed to rule IV only if they had both kinds of help. The 17-year-olds also made their last error much earlier in the training session. Cognitively motivated training helped students in both age groups learn rule IV, but the 13-year-olds needed more help and learned more slowly. This simple instructional manipulation helped high school students learn a rule they had failed to master on two previous occasions in their formal science instruction.

Cognitive Research and Effective Instruction

In a summary of their work with the balance-scale task, Siegler and Klahr (1982, p. 197) conclude that their results "show that acquisition of new knowledge depends in predictable ways upon the interaction of existing knowledge, encoding processes, and the instructional environment." Their summary, like their work, contains all the elements that make cognitive research applicable to educational practice. The work builds on and supports the assumption that humans, like computers, are symbol processors. Task analysis, protocol analysis, response-time studies, and training studies reveal how our cognitive architecture works in solving problems.

The methods tell us about our psychology. They tell us about how we organize knowledge in long-term memory and how this knowledge interacts with our initial problem representations in working memory to guide our behavior. The research suggests that we learn by modifying existing memory structures, such as production systems. Learning can occur when new situations challenge our current theories. In some cases, though, we can learn from new experiences only if we receive explicit instruction about how to represent, or interpret, those experiences.

We want our educational system to help children—universal novices—become reasonably expert within certain domains of knowledge. To do this effectively, we have to know, in some detail, what stages children pass through on their mental journeys from novice to expert. Cognitive science tells us how we can then help children progress from relative naiveté through a series of partial understandings to eventual subject mastery.

Earlier in this chapter, we found it helpful to think of basic cognitive research as trying to solve an equation. If we have values for task demands and observed behavior, we can solve for the subjects' psychology; or with task analysis and psychological hypotheses we can, as Siegler did, predict behavior. Having data for any two variables lets us solve for the third. When we want to apply cognitive psychology to the design of effective instruction, we take the psychology and the behaviors as known and try to solve for the task-demand variable. We want to use what basic research tells us about our cognitive psychology, plus information about the behaviors or competencies we want students to have, to "solve for" (or generate hypotheses about) effective instructional tasks and learning environments. In view of what we know about children's cognitive psychology, what kinds of task environments will result in the expert behaviors we want? Those task environments are the instructional environments we should provide in our schools.

Siegler's work shows how cognitive science "provides an empirically based technology for determining people's existing knowledge, for specifying the form of likely future knowledge states, and for choosing the types of problems that lead from present to future knowledge" (Siegler and Klahr 1982, p. 134). The following chapters describe how researchers and teachers are applying this technology to improve classroom instruction. The tasks, representations, and production systems will become more complex—the progression from novice to expert can't be captured by four rules in every domain. However, our innate cognitive architecture remains the same no matter what domain we try to master, and the methods of cognitive science yield detailed information about how we think and learn. The lessons learned on the simple balance scale apply across the curriculum.

3

Intelligent Novices: Knowing How to Learn

Imagine that a small, peaceful country is being threatened by a large, belligerent neighbor. The small country is unprepared historically, temperamentally, and militarily to defend itself; however, it has among its citizens the world's reigning chess champion. The prime minister decides that his country's only chance is to outwit its aggressive neighbor. Reasoning that the chess champion is a formidable strategic thinker and a deft tactician—a highly intelligent, highly skilled problem solver—the prime minister asks him to assume responsibility for defending the country. Can the chess champion save his country from invasion?

This scenario is not a plot from a Franz Lehar operetta, but a thought experiment devised by David Perkins and Gavriel Salomon (1989). As they point out, our predictions about the chess champion's performance as national security chief depend on what we believe intelligence and expertise are. If the goal of education is to develop our children into intelligent subject-matter experts, our predictions about the chess champion, based on what we believe about intelligence and expertise, have implications for what we should do in our schools.

Since the mid 1950s cognitive science has contributed to the formulation and evolution of theories of intelligence, and so to our understanding of what causes skilled cognitive performance and what should be taught in schools. In this chapter, we will review how our understanding of intelligence and expertise has evolved over the past two decades and see how these theories have influenced educational policy and practice.

Four theories will figure in this story.

The oldest theory maintains that a student builds up his or her intellect by mastering formal disciplines, such as Latin, Greek, logic, and maybe chess. These subjects build minds as barbells build muscles. On this theory the chess champion might succeed in the national security field. If this theory is correct, these formal disciplines should figure centrally in school instruction.

In the early years of the cognitive revolution, it appeared that general skills and reasoning abilities might be at the heart of human intelligence and skilled performance. If this is so, again the chess champion might succeed, and schools should teach these general thinking and problem-solving skills—maybe even in separate critical-thinking and study-skills classes.

By the mid 1970s, cognitive research suggested that general domain-independent skills couldn't adequately account for human expertise. Researchers then began to think that the key to intelligence in a domain was extensive experience with and knowledge about that domain. Expertise was domain specific. This suggested that the chess expert was doomed to failure, and that schools should teach the knowledge, skills, and representations needed to solve problems within specific domains.

In the early 1980s researchers turned their attention to other apparent features of expert performance. They noticed that there were intelligent novices—people who learned new fields and solved novel problems more expertly than most, regardless of how much domain-specific knowledge they possessed. Intelligent novices controlled and monitored their thought processes and made use of general, domain-independent strategies and skills where appropriate. This suggested that there was more to expert performance than just domain-specific knowledge and skills.

Perkins and Salomon call this latest theory or view the "new synthesis," because it incorporates what was correct about the earlier views, while pointing out that none of the earlier theories alone provides an adequate basis for effective educational practice. According to the new synthesis, we should combine the learning of domain-specific subject matter with the learning of general thinking skills, while also making sure that children learn to monitor and control their thinking and learning.

The new synthesis introduces an important new idea into discussions about educational reform. The first three theories of intelligence emphasize *what* we should teach in our schools—formal disciplines, general thinking and learning skills, or domain-specific knowledge and skills. The new synthesis, as we shall see, implies that we should be as concerned with *how* we teach as we traditionally have been concerned with what we teach. The most recent research shows that if we can apply the new synthesis in the classroom, we should be able to teach school subjects as high-order cognitive skills and help children become intelligent novices and expert learners.

Transfer

What connects the chess champion, theories of intelligence, and schooling is a phenomenon psychologists and educators call *transfer*. We generally believe that learning a certain skill or subject area can help us learn a related one. If we first learn tennis, we should be able to learn squash more easily. If we learn Spanish as a second language, we should be able to learn Italian as a third language more easily. Knowledge from the first skill or domain should transfer to the second, so there is less to learn. Notice, though, that in neither of these examples are we simply applying previously learned knowledge. Squash isn't tennis, and Italian isn't Spanish. In these situations, we are using old skills or knowledge in novel situations where we also have to learn new things. One cognitive scientist describes it this way: "Transfer means applying old knowledge in a setting sufficiently novel that it also requires learning new knowledge." (Larkin 1989, p. 283)

If this description is correct, we should be able to tell when transfer occurs. If knowledge transfers from task A to task B, then people who have learned A should be able to learn B more rapidly than people who did not first learn A. A tennis player should be able to learn squash more rapidly than a person with no prior experience at racquet sports.

Transfer is central to designing and developing effective instruction. Problems of transfer pervade schooling. Teachers want to teach lessons so that students can transfer what they have learned during class instruction to solve new problems at the end of a chapter. We want that learning to transfer to the unit, semester, or standardized test. Most important, we want school learning to transfer to real-world problem solving at home and on the job. If this is our goal, what and how should we teach?

If we want to teach so as to promote transfer of knowledge, we have to answer a prior question: What kinds of knowledge and skills, if any, transfer between tasks? What, if anything, might transfer from chess to national security? Theories of intelligence and expertise suggest answers to this question. Theories differ in their claims about what, whether, and when knowledge transfers from one task or knowledge domain to another. Of the theories outlined above, the first says that general mental strength transfers, the second that general skills and strategies transfer, and the third that expertise is domain specific (so that we might find some transfer within a domain, but little or none across domains). The new synthesis suggests that transfer can occur within and across domains, but only if we teach students appropriately.

Formal Disciplines and Mental Fitness

Our oldest theory of expertise and intelligence goes back to the classical Greeks, who believed that mastering formal disciplines, such as arithmetic and geometry, would improve general intelligence and reasoning ability. By the eighteenth century, scholars had added grammar, mnemonics, Greek, and Latin to the list of disciplines that build mental fitness. The theory was that these difficult formal disciplines would build general mental strength, just as rigorous physical exercise builds physical strength. On this theory, if we believe that chess is a formal discipline on a par with logic and geometry, we might favor the chess master's chances.

Edward Thorndike's careful studies of learning and of what knowledge transfers from one subject to another were among scientific psychology's first contributions to education. (See Thorndike and Woodworth 1901.) At the turn of the twentieth century, when Thorndike did his work, the prevailing view, derived from the ancient Greeks, was that learning formal disciplines improved general mental functioning. Thorndike, however, noted that no one had presented scientific evidence to support this view. Thorndike reasoned that if learning Latin strengthens general mental functioning, then students who had learned Latin should be able to learn other subjects more quickly. He found no evidence of this. Having learned one formal discipline did not result in more efficient learning in other domains. Mental "strength" in one domain didn't transfer to mental strength in others. Thorndike's results contributed to the demise of this ancient theory of intelligence and to a decline in the teaching of formal disciplines as mental calisthenics.

However, in some experiments where two subject domains shared surface similarity, Thorndike did observe faster learning in the second domain. He proposed a theory of "identical elements" to explain this. Thorndike suggested that where two domains share common *elements of knowledge*—not formal rigor—a person who has learned one of them might be able to learn the second more quickly. But because psychologists at the turn of the century had no precise way to describe and identify "elements," Thorndike couldn't test his theory rigorously. The methods he needed were those that cognitive psychologists developed more than 50 years later.

Elements, Productions, and Transfer

Once psychologists accepted the assumption that our minds process symbols, and once they realized they could study minds as information-processing devices, it became possible to test theories such as Thorndike's. Psychologists, using the framework of computational theory, could describe "elements" as symbol structures and devise problem-solving simulations and experiments to see which symbol structures two disciplines might share.

Production systems are among the things that allow psychologists to test modern versions of Thorndike's theory. If minds are devices that execute production systems, and if (as on the balance scale) learning occurs when we add new productions to long-term memory, then we might be able to formulate and test Thorndike's claim. We can think of each individual production rule as a piece of knowledge needed for a task; we can think of it as one of Thorndike's elements. If so, the transfer of learning from one task to another should be directly related to the number of productions the tasks share.

M. K. Singley and John R. Anderson (1985) performed an elegant study to test this hypothesis. They studied the way in which secretarial students learned to use three different text editors or word processors. Two of the editors, ED and EDT, were line editors that allowed the user to edit one line of text at a time. EMACS was a screen editor, more like a standard word processor, that allowed the user to edit a document one screen at a time.

As is typical of cognitive scientists, Singley and Anderson first did a careful task analysis of the three editors. The two screen editors used different names for the editing commands and differed in how the user located a line to edit. Once past these superficial differences, however, they found that the production systems used to simulate expert performance on the two line editors were nearly identical. However, the production system that simulated expert performance on EMACS, the screen editor, was almost entirely different from those for the line editors. Thus, there was considerable production overlap between the line editors and almost none between the line editors and the screen editor.

How did this affect learning? Students who learned either line editor first took as long to learn the screen editor as students who started out on the screen editor. Skill on the line editors didn't transfer to the screen editor. In the case of the two line editors, students who learned one learned the second much more quickly. There was considerable transfer between the two line editors. Anderson (1985, p. 241) estimates that learning one of the line editors eliminated up to 90 percent of the work normally needed to learn the second. Singley and Anderson concluded that the amount of production overlap between two skills predicts the amount of transfer between the skills.

Relying on computational theory, production systems, and task analysis allowed cognitive science to make precise scientific sense of Thorndike's hypothesis. The information-processing approach can give us fine-grained representations—in this case, productions—of Thorndike's common elements. Cognitive research gives us methods for stating and testing claims about the transfer of knowledge between tasks.

General Methods and Intelligent Behavior

Cognitive scientists started applying computational insights to issues of expertise, intelligence, and transfer in the late 1950s. To understand their initial approach, recall the model of problem solving presented in chapter 2. As we saw there, problems have initial states and goal states. The solver chooses operators that create a chain of knowledge states linking the initial state to the goal. The operators, themselves composed of basic information processes, combine to form procedures or programs that guide problem-solving behavior.

How do we choose operators when solving problems? Cognitive scientists say that we use *methods* or *strategies* to choose them. Imagine we are playing chess. One method I might use to choose a move, or an operator, is to pick a piece at random or move the first piece I happen to touch. At the other extreme, I might choose my moves by following an opening I have studied in a chess book. An intermediate option would be to use a method based on general chess principles: I might choose my moves so as to control the center, defend my pieces, and attack yours. The same spectrum of methods or strategies is available for balance-scale problems. I might generate a prediction by randomly choosing among left, right, and balance. At the other extreme, I might use Siegler's rule IV, having studied it in a book.

These methods differ in ways that are more interesting than how often I would win the game or make a correct balance-scale prediction. First, they differ in how widely applicable they are. Second, they differ in what I have to know to use them. The method of choosing an operator at random works for any problem: I don't have to know anything about chess or balance scales to use random choice. In contrast, following a line from a chess book or using rule IV works only for chess or balance-scale problems. Furthermore, I have to know a lot about chess or balance scales to use a book or Siegler's rule. Cognitive psychologists call methods that are widely applicable and that require little or no specific knowledge *weak methods*. They call methods that are situation-specific and domain-specific *strong methods*. Random choice is a weak method; rule IV is a strong one. Psychologists see all strategies, procedures, and skills as falling somewhere on the continuum between weak and strong methods.

In the early days of computer and cognitive science, there were divergent views about how to make computers or people more intelligent. Some thought the key to understanding intelligent behavior, for both machines and humans, lay in developing and understanding weak methods that were applicable across many problem domains. Others thought the better scientific bet was to study the knowledge needed in specific domains and find the specific strong methods that experts used.

Initial successes in artificial intelligence research suggested that weak methods were the way to go. Logic Theorist could prove logical theorems. A second-generation machine, called General Problem Solver, could solve problems in a variety of domains, including algebra, geometry, and chess (Ernst and Newell 1969). These programs used weak methods such as *hill climbing* and *means-end analysis*.

Hill climbing is a weak method that chooses intelligent next moves on a problem if the problem requires progress along a single dimension. If you were trying to find the top of a hill in the dark, you would keep taking steps that tended in an upward direction. When you couldn't take any more upward steps, you would stop, assuming you had reached the top of the hill. The children's game of helping a playmate find a hidden object by giving clues of "hotter" and "colder" as the playmate moves toward or away from the object is a hill-climbing game.

Means-end analysis, the method General Problem Solver used, is more complex. Hill climbing considers only one difference between the current and goal states—in the children's game, all that matters is distance from the hidden object. Means-end analysis identifies several differences between the current situation and the goal, then picks an action or an operator that will reduce one or more of those differences. If more than one action or operator could be used, means-end analysis chooses the one whose conditions of applicability best match the current situation. Sometimes, after choosing the action best suited to the situation, one still can't execute the action because the conditions aren't right. In this case, means-end analysis establishes a subgoal to create conditions that permit the chosen action.

The wide applicability of means-end analysis is suggested by the example Newell and Simon (1972, p. 416) used:

I want to take my son to nursery school. What is the difference between what I have and what I want? One of distance. What changes distance? My automobile. My automobile won't work. What is needed to make it work? A new battery. What has new batteries? An auto repair shop. I want the shop to put in a new battery; but the shop doesn't know I need one. What is the difficulty? One of communication. What allows communication? A telephone . . . and so on.

The solver here looks at where he is and where he wants to be, then works back and forth between the ends and the means to achieve those ends until he has a set of actions, or operators, that achieve the goal. His finding a telephone starts a chain of events that results in his son's arriving at nursery school. Students often use means-end analysis to solve school math and science problems.

In the late 1960s and the early 1970s, programs such as General Problem Solver suggested that general skills might be fundamental to human expertise and intelligence. If we could identify and teach such general skills, maybe we could improve human problem-solving performance both in and out of school. If general methods, skills, and strategies are the basis of the chess champion's expertise, maybe he can succeed at solving diplomatic problems.

Experts' Domain-Specific Knowledge

Research to extend the initial insight about the contribution of weak methods to human intelligence met with frustration. The research community soon realized there was a serious limitation on the early successes. The early AI programs, including General Problem Solver, simulated intelligent performance on games or formal, logical problems (e.g., solving number puzzles or proving logical theorems)—but playing games and solving formal problems demand little factual knowledge about the world. To succeed at these tasks requires knowledge of little more than the rules of the game or the rules of the formal system. However, problem solving in other domains, such as physics or medical diagnosis, requires considerably more factual knowledge. Just think about what you have to know to play tic-tac-toe versus what you have to know to solve a physics problem. When cognitive scientists started to explore some of these other more knowledge-rich areas, physics and medicine among them, they found that weak methods didn't work so well. In knowledge-rich domains, they found that strong methods tailor-made to work on specific, well-organized knowledge bases worked better.

Weak methods might work in domains where there is little factual knowledge, but one can't generalize from these puzzle domains to a general theory of human intelligence and expertise. As Marvin Minsky and Seymour Papert (1974, p. 59) wrote, "It is by no means obvious that very smart people are that way directly because of the superior power of their general methods—as compared with average people." Maybe expert, intelligent behavior depends crucially on the knowledge people have, how they organize it, and the specific methods they learn or develop to process it.

Data from psychological experiments also undermined the primacy of weak, general methods for human expertise. One of the most influential experiments was William Chase and Herb Simon's (1973) study of novice and expert chess players, which followed on earlier work by A. D. De Groot (1965). Chase and Simon showed positions from *actual* chess games to subjects for 5 to 10 seconds and asked the subjects to reproduce the positions from memory. Each position contained 25 chess pieces. Expert players could accurately place 90 percent of the pieces, novices only 20 percent. Chase and Simon then had the subjects repeat the experiment, but this time the "positions" consisted of 25 pieces placed randomly on the board. These were generally not positions that would occur in an actual game. The experts were no better than the novices at reproducing the random positions: both experts and novices could place only five or six pieces correctly.

Other researchers replicated the Chase-Simon experiment in a variety of domains, using children, college students, and adults. The results were always the same: Experts had better memories for items in their area of expertise, but not for items in general. This shows, first, that mastering a mentally demanding game does not improve mental strength in general. The improved memory performance is domain specific. Chess isn't analogous to a barbell for the mind. Second, it shows that if memory *strategies* account for the expert's improved memory capacity, the strategies aren't general strategies or weak methods. Chess experts have better memories for genuine chess positions, but not for random patterns of chess pieces or for strings of words or digits. Thus, experts aren't using some general memory strategy that transfers from chess positions to random patterns of pieces or to digit strings.

From long experience at the game, chess experts have developed an extensive knowledge base of perceptual patterns, or chunks. Cognitive scientists estimate that chess experts learn about 50,000 chunks, and that it takes about 10 years to learn them. Chunking explains the difference between novice and expert performance. Reproducing chessboard configurations after 5 to 10 seconds of study is a working-memory task, because there is not enough time to code and store the information in long-term memory. When doing this task, novices see the chessboard in terms of individual pieces. They can store only the positions of five or six pieces in working memory—numbers close to what we found our own working memory spans to be on the basis of the experiment discussed in chapter 2. Experts see "chunks," or patterns, of several pieces. If each chunk contains four or five pieces and if the expert can hold five such chunks in working memory, then the expert can reproduce accurately the positions of 20 to 25 individual pieces. Chase and Simon even found that when experts reproduced the positions on the board, they did it in chunks. They rapidly placed four or five pieces, then paused before reproducing the next chunk.

Expertise, these studies suggest, depends on highly organized, domain-specific knowledge that can arise only after extensive experience and practice in the domain. Siegler's balance-scale study (chapter 2) is another example. Under normal conditions, it takes a child at least 17 years to become expert at balance-scale problems. More knowledge about and experience with the balance scale results in more sophisticated, expert-like performance. Chunking helps children develop more complex rules that contribute to their growing expertise on the balance-scale task.

Other studies of problem solving also argue against general strategies. Try to solve the two problems illustrated in figure 3.1. Philip Johnson-Laird (1983, p. 30) found an interesting difference in individuals' abilities to solve them. This is interesting because formally, or logically, they are the same problem. The same general strategy or formal rule solves both.

The correct answers are "E and 7" and "Manchester and car." Many people answer, incorrectly, that they have to turn only E, or else E and 4, in the first problem. You do have to turn E, because if that card has an odd number on the other side the rule is false. You don't have to turn 4, because even if that card had a consonant on the other side it doesn't matter; the rule doesn't say anything about what is on the other side of a consonant card. You have to turn 7, because a vowel on the other side of that card would make the rule false. The same problem-solving strategy works for the second problem, and for any "if-then" rule as logicians interpret such statements. (According to the laws of logic, an "if-then" statement is false only in the case where the "if" clause is true and the "then" clause is false; in every other case the statement is true.)

The two problems in figure 3.1 differ only in their subject matter. The first problem is an abstract one about letters and numbers, but the second one deals with a possible real-life situation. Johnson-Laird's subjects were much better at the second problem. Only 12 percent of them said they would turn over the "7" card to test the first rule, but over 60 percent said they would turn over the "car" card to test the second rule. Furthermore, he found that giving subjects experience with real-life if-then problems didn't improve their performance on more abstract versions. Apparently, most of

1. Each of the following four cards has a number on one side and a letter on the other side. Pick the cards you have to turn over to find out if this general rule is true or false:

   If a card has a vowel on one side then it has an even number on the other side.

2. Each of the following cards has a destination on one side and a mode of transport on the other side. Pick the cards you have to turn over to find out if this statement is true or false:

   Every time I go to Manchester I travel by train.

Figure 3.1
These two problems are logically the same; they differ only in their content. (From Johnson-Laird 1983.)

us don't use a general rule or strategy to solve these problems. If we did, we would use the same rule to solve all such problems. There would be no difference between performance on number–letter problems and on destination–transportation problems. In other experiments, researchers report that the ability to transfer a solution from one version of a problem to another occurs only if the experimenter *explicitly tells* subjects that the two problems are the same. For some reason, what the problem is about and how familiar we are with that content affects our problem solving. It seems as if domain-specific knowledge *does* contribute to expert performance.

It also appears that the ability to use general strategies at all depends on the subject's having a knowledge base on which the strategies can work. When an experimenter asks subjects to memorize lists of words (e.g., "dog, gold, carrots, diamond, cat, peas"), subjects rarely repeat the words in that order. Usually, subjects say something like "dog, cat, carrots, peas, gold, diamond." To remember the words, subjects group them into meaningful categories—here animal, vegetable, and mineral. Psychologists call this often-unconscious strategy *clustering*. Clustering helps us remember things by exploiting the schema structure of long-term memory; we remember the words by associating them with the appropriate schemas.

When college students and young children were the subjects in such experiments, psychologists found that the college students recalled more words and did more clustering. Initially, psychologists attributed young children's poor performance to their inability to use the clustering strategy. Later it was discovered that if the word list included things young children know more about than college students, the results would be different (Lindberg 1980). If the experimenter used a 30-word list that included names of children's television celebrities, cartoon stars, and comic book characters, young children recalled more and used more clustering than the college students. Thus, there is an interaction between knowledge and strategy use—between facts and skills. Subjects are more likely to use a general memory strategy the more they know about a domain or a topic. Strategies can help us process knowledge, but first we have to have the knowledge to process.

While granting the possibility that strategies might play some role in problem solving, by the mid 1970s many cognitive scientists had come to believe that domain-specific knowledge and strong methods are the bases of expertise and intelligence—that the chess champion would fail to deter the belligerent neighbor nation. If they are right, there may not be a simple way to make people better general problem solvers. Siegler (1985, p. 184) sums up what this means for education: "Seen from this perspective, much of the task of education in problem solving may be to identify the encoding that we would like people to have on specific problems, and then to devise instructional methods to help them attain it." In other words, the educational challenge might be to identify the representations we want students to have in *specific domains* and then develop methods and curricula to teach those representations.

Weak Methods in the Schools

Despite this theoretical shift within the cognitive science community from favoring general strategies to arguing for domain-specific knowledge and skills, some educators still advocate teaching weak, general strategies. If children need thinking and learning skills but don't have them, they argue, the best educational strategy might be to teach those skills directly. Maybe teaching weak, general methods—skills that apply across the curriculum—can serve as a shortcut to higher intelligence and better school performance. Unfortunately, weak methods as they are traditionally taught seem to have little impact on student learning.

Traditional study and learning skills, though less general than means-end analysis, are general, weak methods. These skills are often the staples of junior high language-arts classes—taking notes, outlining, underlining, and figuring out words from context. We all believe that these strategies work, but research on traditional study skills shows that these skills are no more effective than simply reading and rereading a text. (See Anderson 1980.) Other researchers who have looked at the impact of teaching general reading-comprehension skills have found that teaching these skills increases students' awareness of the skills. However, even when students say they use the skills, the skills have little effect on their reading comprehension (Paris and Jacobs 1984). Similarly, the teaching of study or memorization skills in one subject has no impact on students' performance in other subjects. Often, it doesn't even occur to students to use the skills when studying a different subject. Typically, children will use strategies immediately after instruction, but will not use them on later occasions unless explicitly told to do so by the instructor.

Research shows that either the teaching of traditional study skills has no impact on learning or else the skills fail to transfer from the learning context to other situations. Either way, teaching these general skills is not the path to expertise and enhanced academic performance.

A wide variety of books and commercially available courses attempt to teach general cognitive and thinking skills. (For reviews and evaluations see Nickerson et al. 1985, Segal et al. 1985, and Chipman et al. 1985.) Analysis and evaluation of these programs again fail to support the belief that the teaching of general skills enhances students' overall performance.

Most of these programs teach general skills in stand-alone courses, separate from subject-matter instruction. The assumption is that students would find it too difficult to learn how to think and to learn subject content simultaneously. Like the early AI and cognitive science that inspire them, the courses contain many formal problems, logical puzzles, and games. The assumption is that the general, weak methods that work on these problems will work on problems in all subject domains.

A few of these programs, such as the Productive Thinking Program (Covington 1985) and Instrumental Enrichment (Feuerstein et al. 1985), have undergone extensive evaluation. The evaluations consistently report that students improve on problems like those contained in the course materials but show only limited improvement on novel problems or problems unlike those in the materials (Mansfield et al. 1978; Savell et al. 1986). The programs provide extensive practice on the specific kinds of problems that their designers want children to master. Children do improve on those problems, but this is different from developing *general* cognitive skills. After reviewing the effectiveness of several thinking-skills programs, one group of psychologists concluded that "there is no strong evidence that students in any of these thinking-skills programs improved in tasks that were dissimilar to those already explicitly practiced" (Bransford et al. 1985, p. 202). Students in the programs don't become more intelligent generally; the general problem-solving and thinking skills they learn do not transfer to novel problems. Rather, the programs help students become experts in the domain of puzzle problems.

The evaluations of these programs undercut the basic assumption about the power of weak methods in another way, too. If general skills, or weak methods, are the stuff of intelligence, then teaching these skills to students who had not previously used them should improve their performance. This doesn't happen. The programs don't help all students who were initially naive about the general skills taught. Typically, these programs help low-performing students most, average students some, and more able students hardly at all (Nickerson et al. 1985, p. 325).

Although we should not dismiss approaches that might help low-achieving students, this inverse pattern—low achievers benefiting most and high achievers hardly at all—is exactly what we would expect if school performance depends on domain-specific knowledge and strong methods. Low-performing students have neither general cognitive skills nor domain-specific knowledge. Teaching low achievers general skills can only help. The higher the level of initial performance, though, the more domain-specific knowledge a child has. If you have domain-specific knowledge and strong methods to go with it, why use weak ones? If you know all the standard variations on the Queen's Gambit Declined, why choose chess moves at random; why even rely on general chess principles? Teaching general cognitive skills to able students (even able students who haven't heard of those skills) doesn't improve their performance, because they are already relative experts. Able students already have domain-specific knowledge and use strong methods.

Evidence from the laboratory and the classroom argues against a fundamental role for weak methods and general skills in expertise and learning. Weak methods, in the guise of study skills, thinking-skills curricula, or critical-thinking programs, are not a short-cut to improved educational outcomes.

By the mid 1970s, then, most cognitive theorists recognized that domain-specific knowledge and strong methods were keys to expert performance and human intelligence. At that point, many would have bet against the chess champion's having a successful diplomatic career.

This message was picked up by some educators, and it has even reached the general public. E. D. Hirsch's *Cultural Literacy* (1987) is a thoughtful, sustained, and highly popular presentation of how domain-specific knowledge and skills are fundamental to literacy. Chapter 2 of Hirsch's book is an extended discussion of how cognitive research supports this educational philosophy. According to Hirsch, the research should make us skeptical of attempts to teach reading, writing, and critical thinking as general cognitive skills applicable to novel problems. Skilled performance in these subjects, like skilled performance in Simon and Chase's chess studies, demands an extensive store of domain-specific knowledge. "General programs contrived to teach general skills are ineffective," Hirsch argues (p. 61).

Hirsch characterizes the "critical thinking" movement—an attempt to teach weak methods—as a well-intentioned program "to take children beyond the minimal basic skills required by state guidelines and to encourage the teaching of 'higher order' skills" (1987, p. 132). The danger, as he sees it, is that advocates of higher-order thinking tend to ignore the importance of "mere facts." According to Hirsch, "we should direct our attention undeviatingly toward what schools teach" (p. 19).

There are also dangers associated with arguments, such as Hirsch's, for the primacy of domain-specific knowledge and skills. It is easy to oversimplify and misinterpret what the research means for educational practice. Certainly the research implies that we can't ignore "mere facts" in school instruction—domain knowledge is essential. But, conversely, curricula that merely transmit facts aren't desirable either. Cognitive research also implies that we have to be as concerned with how we teach as we are with what we teach. The danger with cultural literacy is embracing the what to the detriment of the how. Lists of proper nouns, such as appear in the appendix to Hirsch's book, might help outline curricular content, but they say nothing about how to teach that content effectively. Researchers have known for a long time that teaching word meanings to children can increase vocabulary knowledge, but more vocabulary knowledge doesn't necessarily improve reading comprehension. If better reading comprehension is the goal, how one teaches vocabulary matters. Similarly, current social studies texts may present the facts about geography or history, but fail to teach course content so that students have an understanding of geography or history. As we will see, how texts present the facts is vitally important.

Finally, the majority of the cognitive research Hirsch cites was done in the 1970s. But cognitive research didn't stop then. The prevailing view of 20 years ago was not the final word, nor should it necessarily guide educational practice. Research that started to appear in the early 1980s suggests that domain-specific knowledge and skills are necessary for expert performance but may not be sufficient. There is more to intelligence and expert performance than domain knowledge.

Metacognition

Around 1980, cognitive scientists introduced a new element, called *metacognition,* into discussions of intelligence and expert performance. Metacognition is the ability to think about thinking, to be consciously aware of oneself as a problem solver, and to monitor and control one's mental processing.

John Flavell, one of the developers of this notion, described metacognition as the fourth and highest level of mental activity

(Flavell and Wellman 1977). At the lowest level are the hard-wired, basic processes such as matching the contents of working memory to conditions on production rules. At the next level are things like knowing $9 \times 7 = 63$, being able to recall your mother's maiden name, and having command of sufficient schemas or facts to be culturally literate. At the third level are strategies, weak or strong methods, which we voluntarily and consciously use. For example, you might repeat a phone number silently to keep it active in working memory, or you might use Siegler's rule IV to solve a balance-scale problem. The fourth level is the metacognitive level—the knowledge, awareness, and control of the three lower levels. It is our conscious awareness of ourselves (and, by extension, others) as problem solvers.

Research on metacognition has shown that knowledge, awareness, and control of mental abilities develop with age and experience. As children mature, for example, they develop a much better sense of how many items they can hold in short-term memory. Four-year-old children can usually hold about three items, but will predict they can remember eight. Adolescents have a short-term memory capacity of about six items and accurately predict this capacity (Yussen and Levy 1975).

Children's performance on other memory tasks also provides evidence for metacognitive development. When experimenters give children a list of items to study and tell the children they can take as much time as they need to memorize the list, older children perform better than younger children (Flavell 1979). Although young children might lack effective memory strategies or lack background knowledge needed for the task, there is an independent metacognitive trend as well. Preschool children, after taking as much time as they want to study the list, think they have learned it completely but do very poorly when tested. In contrast, when elementary school children say they have learned the list, they can recall it accurately. The younger children don't know how to use study time effectively and have no idea if they have learned the list or not. It seems that the younger children don't know how to learn and don't know when they have learned.

Children's understanding of texts and stories shows a similar developmental trend. Even young children grasp the essential gist of a story. If given sufficient time to study a text, children at every age can remember more about it. Children younger than about 12, though, do not use the study time effectively. They remember more about the text, but tend to remember more details or isolated ideas from the text. They don't remember more about the text's themes or about how those themes interrelate. In short, before age 12 children don't seem to know what kinds of things are important for better understanding of texts and can't direct their mental energy to those things. The younger children lack important reading comprehension strategies, or, if they have the strategies, they lack control over them. They have weaknesses at Flavell's third and fourth cognitive levels. In contrast, children of age 12 and older usually remember more of the text's important ideas after additional study. The older children know what is important in texts, have strategies for reading texts and studying that are directed at those important features, know how and when to use the strategies, and can monitor their use of them. They can control their cognitive activity—they have metacognitive skills. Ann Brown and Judy Deloache, who reported some of these results, conclude that "one main aspect of 'what develops' is metacognition—the voluntary control an individual has over his own cognitive processes," and that "the growth of metacognitive abilities underlies many of the behavioral changes that take place with development" (Brown and DeLoache 1978, p. 26).

Hirsch emphasizes the necessity of domain-specific knowledge in learning and doesn't mention metacognition explicitly. Nonetheless, the importance of metacognition is implicit in his diagnosis of literacy problems. Although domain-specific knowledge contributes to expertise in all domains, in reading (as Hirsch carefully explains) background knowledge—knowledge that goes beyond what is literally printed on the page—is crucial for comprehension. Teaching the schemas of cultural literacy is intended to give students the background knowledge needed to be culturally literate. Note that such knowledge would fall into level 2 of Flavell's taxonomy: facts stored for recall in long-term memory.

But Hirsch alludes to knowledge that literate individuals have that would fall into Flavell's fourth level: "In effective reading, one must not only call up one's own schematic associations but also *monitor* [my italics] whether they are appropriate ones shared by the wider speech community." Literate adults do this automatically, but "young children and other semi-literates do not confidently know what other members of the speech community can be expected to know." They lack "readily accessible information about what is shared by others" (p. 68).

Calling up one's one schematic associations is a level-2 cognitive process. Monitoring their appropriateness, on the other hand, is a level-4, metacognitive process. Similarly, knowing about or estimating what other members of the speech community might know is also a metacognitive task; it involves the ability to envision other people as problem solvers whose minds work similarly to one's own. This is just to say that reading comprehension involves more than extensive cultural background knowledge. Minimally, reading comprehension also requires metacognitive monitoring skills. If students lack these skills, no amount of cultural knowledge on its own can make them literate.

Metacognition and Intelligent Novices

Metacognition is an important addition to a theory of expertise and intelligence. The results of the research discussed so far—the studies of memory, learning skills, and reading—are consistent with the contention that metacognitive skills are high-order skills but domain-specific skills nonetheless. Clearly, it is possible for a person to be expert and metacognitively sophisticated in one domain but not in others. Our cultural stereotype of the absent-minded professor—a scientist or scholar who is expert and metacognitively capable in an academic domain but inept and unaware outside that academic specialty, particularly in everyday life—derives from this possibility.

Other results, though, suggest that metacognitive skills are general skills—skills that some people can apply across domains and in domains where they have little prior background knowledge. Everyday experience suggests that there are *intelligent novices:* some novices learn new domains more quickly than other novices. Research tells us that one thing that makes some novices more intelligent than others is their metacognitive skills.

As part of an experiment, John Bransford, an expert cognitive psychologist who has done work on math learning, tried to learn physics from a textbook with the help of an expert physicist. He kept a diary of his learning experiences and recorded the skills and strategies most useful to him (Brown et al. 1983). Among the things he listed were (1) awareness of the difference between understanding and memorizing material and knowledge of which mental strategies to use in each case; (2) ability to recognize which parts of the text were difficult, which dictated where to start reading and how much time to spend; (3) awareness of the need to take problems and examples from the text, order them randomly, and then try to solve them; (4) knowing when he didn't understand, so he could seek help from the expert; and (5) knowing when the expert's explanations solved his immediate learning problem. These are all metacognitive skills; they all involve awareness and control of the learning problem that Bransford was trying to solve. Bransford might have learned these skills originally in one domain (cognitive psychology), but he could apply them as a novice when trying to learn a second domain (physics).

This self-experiment led Bransford and his colleagues to examine in a more controlled way the differences between expert and less-skilled learners. They found that the behavior of intelligent novices contrasted markedly with that of the less skilled. Intelligent novices used many of the same strategies Bransford had used to learn physics. Less-skilled learners used few, if any, of them. The less-skilled did not always appreciate the difference between memorization and comprehension and seemed to be unaware that different learning strategies should be used in each case (Bransford et al. 1986; Bransford and Stein 1984). These students were less likely to notice whether texts were easy or difficult, and thus were less able to adjust their strategies and their study time accordingly (Bransford et al. 1982). Less-able learners were unlikely to use self-tests and self-questioning as sources of feedback to correct misconceptions and inappropriate learning strategies (Brown et al. 1983; Stein et al. 1982).

Hirsch, in his discussion of reading, notes how expert readers "monitor" their schematic associations. Monitoring comprehension is also a metacognitive skill. Ellen Markman (1985) studied this skill by having students in grades 3 through 6 read short passages which they had never seen before and which contained obvious contradictions. For example, a passage about ants might say in one place that ants navigate by leaving a chemical trail which they can smell and in another place that ants have no sense of smell. Most of the younger children and even a few of the older ones were oblivious to the inconsistencies; they weren't monitoring their comprehension. Children did improve on the task with age, so Markman first interpreted the results in terms of developmental differences between younger and older children. Subsequent research supported a more general conclusion: that the ability to apply this metacognitive skill differentiated strong from weak learners at all ages.

The ability to monitor comprehension is an essential learning skill. Often poor students are totally unaware that they don't comprehend class material. If they aren't aware that they have a learning problem, they can't take steps to overcome it.

Everyday experience suggests there are intelligent novices. Research tells us that metacognitive skills contribute to these expert learning performances. Some people develop these skills naturally; others do not. Those who do can become intelligent novices; those who don't may have difficulty learning.

Metacognition and Education

The importance of metacognition for education is that a child is, in effect, a universal novice, constantly confronted with novel learning tasks. In such a situation it would be most beneficial to be an intelligent novice. What is encouraging is that the research also shows that it is possible to teach children metacognitive skills and when to use them. If we can do this, we will be able to help children become intelligent novices; we will be able to teach them how to learn.

Just as there are basic math and reading skills, there are basic metacognitive skills. Among the basic metacognitive skills are the abilities to predict the results of one's own problem-solving actions, to check the results of one's own actions (Did it work?), to monitor one's progress toward a solution (How am I doing?), and to test how reasonable one's actions and solutions are against the larger reality (Does this make sense?). For example, a metacognitively adept chess player tries to predict the consequences of a series of moves, checks the results of those moves, and monitors whether those moves might contribute to a possible checkmate. Such a player also checks possible strategies against the larger reality. In a game against a higher-rated opponent, a metacognitively aware player would not look for an easy mating combination early in the game; a quick reality check would convince him that such a strategy doesn't make sense. Brown and DeLoache (1978, p. 15) call these skills "the basic characteristics of efficient thought." To become efficient thinkers—intelligent novices—students have to learn the skills and learn when to use them. Although a student might first learn the skills in the context of some specific subject matter (as Bransford first learned them in psychology), once he or she has learned them, the student can apply the skills in any learning situation—*if* the student has also learned that these skills are applicable and useful in any learning situation. Cognitive scientists call instruction that teaches students metacognitive skills and when to use them *metacognitively aware* instruction.

How does one teach like this? One can think of metacognitive skills as the ability to be critical of one's own problem solving. Metacognitively aware instruction attempts to transfer the critic's role from the teacher to the student. The transfer occurs in stages. Initially the teacher models the critic's role for the students. Gradually, the students begin to share this critical, metacognitive role with the teacher; eventually they can take on the role themselves, with the teacher standing by to provide coaching when the students falter. As the children become more metacognitively adept—more self-critical—the teacher cedes the critic's role entirely to them. Researchers describe this transition from the teacher's modeling and control to the students' control as *scaffolding*. Instruction creates a scaffold to support learning, and then the scaffold is gradually dismantled as the students become increasingly self-critical.

One problem with metacognitive skills is that they are usually covert and implicit in expert performance. To teach these skills and when to use them, the instructor has to make metacognition overt and explicit. One effective way to do this is in group learning situations where teachers and students engage in dialogues about their joint learning and problem solving. Almost all children are able conversationalists and can play the dialogue game. Appropriately guided by the teacher, the dialogue can become a social, collaborative form of "thinking aloud" in which each member of the group makes his or her thinking overt. In such situations, first the teacher and then the students describe their problem-solving strategies, present their reasoning to the group, and then defend and justify it against criticisms. These group dialogues make reasoning, planning, and monitoring public and shared. The children begin to see cognitive processes in action and understand how they can be monitored and controlled.

In experimental situations, Brown, working with various collaborators, has used metacognitively aware instruction to teach memory strategies to mildly retarded students (Brown et al. 1979), text-summarizing skills to college students (Brown et al. 1981), and analogical reasoning to children as young as 3 and 4 years (Brown 1989), all with great success. As we will see, the approach also works in the classroom, where metacognitively aware instruction can improve students' understanding of scientific reasoning, reading comprehension, and the writing process.

The Final Element: General Skills Again

The final element leading to the new synthesis is general skills—they just won't go away. Besides metacognitive ability, there is another trait that intelligent novices show. Research scientists are an extreme but illustrative example. Scientists don't just apply their extensive domain knowledge to solve standard, textbook problems; rather, they formulate new problems and discover new solutions. Deep, domain-specific knowledge is fundamental to their performance, but so are general skills and strategies. Einstein attributed his interest in Brownian motion to childhood experiences watching the patterns formed by smoke rising from his uncle's pipe. My graduate adviser, a biophysicist, would help us graduate students understand an abstract geometrical theorem about how objects can move in space by referring to it as "the hatpin-through-the-grapefruit theorem."

On the frontiers of science, or in any creative endeavor, everyone is a novice in the sense that prior knowledge is not directly applicable. Here, too, it helps to be an intelligent novice. Scientists, scholars, artists, and skilled managers all have to take what they know and stretch it to pose and answer novel problems. They have to transfer prior learning to new situations. Intelligent novices, like Einstein and my adviser, often use general strategies to do this. They use strategies such as modeling and analogy—weak methods applicable across many domains—in their attempts to apply what they know flexibly and creatively in new ways. Their extensive domain-specific knowledge interacts with general strategies to help them acquire new knowledge. General strategies do seem to have a role in intelligence and in expert performance.

General strategies should also be helpful to those universal novices, children. Although research on the teaching of such study skills as memory strategies, underlining, and note taking has shown that after instruction children do not apply these skills spontaneously, it is still hard to accept that such skills are not useful. Maybe the problem is not with general skills but with how we have traditionally tried to teach them.

Let us review briefly what we think we know about intelligence and expertise. First, we have seen the importance of domain-specific knowledge for expert performance. The scientist's use of general strategies is based on deep understanding of at least one scientific domain. We can agree with the advocates of domain specificity that general programs contrived to teach general skills are ineffective, but that leaves open the possibility of teaching general skills within specific subject-matter instruction. General strategies do need a knowledge base on which to work, but once learned in a specific context they should be applicable in other domains. Second, both from the Johnson-Laird experiment (figure 3.1) and from research on study skills, we have seen that adults and children have difficulty transferring a skill or a strategy from one context to a similar context. In some cases, subjects could make the transfer between contexts only after the experimenter *told* them that the strategy applied in the new situation.

Perhaps, just as children have to be taught metacognitive skills and when to use them, they have to be taught general learning strategies and when to use them. Perhaps, then, previous attempts to teach general skills failed because course designers and instructors overestimated children's ability to generalize from one learning situation to another. Maybe children don't see how and why the situations are similar. In general-strategy and learning-skill instruction, rather than assume that students see the similarities between various learning situations, perhaps we should explicitly tell them how and why the situations are similar. This has led cognitive scientists to think that general-strategy instruction has a place in schools, but that strategy instruction has to be *informed*. By this they mean that strategy instruction should include explicit descriptions of the strategies, instruction about *when* the strategies are useful, and an explanation of *why* they are useful.

Paris et al. (1982) ran an experiment in which they compared informed instruction with a more traditional approach to strategy instruction. On each of the first two days of the experiment, they had 7- and 8-year-old children study sets of 24 pictures. After a period of study, they asked the children to remember as many of the pictures as they could. On average, the children could recall 12 or 13 pictures. On the third day, all the children were taught memory strategies: naming or labeling each item, sorting the items into related groups (clustering), learning the items one group at a time, and then testing themselves by trying to recall the items in groups (a meta-cognitive skill).

Half the children (the control group) saw the instructor demonstrate the memory strategies and were permitted to practice them, but were given no explanations of why the strategies worked and no feedback on their performance when they tried to use them. In short, the control group received traditional strategy instruction.

The other children (the experimental group) received the same instruction as the control group but in addition were told why the strategies worked and when to use them. Also, when the children in this group used a strategy they received immediate feedback on how successful they had been with it. This group received informed instruction.

Immediately after learning the strategies, children in the control group could recall on average 16 pictures and children in the experimental group 19. The experiment was continued for two more days. By the fifth day, children in the experimental group could still recall 16 items. These children continued to use the memory strategies spontaneously. Without being told, they continued to label, sort, cluster, and self-test. In contrast, by the fifth day children in the control group had fallen to the pre-instruction level of 12 to 13 items and had reverted to passive, pre-instruction learning strategies, such as looking at the pictures and trying to remember them. This experiment shows that children will use a strategy spontaneously—they will transfer it to a new situation—if they understand why it works and when it can help them learn. Informed strategy instruction works; traditional instruction doesn't.

General thinking, learning, and study strategies are important elements of intelligence and expert performance, and now it seems we may know how to teach them. According to Brown (1985, p. 335), "ideal cognitive skills training programs include practice in the specific task-appropriate strategies, direct instruction in the orchestrating, overseeing and monitoring of these skills, and information concerning the significance of those activities." Such instruction recognizes the necessity of domain-specific knowledge in that the strategies are specific, task appropriate, and integrated into subject-matter learning. The instruction is also metacognitively aware, in that the children receive direct instruction about how to monitor and control their problem solving. It is informed in that children learn why the strategies work.

The New Synthesis and the Teaching of High-Order Skills

The new synthesis suggests that domain-specific knowledge, meta-cognitive skills, and general strategies are all elements of human intelligence and expert performance.

Where does this leave our chess champion? His detailed knowledge of chess won't help him in his new diplomatic career, because by definition it is domain specific. On the other hand, even if he has some potentially relevant general skills, he may not be able to transfer them readily to new problem domains—not everyone can do that. Much depends on whether the champion is an intelligent novice or not. Is his expertise narrowly confined to chess, or does he have the metacognitive insight to be an effective, rapid learner? If the latter, then maybe with some tutoring in foreign affairs and some on-the-job experience he could rapidly become a national security expert. Some chess champions—like some college professors and some school children—are naturally intelligent novices; others aren't. Whether our chess champion will succeed depends on what cognitive skills he has beyond his chess expertise.

We are just beginning to see what the new synthesis might mean for educational practice. Many of the examples in the following chapters illustrate how this latest theory of human intelligence might be applied in the classroom. For education, the most important implication of the theory is that how we teach is as important as what we teach. Domain-specific knowledge and skills are essential to expertise; however, school instruction must also be metacognitively aware and informed.

Most important, innovative classroom practices based on the new synthesis can help us achieve our goal of teaching high-order skills to all students. In chapter 1, we initially identified high-order skills as the skills that students need to achieve the higher NAEP proficiency levels. We observed that these higher proficiencies demand that students solve complex problems, for which there often are no standard solution procedures and no single correct answer. Students with high-order skills can use their knowledge flexibly to solve ill-structured, novel problems.

This characterization of high-order skills relies primarily on the kinds of problems students can solve and on students' observed behaviors. But "high-order" also refers to the thought processes needed to solve such problems and guide such behaviors. Susan Chipman, Program Manager for Cognitive Science at the Office of Naval Research, argues that "behind our choice of the term 'higher-order,' there are strong intuitions about the way in which our cognitive activities are structured and controlled" (Chipman 1992). These intuitions link high-order skills with our current theory of intelligence and expert performance.

First, Chipman points out that higher-order skills in a subject domain, such as those needed to solve ill-structured complex problems, are skills grounded in deep factual and procedural knowledge of the domain. As the new synthesis implies, high-order skills require extensive domain knowledge.

Second, she notes that students who genuinely possess high-order skills in a subject domain not only have the requisite factual and procedural knowledge, they also can recognize *when* the knowledge is applicable and can use it appropriately. It is this feature of high-order skills that accounts for the flexible, spontaneous use of knowledge in novel situations. This connects high-order skills with the notion of transfer. High-order skills should transfer from school learning to real-world situations and allow students to use what they already know to learn new things more rapidly. The key to transfer, and so to high-order skills, is knowing when to use knowledge. If we want to teach high-order skills, then, as the new synthesis says, the instruction should be informed.

Third, implicit in our use of "high-order," according to Chipman, are intuitions about how students control and monitor their cognitive skills. High-order skills, in this sense, involve awareness of what is happening in working memory, of how those processes determine eventual action, and of how to control those processes. Thus, metacognitive abilities are implicit in our notion of high-order skills. For this reason, if we want students to acquire high-order skills, instruction must be metacognitively explicit.

In short, high-order skills require extensive domain knowledge, understanding when to use the knowledge, and metacognitive monitoring and control. Students who have these things can solve novel, ambiguous problems; students who have high-order skills are intelligent novices.

For these reasons, instruction based on elements of the new synthesis is our best educational bet if we want all students to have the knowledge and skills that in past generations have been confined to the college-bound elite—if we want all students to acquire high-order skills. Educational practice grounded in cognitive theory, Lauren Resnick (1986, p. 43) writes, "would transform the whole curriculum in fundamental ways. It would treat the development of higher-order skills as the paramount goal of *all* schooling."

Transforming the curriculum to meet this goal won't be easy. We will have to rethink, or at least reevaluate, much of our received wisdom about educational policy, practice, and standards and about teacher training. We will have to restructure our schools—starting in the classrooms, where teachers interact with students. We will need teachers who can create and maintain learning environments where students can become intelligent novices. Many of us will have to change our representations of what schools and schooling are.

Admittedly, there is much we still don't know about how our minds work, how children best learn, and how to design better schools. Nonetheless, as a first step, we can start applying what we already know to improve instruction in what Resnick calls the "enabling" or "tool" domains: mathematics, science, reading, and writing. Mastery of these domains is necessary for advanced learning in more specialized subjects. We can teach these enabling domains as high-order cognitive skills to all students, as the following chapters will show.

4

Mathematics: Making It Meaningful

When I was in third grade, Sister Mary Carl taught us a procedure for checking multi-digit multiplication called "casting out nines." It works like this:

$$\begin{array}{cc} 237 & 3 \\ \underline{\times 29} & \underline{\times 2} \\ 6873 & 6 \end{array}$$

In the multiplicands and the product, cross out all nines and any numbers that add up to 9. Then add the remaining digits in each number and divide each total by 9. In the above example, casting out the nines leaves 3, 2, and 6. Next multiply the results of casting out nines in the multiplicands (here, $3 \times 2 = 6$), divide that product by 9, and keep the remainder ($6 \div 9 = 0$, remainder 6). If you multiplied correctly, then the remainder should equal the result of casting out nines in the original product (here, 6). Casting out nines is a method for checking multiplication that requires only cancellation, addition, and division by 9. I used this mysterious trick all through school, and I still cast out nines on every license plate I see. Until recently I had no idea why casting out nines works.[1]

The results of the National Assessments of Educational Progress suggest that for many students much of mathematics is as meaningless as casting out nines was for me. Many students don't know why the math procedures they learn in school work. Students leave school having the computational skills to solve standard problems but lacking the higher-order mathematical understanding that would allow them to apply their skills widely in novel situations. Too often, math instruction produces students who can manipulate number symbols but who don't understand what the symbols mean.

This situation is symptomatic of a gap between our professed educational goals and our educational practice. As Sandra Marshall, a psychologist at San Diego State University, told me, "We are just paying lip service to thinking skills. In reality, everything flips back to what algorithm to use when." Too often math instruction emphasizes rote learning and number recipes over reasoning. For many students math is a mysterious, meaningless, abstract activity with little relevance to daily life.

Cognitive scientists have developed explicit models of expert knowledge and skills in a number of mathematical domains. Using these models to design instruction in elementary school arithmetic, middle school word problems, and high school geometry could help teachers make mathematics a meaningful, rather than mindless, activity for their students.

Preschool Children and Number

A major contribution of cognitive psychology to math instruction has been to show that preschool children have what might be an innate interest in number. Before entering school, children informally absorb much number knowledge. They enter school not as mathematical blank slates but as intuitive, informal mathematicians. Cognitive research shows that the educational challenge is to help children link their informal number knowledge and skills to the formal rules, notations, and procedures they first encounter in the classroom. Success in this transition demands that children master such number procedures as counting and comparing numbers and that they have a representation of number and quantity they can use to justify and motivate these procedures.

Before 1980 many psychologists and educators, following Jean Piaget's pioneering work on children's cognitive development, believed preschool children had an extremely limited understanding of number and counting. Young children look as if they might be counting, many educators thought, but it is just a rote performance—saying number words while pointing at things. Young children don't really understand the counting procedure or what it means.

According to Piaget's developmental theory, children from ages 2 through 7 are in the *preoperational* stage; they can think about physical objects but they can't reason about abstract things such as numbers. Piaget based his theoretical claims on the way children

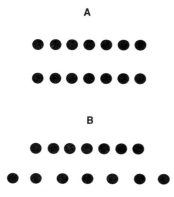

Figure 4.1
Jean Piaget's number-conservation task. Young children will say that the two rows in panel A contain the same number of objects, but will also say that the lower row in panel B contains more objects than the upper row.

solved standard tasks, such as the balance-scale task discussed in chapter 2. He argued that children's performance on the task he called *number conservation* showed that they had, at best, only a limited understanding of numbers and counting.

In the number-conservation task, a child sees two rows of objects (as in figure 4.1). Each row contains the same number of equally spaced objects, and the rows are first arranged so that the objects in them are aligned (as in figure 4.1A). If the experimenter asks whether the two rows contain the same number of objects, a preschooler will say yes. If the experimenter, while the child is watching, moves the objects in one row farther apart, so that one row is longer than the other (as in figure 4.1B), the child will then say that the longer row has more objects. According to Piaget, children in the preoperational stage don't know that rearranging a set of objects doesn't change the number of objects in the set. If children don't know this, Piaget reasoned, they don't understand numbers and counting.

Science advances by extending, refining, or refuting earlier theories, and cognitive science is no exception. Since the mid 1970s developmental psychologists have scrutinized Piaget's claims, using the assumptions and methods of cognitive science. They have found that young children (even infants), when tested carefully, show evidence of understanding numbers and counting.

Infants as young as 7 months notice differences in the numbers of objects they are shown in experimental displays. They can notice the difference between displays containing one, two, and three objects (Starkey et al. 1983; Starkey et al. 1990). At 2½ years, children start to use number words in strings. By age 3 they can accurately count small and medium-size sets of visible objects. However, at this age, if they watch a puppet count small sets, they can't reliably tell whether the puppet has counted correctly; they are better at executing the counting procedure than at knowing when the procedure has been used correctly (Briars and Siegler 1984; Siegler 1991). By age 4 to 5, children have a more sophisticated understanding of the counting procedure; they are aware of the puppet's counting errors and they are less tolerant of them. Thus, preschool children can both count and have some understanding of the principles involved.

By age 5, most children develop other number skills in addition to counting. First, they learn to compare two numbers for size and can reliably report which number is larger or smaller (Resnick 1983). Next, they spontaneously combine their counting and comparing skills to invent methods for solving simple addition problems. Groen and Resnick (1977) taught 4½-year-olds to do simple addition by using only their counting knowledge. To add 4 + 2, they taught children to count out one group of four objects and one group of two objects, combine the two groups, and count the entire set. Teachers call this method *counting-up*. Utilizing a task analysis of methods children might use, Groen and Resnick analyzed children's response times on the problems and discovered that after several practice sessions half the children began to use a different method—one they hadn't been taught. The new, invented method was noticeably faster. Groen and Resnick called the method the children invented for themselves *counting-on*. It exploits the ability to compare numbers for size. In counting-on, children pick the larger of the two addends, here 4, and count up from there. Using this method, a child might say aloud, or under her breath, "four (pause), five, six" rather than "one, two, three, four, (pause) one, two (pause) one, two, three, four, five, six." The fact that children combine counting and comparing in order to invent counting-on shows that they understand both procedures. We can't explain such number skills as mere rote performance.

What about Piaget? It is true that children can't do the conservation task, but cognitive research shows that by age 4 or 5 children can indeed count and have a solid, though informal, understanding of numbers. These new insights came after researchers performed careful task analyses of the counting task and could specify what knowledge and skills the task demands. With the task analysis in hand, they could design simple experiments to find out when children acquire the knowledge and skills. Preschool children have number knowledge, cognitive scientists say, but Piaget's task requires more knowledge than children have—knowledge that goes beyond what they really need in order to count.

The Mental Number Line: The Heart of Math Readiness

Children bring their informal, invented number knowledge to school. It is the background knowledge they use to understand their first formal math instruction. It is obvious to any teacher that children vary in mathematical background knowledge when they start school. Even in first grade, Siegler (1988) found differences between strong and weak math students in the strategies used to solve simple arithmetic problems. Successful students had already mastered some basic number facts, could easily retrieve the facts from long-term memory, and used effective strategies (such as counting-on) in tackling unfamiliar arithmetic problems. Weak students were poor at retrieving answers from long-term memory and poor at using counting strategies. How do the two groups of students differ in their initial knowledge?

Robbie Case and Sharon Griffin, developmental psychologists, noticed a connection between children's ability to solve balance-scale problems and their early math skills (Case and Griffin 1990). On balance-scale problems where one side of the scale obviously has more weight than the other, 4-year-olds can make the "more or less" judgment and predict that the side with more weight will go down. Four-year-olds, as we have seen, can also accurately count small sets of objects. However, they cannot solve balance-scale problems where the numbers of weights on the two sides are sufficiently close that a child has to count to find out which side has more. They can count and make qualitative comparisons in isolation, but they can't combine counting with comparing to make quantitative comparisons. They can do "more or less" but not "*how much* more or less.*"

By age 6, though, most children are using Siegler's rule I, which does require quantitative comparisons. Something happens between ages 4 and 6 that enables children to combine counting and comparing. As Groen and Resnick showed, these are just the two procedures that children combine to invent methods such as counting-on. A child who cannot combine the counting and comparing procedures can't invent these methods and can't generate basic number facts, such as 4 + 2 = 6, to store in long-term memory. Such students perform just like Siegler's weak first-grade math students.

There are further similarities between performance on balance-scale problems and learning arithmetic. Siegler's four rules are procedures for finding answers to balance-scale problems. Counting, comparing, and counting-on are procedures for finding answers to number problems. Using the balance scale, Siegler showed that sometimes children can't learn new rules if they don't have the proper underlying representations to support and motivate the new rules. The same is true for children who have difficulty learning school arithmetic. They lack the initial representations of number and quantity they need to understand counting and comparing. If they don't understand counting and comparing, they can't combine them to invent counting-on.

Cognitive research has also given us insight into how children represent basic number knowledge. Researchers call the representation that children use the *mental number line*. As figure 4.2 shows, it is actually three interconnected lines. The top line is the series of number names connected by "next" links. The middle line symbolizes objects to count. Each time you touch an object in the set, you say a number name. The bottom line represents the number quantities themselves. These are linked by +1 or -1 links, symbolizing that one moves up or down the line in increments of 1. The number-line structure is anchored on the left by "a little" and on the right by "a lot," indicating that the number line elaborates on the 4-year-old's ability to make qualitative "more or less" comparisons. The number line allows a child to make *quantitative* comparisons and to combine counting and comparing in learning arithmetic.

This representation gives children the conceptual knowledge they need to understand and meaningfully apply basic number skills. Counting is a procedure that takes a list of symbols for objects and the list of number names. If you assign one and only one number name per object, the last number name you say is the number of objects in the set you are counting. This procedure operates on the mental number line. You can get a sense of how it works by pointing to the object symbols in figure 4.2 with your left hand and to the number names with your right hand. Begin by a locating a thing to

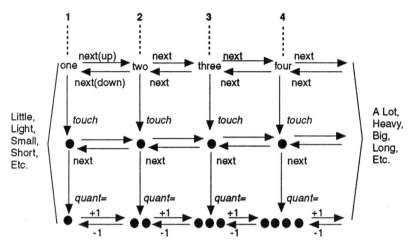

Figure 4.2
The mental number line is the central conceptual structure for early number skills. The number line elaborates the child's earlier qualitative understanding of "a little" versus "a lot" by allowing him to assign number names to sets of objects he counts. The top line shows how number names are correctly ordered. The middle line symbolizes how a child assigns a number name to an object in a set by pointing to it or touching it while saying the number name. The bottom line shows the number named by the numeral and how one moves up or down the number line by adding or subtracting 1. (Used with permission of Robbie Case.)

be counted. Store a symbol for it in working memory (point to the first object symbol). Recall the first number name, "one," from long-term memory into working memory (point to it with your right hand). Thereafter, follow a cycle: See if there is another thing, store a symbol for it in working memory (move your left hand along the bottom line) and retrieve the next number name into working memory (move your right hand). Stop when there are no more things. The last number name stored in working memory, the number name your right hand is pointing at, is the number of things in the set. Counting works by moving "pointers" through two lists in a way that ensures that each object gets a unique number-name tag. Using the number-line representation and this counting method, cognitive scientists have written computer simulations that mimic children's performance on a variety of counting tasks (Greeno et al. 1984).

The mental number line also motivates quantitative comparisons. Knowledge of how "next" links work allows children to infer that positions farther up the line are "larger"—they are closer to the "a lot" end. Response-time studies suggest that children use this representation to compare numbers. Suppose a child is trying to decide whether 4 or 2 is larger. He doesn't count up the number line until he reaches the first number and then say that the other one is larger. If children did this, then all comparisons where (e.g.) 2 is the smaller number would take the same amount of time. Response times show that children, like adults, take longer to decide about numbers that are closer together on the mental number line. It takes longer to decide if 3 is larger than 2 than it does to decide if 5 is larger than 2. It is as if we view the number line in our mind's eye, like a ruler; positions closer together are harder to distinguish than those farther apart. Apparently, when children hear a number name, they can "see" it on the number line and go directly to that position.

This mental structure also motivates and justifies counting-on. In adding 4 + 2, children can go directly to the 4 position, count up two positions from there, and say "6." This structure also shows why counting-on is a faster method than counting-up. To see why, go back to the counting procedure that involves pointing with your fingers. If each move of your fingers along the number line stands for a mental operation that takes a similar amount of time, then you move your fingers many less times when you count-on (two moves—start at 4, then move to 5 and then 6) than when you count-up (eleven moves—count 4, count two more, then go back to the beginning and count up to 6).

Case and Griffin observed that most first-grade math curricula do not directly teach the number line and its properties. A child who has not figured it out for himself is not taught it in school. In exploring this further, Case and Griffin concentrated their efforts on children known to be at risk for math failure: children from low-socioeconomic-status (low-SES) homes. They worked with children of rural Portuguese immigrants in Toronto, with children attending inner-city schools in Worcester, Massachusetts, and with Hispanic and inner-city children in the San Francisco Bay area. Case and Griffin developed a test that assessed knowledge of number words, ability to count small sets of objects, ability to visualize the mental number line in making comparisons, and skill at simple addition. At each research site the results were the same (Case and Griffin, n.d.). Performance on the test indicated that 67 percent of the high-SES 6-year-olds had an adequate grasp of the number-line representation, but only 32 percent of the low-SES children performed to the same level. There were no differences in counting ability between the two groups, but there were big differences in the ability to compare numbers and to visualize the number line. All high-SES children could accurately compare two numbers; only 60 percent of the low-SES children could do so. Thus, if counting *and* comparing are needed to construct efficient addition strategies, it is not surprising that only 25 percent of the low-SES children, versus 71 percent of the high-SES children, could solve simple addition problems, such as finding the sum of 4 and 2.

If lack of the mental-number-line representation is the problem, then the simple solution is to follow Robert Siegler's advice (chapter 2 above): teach the necessary representation.

The Readiness Module

Case and Griffin designed a math readiness module to teach the number line and the basic operations on it. The module teaches forward and backward counting, making one-to-one correspondences, comparing numbers, and simple arithmetic (limited to moving up or down one unit on the number line). It consists of a series of number games that groups of up to five children play with the teacher's help. One lesson teaches number comparison by having pairs of students roll dice and determine who has "more." Whoever gets the higher number moves a playing token that number of spaces along a number-line game board. Another lesson teaches moving up the number line by ones. The teacher shows the children a lunch bag containing between five and nine cookies. The teacher takes the cookies out of the bag, counts them while putting them back in the bag, and tells the children how many there are. She then asks "If the Cookie Fairy comes and leaves one more, how many will be in the bag?" To move down the number line, the teacher plays the same game but replaces the fairy with the Cookie Monster. The module contains 20 lessons taught in 40 half-hour sessions.

Case and Griffin divided the poorest-performing low-SES students into two groups. They had an experienced teacher use the module with one group—the experimental group. The students in the second (control) group received only the standard classroom math instruction. After the readiness module, all children took another number-skills test, and Case and Griffin compared the post-instruction performance of the experimental group with that of the control group. At the Worcester study site (the results were similar for the Bay Area study), 87 percent of the readiness group, versus 25 percent of the control group, passed the posttest. On specific test items, 93 percent of the readiness group but only 37 percent of the control group could determine which of two numbers was smaller, and all those in the training group but only half of those in the comparison group could tell which of two numbers was bigger. On simple addition, 87 percent of the readiness group but only 29 percent of the control group gave correct answers. The readiness group also showed significant improvement on other number tasks, such as telling time, making change, and solving balance-scale problems. Children in the readiness group also surpassed the children in the control group in understanding first-grade arithmetic. Over 75 percent of the children who had completed the readiness module, but only half of the children in the control group, mastered a first-grade math unit (Case, n.d.). The children in the experimental group had learned the number-line representation.

In early math, the mental number line is the representation that guides children's conceptual understanding. It is the representation they need to combine and exploit the power of their counting, comparing, and informal adding skills. Without this understanding, their basic number skills remain recipes, rather than rules for reasoning. If they don't understand how number concepts and structures justify and support these skills, their only alternative is to try to understand school math as a set of arbitrary procedures. Why arithmetic works is a mystery to them, just as casting out nines was a mystery to me. For mathematics to be meaningful, conceptual knowledge and procedural skills have to be interrelated in instruction.

Knowing Your Places: Learning Multi-Digit Arithmetic

In second grade, children move on to multi-digit arithmetic and need the new skills of carrying and borrowing. These skills require children to understand that numbers are related to one another in ways other than their places on the number line. Children have to understand that a number can be decomposed into parts—ones, tens, hundreds—in a variety of ways. Getting children to understand this is a central goal of early math instruction and, math teachers say, one of the hardest to achieve. Children have to construct a more complex representation of number.

Most children develop the representation they need to understand multi-digit arithmetic by elaborating a schema they acquire at an early age: the part-whole schema (Resnick 1983, 1984). Very young children understand parts and wholes in a qualitative way. When sharing a cookie, a two-year-old clearly prefers to get the larger part, even though he can't say how much larger one part is than the other. Children's developing number-line knowledge and counting strategies gradually result in their attaching numbers to wholes and parts. They can begin to say how much larger one part of the cookie is than the other.

In early elementary school, children further elaborate their understanding of number parts and wholes, usually in two stages. First, in manipulating two-digit numbers children begin to act as if they are dividing numbers into a "tens" part and a "ones" part. Children use numbers' decimal structure in their invented math procedures. At this stage, if the teacher asks "What is 57 minus 33?" a child might answer: "50 minus 30 is 20, then take away 3 is 17, plus 7 is 24." Children can also use color-coded blocks to make visual representations of numbers, although at this stage they believe that a multi-digit number can have only one correct block representation or part-whole decomposition: 57 can only be 5 tens and 7 ones.

Next, children elaborate their part-whole schemas to allow a number to be divided into hundreds, tens, and ones in a multitude of equivalent ways. This again becomes obvious as one watches children use colored blocks to represent numbers. The children realize they can have more than nine blocks of a particular denomination, and that they can trade ten blocks for one block between adjacent "parts." They realize, in other words, that 57 can also be 4 tens and 17 ones. This realization provides the conceptual basis for understanding borrowing, carrying, and other conventions of written multi-digit arithmetic. The elaborated part-whole schema plays the same role for multi-digit arithmetic that the number line does for elementary arithmetic.

Buggy Arithmetic

A major instructional problem in multi-digit arithmetic is that, although children might have the part-whole schema, they don't always connect the schema with the written math procedures. When this happens, the written procedures—what they mean and why they work—remain a mystery to the students.

Multi-digit subtraction provides a good example. In the late 1970s John Seeley Brown, Richard Burton, and Kurt Van Lehn analyzed children's performance on multi-digit subtraction in the course of developing a diagnostic program to help teachers identify and correct children's math errors. They found that multi-digit subtraction is "a virtually meaningless procedure" for most school children, totally divorced from any understanding of the number system (Van Lehn 1983).

After analyzing tens of thousands of arithmetic problems done by thousands of students, Brown, Burton, and Van Lehn also found something else: Most teachers assume that children's subtraction errors are random, careless, or the result of the child's not having mastered the subtraction procedure; the remedy is assigning more problems, urging the child to be more careful, or reteaching the entire procedure. But children's errors are not random; they are systematic. In a group of 1138 American third- and fourth-graders, fewer than 10 percent made no errors on multi-digit subtraction. Among children making mistakes, 40 percent made systematic errors. The 40 percent figure was also found among Nicaraguan fifth- and sixth-graders and among British 10-year-olds (Van Lehn 1983). It's not that children can't follow procedures very well; rather, "students are remarkably competent procedure followers, but . . . often follow *the wrong procedures*" (Brown and Burton 1978, p. 157). Many children have "bugs" in their math procedures.

It is not easy to identify a bug by looking at a few answers, which is to say it is not easy for a teacher to diagnose a student's misunderstanding. Each of the three rows of subtraction problems below illustrates one of the three most frequent bugs. Can you identify them? When you think you have discovered the bug, answer the last problem in the row as the buggy student would. Then compare your answers with the buggy answers given in note 2.

(a)	930	637	326	542	731
	−563	−415	−117	−389	−452
	433	222	211	247	???
(b)	427	602	515	802	307
	−293	−437	−204	−396	−168
	234	265	311	506	???

(c)   602   326   707   402   504
       −327   −117   −139   −123   −199
       225   209   538   229   ???

Brown, Burton, and Van Lehn identified 80 simple bugs like the three above, some of which could occur in combination to generate approximately 300 common bugs. They used this model to design two computer games, BUGGY and DEBUGGY, which they tested on both teachers and students. The computer plays the part of a buggy student. The teacher gives the student problems to solve. Then the teacher has to be a mathematical Miss Marple and use clues from students' answers to find the bug. When teachers play this game, they quickly see that the errors are not random; they realize that students have buggy procedures that can be identified and fixed with appropriate instruction. More generally, the game suggests how teachers might design math lessons to lower the chances of students' developing bugs in the first place. Teachers can choose instructive sequences of example problems, give students informed feedback about errors, and warn students about where bugs might arise.

When students play the game, they come to the same realizations as the teachers. More important, students begin to appreciate that their own mathematical deficiencies often arise from specific misunderstandings, not from lack of mathematical aptitude. They can say "I have a buggy rule" rather than "I'm bad at math." What appeared before cognitive analysis to be careless or unintelligent behavior turns out after cognitive analysis to be sensible and intelligent, but buggy, behavior.

Brown and Van Lehn also theorized about how children generate buggy procedures. Multi-digit subtraction involves three subprocedures: subtracting within a column, borrowing from an adjacent column, and borrowing from two columns to the left when there is a zero at the top of the adjacent column. A student would have to use all three subprocedures in this problem:

    4202
   −2879
    1323

The student has to borrow from the third column to do the rightmost column. In the next column, after the first borrow the student can do single-digit subtraction. The third column from the right requires borrowing, and the final column is another single-digit subtraction. When doing multi-digit subtraction, sometimes children forget a step in one of these subprocedures or don't know how to do the subprocedure at all. If they can't proceed to a solution, they use their inventive skills and background knowledge to repair their procedure. What is educationally revealing is the kind of knowledge children use in their repairs.

When students learn multi-digit subtraction in school, it requires very little number knowledge. Students have to know when one digit is greater than another to know when to borrow. They also must know simple subtraction facts, such as $12 - 9$ and $7 - 2$. Everything else is symbol manipulation. "Borrowing" is writing a small 1 next to the number in the column the student is trying to solve and decreasing the top number in the neighboring column to the left by 1. The procedure honors the decimal system but does not require the user to understand it.

Brown and Van Lehn identified eight repair rules children use to fix their procedures when stymied, including "skip to the next column," "skip an action entirely," "copy a number," and "switch a number in an operation (e.g., change $x - y$ to $y - x$)." Children use the rules to generate possible repairs, but they realize that not all possible repairs are good ones. They choose good repairs by considering how the results of the repair would look. They use criteria such as "Don't leave a blank in the middle of an answer" and "Don't write more than one digit per column." What the theory suggests is that children use only their knowledge of how written subtraction should *look* to fix their procedures, not knowledge of what subtraction *means!*

This theory explains how children invent the bugs, including the three you tried to find above. Bug *a* is called Smaller-from-Larger. The child sees that the top number in a column is smaller than the bottom number but doesn't know how to borrow; thus, the child uses the "switch numbers" rule, which ensures that a smaller number is available to subtract from a larger one. The result looks right, but it systematically gives wrong answers: it treats each column as an isolated single-digit subtraction. This violates the meaning of multi-digit subtraction, which requires that the entire bottom number be subtracted from the entire top number.

Bug *b* is called Borrow-from-Zero. The child knows that in borrowing from 0 the 0 becomes 9, but doesn't understand where the 9 comes from. In the second problem, 602 should become 59^12: with this bug it becomes 69^12. The patched procedure works and looks all right, but it systematically gives wrong answers.

Bug c is called Borrow-Across-Zero. Here the student doesn't bother to change the 0 to a 9 when borrowing, but does everything else. This bug also requires that the child invent a special rule for subtracting from zero, either $0 - N = N$ or $0 - N = 0$. Again, the fixed procedure generates answers to multi-digit subtraction that look right to the student.

We can explain children's bugs entirely in terms of symbol manipulation and how the results look. Children's repair rules and their criteria of choosing good repairs have little to do with what numbers and arithmetic symbols mean. The background knowledge that children use in their repairs refers only to symbol-manipulation strategies. If children have knowledge of the number system, as found in the elaborated part-whole schema, they aren't using it here. An understanding of borrowing based on the part-whole schema would rule out all three bugs as acceptable repairs. In buggy arithmetic, procedural skills are divorced from mathematically meaningful concepts.

Marrying Concepts to Procedures

Buggy arithmetic does not necessarily arise because children lack understanding of the number system. More often the problem is that children make no connection between their number knowledge and written arithmetic procedures.

Resnick (1982) discovered this when she studied how four second- and third-graders—Sandra, Anton, Alan, and Amanda—developed number knowledge and computational skills over the course of a school year. The children used color-coded blocks to construct visual representations of number; how they used and grouped blocks gave Resnick some insight into how their part-whole schemas developed. The children also learned multi-digit addition and subtraction procedures. Understood correctly, the blocks and the written procedures are two different codes, or representations, of the same underlying concepts.

In September, at the start of the school year, the children could use blocks to represent tens and ones, could count by tens and ones, and knew that, in the standard block representation of a two-digit number, the number with more tens blocks is larger. By May, the children seemed to have an understanding of how the blocks could be used to represent multi-digit addition and subtraction; they seemed to understand the decimal number system. During the year, they also gradually learned the written procedures for multi-digit arithmetic, including borrowing and carrying.

However, Resnick found no correlation between children's number knowledge and their computational skills. Sandra had the poorest understanding of the number system, but could carry by February and could borrow by May. Alan and Amanda showed the deepest understanding of the number system when using the blocks, but had the weakest grasp of written procedures. Alan was still having difficulty with carrying and borrowing in May. Amanda first used the borrowing procedure, but with difficulty, in May. She never mastered the written addition procedure. None of the children figured out spontaneously that there was a connection between the block representations and written arithmetic. They knew that colors coded the same information as column position in written numbers, and they could translate between the codes but none expected exact correspondence between the codes, or realized that the block displays might help in doing written arithmetic. All the children had some understanding of the number system, but did not see how this knowledge was linked to, and justified, the written procedures. Their conceptual number knowledge was isolated from their procedural number skills.

Resnick developed a method called *mapping instruction* to help children to see the correspondence between block representations and written procedures. This method, illustrated in figure 4.3, has children work with both blocks and number symbols in solving multi-digit problems. The children see that written computation is a way to keep track of block procedures and, conversely, that block procedures justify steps in the written computations.

In mapping instruction, the teacher presents a problem—for example, "300 − 139 = ?". The child uses the blocks to make a physical representation of the larger number, here 300, then writes the problem in column format (steps 1 and 2). The student then makes trades on the blocks using the 10-for-1 rule and records the trades as borrows on the written numbers (steps 3–6). Then, within each block denomination, the child removes the number of blocks specified in the bottom number (step 7) and records the number of

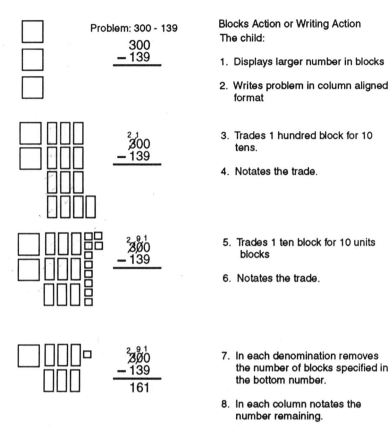

Figure 4.3
Lauren Resnick's mapping instruction has children work with blocks and number symbols simultaneously to solve multi-digit arithmetic problems. This helps the children to see explicitly the relation between the block and numeric representations: written computations record block procedures, and block procedures justify the written computations. (From Resnick 1982, p. 149. Used with permission of Lawrence Erlbaum Associates.)

blocks remaining in the appropriate column (step 8). After 40 minutes of instruction, children can do the procedure flawlessly on their own. The teacher then removes the blocks and the children do only written arithmetic.

Mapping instruction corrected children's buggy algorithms, such as using smaller-from-larger and borrow-across-zero, and after instruction no new bugs appeared. The children had a correct and deeper understanding of multi-digit arithmetic. Interviews with the children indicated that they knew why the standard subtraction procedure works, and they could explain why their previous bugs were wrong. With appropriate, explicit instruction to marry concepts and procedures, the children learned to manipulate symbols meaningfully. They could use their number understanding to repair their procedures on the basis of what numbers mean, not just on the basis of how written arithmetic should look.

The Bug Picture

Buggy rules and lack of conceptual understanding are not confined to multi-digit subtraction. Similar stories can be told for multi-digit multiplication and addition (Resnick 1980), decimal fractions (Hiebert and Wearne 1985), and even high school algebra (Matz 1982). Examples from my own elementary education are still with me. Why, when I multiply two decimal fractions, do I perform whole-number multiplication and then "point off" the total numbers of decimal places found in the two multiplicands (e.g., $4.73 \times 2.651 = 12.53923$)? Why, when dividing by a fraction, do I "invert and multiply" (e.g., $\frac{2}{3} \div \frac{1}{4}$ becomes $\frac{2}{3} \times \frac{4}{1} = \frac{8}{3}$)? In school I learned to execute these procedures flawlessly, but I never learned why they work. These procedures are much less exotic than casting out nines, yet for many adults there is little connection between conceptual knowledge and procedural skills. Mathematics as a high-order cognitive skill, a skill that can be flexibly applied to novel problems, requires that concepts and skills be interconnected.

What does this mean for current American educational practice? Although some children have difficulty mastering elementary math, most learn basic arithmetic facts and operations. Yet, according to national assessments, one-quarter of our seventh- and eighth-graders do not have sufficient grasp of multi-digit arithmetic to do everyday tasks. Only half of our high school students develop an understanding of number systems, and many have difficulty applying numerical concepts in nonroutine situations (Dossey et al. 1988). In other words, students have reasonable basic procedural skills, but their understanding of number concepts is weak.

The debate on how to improve elementary math instruction often pits those who argue for more number facts and computational fluency (primacy of procedural knowledge) against those who argue for more knowledge about the number system (primacy of conceptual knowledge). The NAEP results, and the data on Resnick's subject Sandra, show that computational skill doesn't ensure conceptual understanding. However, conceptually oriented instruction, although it recognizes the importance of relating underlying concepts to computational rules, sometimes leaves *too* much to children's inventive minds. Resnick's subjects Alan and Amanda demonstrate that we can't assume, as some conceptual approaches do, that with conceptual understanding children can invent or master the computational procedures. The power of a technique such as mapping instruction is that it *explicitly* combines the two kinds of knowledge that children need to build their mathematical expertise.

Most school math does not do this. Instruction either doesn't teach the underlying representations (such as the mental number line and the part-whole schema) or doesn't make the link between concept and procedure explicit. Some children make the connection on their own, but many do not. Without the link, mathematics is meaningless.

All children would benefit from understanding how number concepts support and give meaning to procedural skills. Some educators and critics may find this a painfully obvious conclusion. If so, it is an obvious conclusion that many schools apparently find hard to implement.

Word Problems: The Black Hole of Middle School Math

"While exploring a haunted house, Peter saw three cobwebs on the first floor and two on the second. How many cobwebs did he see altogether?" Word problems, such as this one, are supposed to teach problem solving and show how math is useful in everyday life, but as typically taught they do neither. Word problems are the black hole of middle school math: a lot of energy goes in and no light comes out.

Often the simplicity and artificiality of word problems undermine their purported educational purposes. Consider the cobweb problem. Its solution requires one operation applied to two given quantities. This is very unlike real-world quantitative problems, such as balancing a checkbook or making a budget, which are complex and which require multiple steps. Furthermore, the problems are posed *for* the students rather than *by* the students. If our goal is to teach problem-solving skills, we should remember that posing problems is one important such skill.

Also, word problems are typically presented without any context, except where they happen to be placed in the textbook. Problems about birds on fences, cobwebs in houses, and cookies in jars follow one after another. Rather than fostering a link to everyday experience, the problems insulate math from reality. Word problems become as meaningless as multi-digit subtraction. For example, when given the problem "One bus can carry 60 people. If 140 people have to be carried, how many buses must be rented?", children—who know you can't rent part of a bus—often answer $2\frac{1}{3}$ (Silver 1986).

Children hate word problems, don't understand their purpose, and see them as just another weird school task (Cognition and Technology Group 1991). However, being clever, they approach these tasks appropriately. The trick is to figure out which math operation to apply to the quantities stated in a problem to get the correct answer. Children use a superficial but adequate strategy: they look for a key word that reveals which operation to use. For example, "altogether" means add, "take away" means subtract, and "each" means multiply. Students pick an operation on the basis of the key word and apply it slavishly to every number in the problem, whether it makes sense or not. Because many texts group (say) rate problems together, once a student finds the key for one problem, he or she can do all the others the same way. Sometimes textbooks put even lower demands on students. Sandra Marshall analyzed math texts used in California and often found instructions like "Use addition to solve the following problems." With problems and texts like these, Marshall observed, "the idea that there is *any* meaning out there is lost."

The Adventures of Jasper Woodbury: Invitations to Thinking

Jill Ashworth is a fifth-grade teacher in the Franklin Middle School. Though it is in a rapidly growing satellite suburb of Nashville, this is a Title 1 designated school where over 50 percent of the children qualify for free lunches. On word problems, Ashworth's students are typical. "The children don't like word problems and certainly don't understand them," she says. Their lowest scores on standardized tests are on math applications. Fifteen minutes into her math class, children are gathered around a video monitor engaged in a noisy discussion of what information they need and what calculations they must do to develop a business plan for recycling aluminum cans. Children are recording data, spontaneously taking notes, and doing various calculations at their seats and at the board. Ashworth prompts and coaches.

In the afternoon, in Nancy Johnson's fourth-grade class at Franklin Road Academy, a private school in Nashville, groups of three students present their solutions for the quickest way to rescue a wounded eagle from Boone's Meadow using an ultralight aircraft. They are doing calculations about fuel consumption and payloads. Johnson describes her students as "emerging independent, yet accurate thinkers."

Jeff Swink's sixth-graders at Nashville's public Carter-Lawrence School discuss the effect of head and tail winds on an ultralight aircraft's ground speed. He comments: "The children like the challenge. They like to think, but don't often get a chance to."

Ashworth, Johnson, and Swink are participating in an experimental math curriculum, "The Adventures of Jasper Woodbury," developed by Vanderbilt University's Learning Technology Center (LTC). "Jasper" combines cognitive research and videodisc technology to create what the research team calls "invitations to thinking"— a meaningful alternative to word problems in the middle school math curriculum.

Jasper's Theoretical Basis: Representations and Inert Knowledge

The Learning Technology Center is a 30-member multi-disciplinary research group. Its co-directors, John Bransford, Susan Goldman, Ted Hasselbring, and Jim Pellegrino, bring decades of experience in basic cognitive research to their research on effective classroom instruction. One focus of the applied research at LTC is how to teach mathematical thinking as a high-order cognitive skill—to help children learn mathematical problem-solving skills, understand why they work, and know when to use them.

Bransford and his colleagues have contributed to the research, reviewed in chapter 3, on how hard it is to teach study skills and problem-solving strategies. In general, children will use the skills or strategies immediately after instruction but won't spontaneously use them later. They may even be able to describe a problem-solving or memory strategy in their own words, but they can't use it to solve problems. Yet if they can describe the strategies, the knowledge is in their memories. Therefore, being able to recall information from long-term memory when asked does not ensure spontaneous use of that information when it is useful. Cognitive scientists call knowledge that is in memory but is not active when it should be *inert knowledge*. The knowledge may be in long-term memory, but it is not triggered when it should be by conditions that are active in working memory. Many traditional educational practices produce inert knowledge—knowledge that is not accessible when it should be.

The difference between recalling information when asked and using it spontaneously when appropriate depends on how the knowledge is stored in memory. Often inert knowledge is stored as verbal propositions or memorized facts. As we have seen, some cognitive psychologists characterize active knowledge—knowledge available for use—as productions or condition-action pairs. The condition specifies when the knowledge encoded in the action is applicable. Some failures of traditional instruction might be characterized as overemphasizing the action part (the rote learning of facts) and underemphasizing the condition part (when to use the facts).

How we store knowledge depends on how we learn it. In 1989 Bransford and his colleagues ran an experiment in which they contrasted *fact-oriented* with *problem-oriented* learning. They had students read passages similar to those found in middle school science texts—passages on the nutritional values of the food groups, the use of water as a standard density for liquids, the design of solar-powered airplanes, and the way in which Bronze Age humans made oil lamps. The researchers told the students they would be tested on how much they remembered after reading the passages.

The researchers told one group of students, the "fact-oriented group," to remember as much as they could. A second group, the "problem-oriented group," read the information in a problem-solving context. The researchers told the problem-oriented subjects to read the passages as if they were preparing for a trip down the Amazon. Before the retention test, the students did a "filler" task to test spontaneous recall. This task was actually the heart of the experiment. Students were told to imagine they were planning a trip to the desert Southwest, and to list and discuss ten issues they would have to address in planning the trip. They were to be as explicit as possible: What kind of food should they take? How much water would they need?

The fact-oriented subjects never mentioned any of the information they had just read, and gave vague answers (such as "Take enough food and water"). The problem-oriented students spontaneously used information from the passages they had read and specifically mentioned kinds of food, the weight of water, and the availability of solar versus gasoline power in the desert. The students who had learned in a problem-oriented manner associated applicability conditions with the facts they had read. This helped them recall and use the facts on a new, but related, problem.

Problem-oriented learning works because students learn in a context that is similar to the eventual problem-solving situation, which helps them associate the new knowledge with conditions in which they might use it. If students learn and work with knowledge in a variety of contexts, they should associate the knowledge with all those contexts. This should help them use the knowledge more flexibly—even in novel situations. This research result led the LTC group to consider how they might create invitations to thinking for classroom use.

The goal of the LTC researchers became the creation of shared problem-solving contexts that students and teachers could explore to acquire active, rather than inert, knowledge—contexts that would invite students and teachers to think. They called their theory-based approach *anchored instruction*. Their hope was that problem-solving environments would create an "anchor" for learning that would generate interest and allow students to define problems. If the contexts were public and shared, students would have to explain and justify their problem-solving strategies to their peers, which in turn would encourage students to monitor their thinking and help them acquire metacognitive skills. Decades of research suggested to the LTC team that changing the learning situation would change students' performance.

Theory into Prototype

Much of the LTC's applied research had addressed the needs of middle school students with learning disabilities. In particular, the team saw the difficulties these students had with word problems (Bransford et al. 1988). Students with learning disabilities have the usual responses to word problems: they don't understand them, and they often use key-word strategies to guess which mathematical operation to apply. But these students also have other difficulties. In sixth grade, many have not learned elementary math facts and use counting procedures, like preschool children, to solve simple problems. Many of these children are poor readers, which makes word problems even more difficult. Often teachers think that solving word problems is beyond these students' capabilities.

To help these students, the LTC researchers realized they needed a rich problem context, yet one accessible to poor readers. They satisfied both requirements by "repurposing" (their word) the first 12 minutes of the movie *Raiders of the Lost Ark* as an invitation to think. In this segment, Indiana Jones treks from the river through the jungle to a cave where he finds the golden idol. Using the video, a group of learning-disabled students were encouraged to solve problems that Indy might have to solve: How wide is the pit Indy must jump over? How big is the idol? How long is the airplane? All the information the students needed could be found in the video. For example, on the pit problem students might observe that if Indy is 6 feet tall, then the pit is about 2 Indies, or 12 feet, wide. For comparison, a second group of learning-disabled students were given individual and intensive, but traditional, instruction on word problems.

Before instruction, both groups scored less than 20 percent correct on a word-problem test. After instruction, the video group raised their score to 50 percent, but the group receiving traditional instruction showed no improvement (Bransford et al. 1988). The researchers also tested for transfer by having students in both groups do word problems taken from a "non-Indy" context. Here the video students scored 60 percent correct, while the traditional students showed no improvement from the pretest. Anchored, video-based instruction more than doubled the scores on word problems, and in addition helped these children transfer the skills to novel, "non-Indy" problem contexts.

While encouraged, the LTC researchers also realized the limitations of using movies for instruction. *Raiders* was not made with math instruction in mind. One can teach only so many concepts and problems using *Raiders,* and what one can teach doesn't make a curriculum. In early 1988, the LTC produced its own video, *River Adventure.* In the video, students were told that they had won the use of a houseboat for a week and had to plan all the details of their one-week cruise. Among other things, they had to figure out the boat's cruising speed, how much fuel and water to take, and even the boat's length (so they could rent a suitable dock)—all by using information embedded in the video.

When they repeated the *Raiders* experiment with *River Adventure,* the LTC researchers obtained similar results (Van Haneghan et al. 1991). But with *River Adventure,* they also collected pre-instruction data on college students and on both high- and low-achieving fifth-graders. The college students performed adequately on the planning problem, but the middle school students (both high and low achievers) performed poorly. The fifth-graders often failed to consider crucial planning categories and seldom found the specific information they would need to plan their trip. They showed little inclination to use math at all, and when they did they produced wildly inaccurate numerical solutions. This was true even of the high-achieving students, who scored in the top 20 percent on standardized math tests (Bransford et al., n.d.).

This suggested to the LTC research team that video learning contexts might be of educational value for all students, regardless of measured math ability. They shared that insight with a group of classroom teachers, who provided advice and criticism. The teachers recognized the difficulties students have with multi-step problems and were excited about the idea of using video learning contexts in the classroom. They were, however, concerned about the effectiveness of *River Adventure.* Knowing what matters to children, the teachers pointed out that *River Adventure* was a home video, lacking the professional quality children expect. They also noted that it had no story line or narrative structure. The teachers feared that the video wouldn't hold students' attention.

This could have been a major setback but for the support of Bill Hawley, then Dean of Vanderbilt's Peabody College. Hawley supplemented the LTC's research budget with college funds to pay for professional videodisc production. The LTC team hired Tom Sturdevant to work with them on scripting and producing a problem-rich movie. Thus were Jasper Woodbury and his adventures conceived.

Jasper's Debut

With Sturdevant, the LTC researchers began to explore the ways in which videodisc technology might support rich, complex problem-solving contexts. In response to the teachers' criticisms, they decided that the learning contexts would have a strong story line to hold students' attention and to exploit as a memory aid what children know about the structure of stories. The stories would involve a character called Jasper Woodbury and his friends, all of whom live in Cumberland City. The video format would make complex problems accessible to weak readers and would provide believable connections between everyday experience and school math. The videos would be like good mysteries; all the clues are there, but you have to notice and interpret them to solve the problem.

In the summer of 1988, the first Jasper Woodbury video, *Journey to Cedar Creek,* was completed. One morning while reading the newspaper, Jasper, who is thirty-something, sees an ad for a 1956 Chris-Craft cruiser that needs work. He takes his aluminum fishing boat, the *Sweetie Pie,* up the Cumberland River to Cedar Creek, where he meets the cruiser's owner, a woman named Sal. Jasper tries the cruiser, buys it, and then learns that the running lights don't work, which means he must be off the river by sunset. The 15-minute video ends with Jasper still at Cedar Creek and mid-afternoon approaching. The students are given a challenge: Can Jasper get the cruiser home before sunset?

Answering the challenge requires that the students find in the video all the information they need to solve a lengthy time-rate-distance problem. They must solve at least 15 math problems and consider two major plans in the light of constraints presented in the video.

Figure 4.4 characterizes what students have to think about, know, and do to solve the problem. Can Jasper make it home? First, students must figure out from the video how much time and fuel Jasper needs to go from Cedar Creek to his home dock. Solving this problem, students find that Jasper has enough time but that the

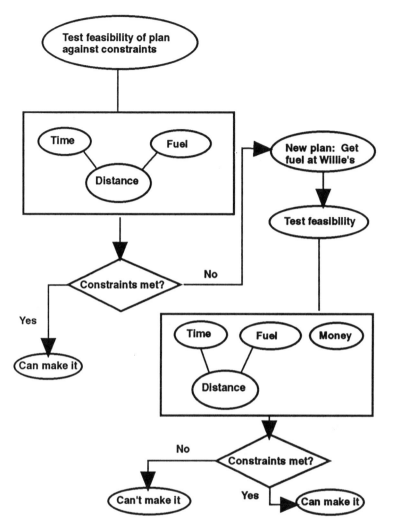

Figure 4.4
The solution path for *Journey to Cedar Creek* illustrates the problem's complexity. To solve it successfully, students have to consider two time-rate-distance problems. First (left box) they must figure out if Jasper has enough time and fuel to reach his home dock. They find that he has time but will have to refuel. This forces the students to evaluate an alternative plan of buying fuel at Willie's (right box). (From Goldman et al. 1991, figure 1. Used with authors' permission.)

cruiser will have to be refueled. So Jasper can't make it home without stopping for gas.

Students then have to consider a second problem. On the trip to Cedar Creek, Jasper stopped at Willie's marine gas station for repairs. But Willie's closes at a certain hour, Jasper left home with only $20 in cash, and Willie's doesn't take American Express. Does Jasper have enough time and fuel to reach Willie's? Does he have enough money to buy the fuel he needs? Working through this problem, students eventually find that Jasper can get to Willie's, can buy enough gas, and can get off the river before sunset. Middle school students rarely have to solve such complex problems.

In preliminary studies, *Journey to Cedar Creek* presented a for-midable challenge to both college and middle school students (Goldman et al. 1991). Without hints or prompting, about half the college students could figure out that Jasper had enough time to get home, but that he would have to refuel on the way. With hints about which subproblems had to be solved, 70 percent of the college students could solve both the time and the fuel problems. Among a group of 11 above-average sixth-graders (mean score on the Stanford Achievement test: 83 percent), only one could solve the time and fuel problems without hints. Even with explicit hints to consider time and fuel, only 18 percent of the sixth-graders solved the time problem, and none solved the fuel problem. Both groups, although expert at ready-made, one-step word problems, had difficulty posing and then solving a multi-step problem (Learning Technology Center 1990).

The true test of Jasper took place in classrooms. Several middle school teachers, Jill Ashworth and Jeff Swink among them, agreed to use Jasper on an experimental basis. The evaluation study involved both high- and low-achieving fifth-graders. The students in the ex-perimental groups worked on solving *Journey to Cedar Creek* for four to five consecutive days, devoting 50 minutes to Jasper each day. These students also had instruction on how to organize and plan solutions to multi-step problems. Students in the comparison groups received traditional word-problem instruction.

Students in the experimental groups liked learning with Jasper and felt that Jasper helped them learn more (Learning Technology Center 1990). Both high- and low-ability students improved at plan-ning and generating solution strategies for multi-step problems. After four Jasper sessions, the high-achieving fifth-graders matched or surpassed the college students' performance on each of the five main subproblems (Goldman et al. 1991).

On a standard one-step word-problem test, there was no significant difference between Jasper and traditional instruction for high-achieving students, but these students were already expert at such problems. Jasper did improve, from 34 percent to 43 percent correct, the performance of low-achieving students on traditional word problems (Learning Technology Center 1990). After Jasper, low-achieving students understood word problems better and made fewer mistakes in choosing which mathematical operation to use. In short, Jasper worked in the classroom, providing benefits for students at all achievement levels.

Jasper had other desirable effects. All the teachers commented on how video-based instruction reached out to nontraditional learners and weak readers. Children who had previously contributed little in the classroom became deeply involved. Reluctant students became highly motivated. Because of the strong story line, students recalled the details of the adventure from day to day and continued to work on the problems outside class time. Nancy Johnson's fourth-graders worked on Jasper for nearly two straight hours, a long time for children this age, and enjoyed the challenge. It also became evident that teachers with very different classroom styles—whole class versus small group, direct instruction versus discovery learning—could adapt to using Jasper.

The Jasper Implementation Network

Vanderbilt's chancellor, Joe B. Wyatt, is an educator committed to combining the expertise of higher education with that of the corporate world to improve America's schools. A pioneer in computer science, Wyatt believes that technology, intelligently applied, can improve productivity in both schools and industry. Wyatt saw the Jasper videos and asked the LTC group to make a presentation to Vanderbilt's trustees in the autumn of 1989. The trustees ended up sharing Wyatt's enthusiasm for Jasper and several of them offered to sponsor its use in their local schools. Wyatt encouraged the LTC research team to develop an implementation network that would disseminate and test Jasper in schools at a distance from Nashville.

Wyatt committed funds to allow collaboration with teachers at the Carter-Lawrence School and to produce two more Jasper adventures, *The Big Splash* and *A Capital Idea*. These videos challenge students to use math skills, statistics in particular, to develop business plans. And Wyatt prepared his own video describing the Jasper Implementation Project and its educational importance, which he distributed to business leaders throughout the Southeast. Ten corporations responded by sponsoring schools at a cost of $50,000 each. The sponsors purchased the Jasper materials and equipment for a school of their choice, named a corporate representative to work 20 hours per week with teachers in the school, and provided support for two teachers and the representative to attend a two-week training course.

Currently, the Jasper Implementation Network includes more than 1500 students in 16 schools in nine states, from Georgia to Indiana to Texas. Dozens of teachers are experimenting with Jasper in diverse settings and within a variety of standard curricula.

The Implementation Network is playing an important role in assessing how Jasper works and how it can be used in real school situations. In cooperation with Network schools and teachers, the LTC group has developed ways to assess Jasper's impact on thinking and problem-solving skills—skills not measured by current standardized exams. When data on nearly 1000 students in 16 different schools began flowing into the LTC from the implementation sites, even the researchers, who thrive on data, were momentarily overwhelmed. They decided to concentrate their data analysis on five sites where they could compare two Jasper and two non-Jasper classrooms per site (Learning Technology Center 1991). This involved looking at the data from tests given at the beginning and the end of the year to a total of 221 Jasper students and 214 comparison students. On all the pretests, the Jasper and non-Jasper students were equal; thus, year-end differences had to be attributable to what happened in the classrooms during the year.

The Jasper students showed improved attitudes toward math and math instruction at year's end. They showed more interest in math and a greater willingness to tackle challenging problems. The non-Jasper students showed decreased interest in math and less willingness to attempt hard problems. Jasper students improved more than non-Jasper students in appreciating the usefulness of math. Most important, Jasper students' math anxiety decreased over the year, while non-Jasper students' anxiety increased.

Jill lives in Carson City. She wants to drive her car from her house to a friend's house in Meridian. As shown on the map, Jill can take the road from Carson City to Johnstown and Johnstown to Meridien. Her car is filled with gasoline and ready to go. There are gas stations in Carson City, Ceymore, and Meridien, but there is not one in Johnstown. Jill plans to leave at 8:00 in the morning.

Top-Level Planning Challenge: What does Jill need to think about to figure out how long it will take to make the trip?

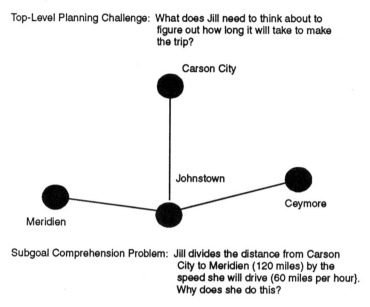

Subgoal Comprehension Problem: Jill divides the distance from Carson City to Meridien (120 miles) by the speed she will drive (60 miles per hour}. Why does she do this?

Figure 4.5
This problem, which involves planning a trip, forces students to formulate subproblems (a top-level planning challenge) and asks them to specify the subproblem which a specific calculation answers (a subgoal-comprehension problem). (From Learning Technology Center 1991. Used with authors' permission.)

On word problems, the Jasper students did significantly better than the comparison students on one-step, two-step, and multi-step word problems. The LTC team designed special problems to test students' planning skills and their understanding of how subproblems fit into the solution path. Figure 4.5 shows a sample problem. On these problems, solving the planning problem requires the students to formulate the subproblems that have to be considered in a solution. The subgoal comprehension question gives a calculation, and the students have to specify the subproblem the calculation answers.

The Jasper students improved their planning performance by over 20 percent during the year; the comparison students improved only 5 percent. On understanding subproblems, the Jasper students also improved over 20 percent, the comparison students just over 10 percent. The LTC researchers had not developed Jasper with standardized math tests in mind, but they were able to get achievement-test scores for Jasper and non-Jasper students at four schools. Jasper classes met or surpassed the standardized test scores of non-Jasper classes at three of the four sites.

Assessment of new curricula and teaching methods on an even larger scale will become increasingly important if we are to identify methods that help students from diverse populations master mathematics as a high-order skill. For now, the LTC researchers can take satisfaction from the early returns on Jasper. As they wrote in a newsletter to the Jasper Implementation Network schools: "By any possible set of realistic standards and expectations one could not have asked for a more positive set of assessment outcomes. At five different sites, located in five different states, with varying curricula and with widely different levels of academic achievement, the children in Jasper classrooms performed better than children in non-Jasper classrooms on an array of attitude, conceptual, computational, and problem solving measures." (Learning Technology Center 1991, p. 4)

Jasper is a model for how research can lead to effective practice when all the pieces fall into place—a talented, multi-disciplinary research team with real-world concerns, interested and committed classroom professionals, influential university administrators, and public-minded business leaders. These groups, working together, moved Jasper from inception to implementation testing in only 4 years, and the Network continues to grow.

Jasper shows that school reform should begin with a consideration of how children learn. Jasper provides anchored instruction, a concept based on years of cognitive research which helps middle school students reach a level of mathematical proficiency—the ability to solve multi-step problems—that most students fail to attain in our schools. Jasper is a tool that can help us teach math as a high-order skill.

Geometry Proof Tutor: An Underground Classic

John Anderson is the Walter van Dyke Bingham Professor of Psychology at Carnegie Mellon University, a past president of the Cognitive Science Society, and a leading cognitive theoretician. Aware that geometry is one of the least-liked high school subjects, Anderson decided, around 1980, to test his cognitive theory by building the Geometry Proof Tutor (GPTutor). Anderson calls it an "underground classic," famous within the cognitive community but unknown outside. GPTutor is an example of intelligent computer-assisted instruction, in which interactive computer technology implements an underlying expert model as a teaching tool.

Since his graduate student days at Stanford in the 1970s, Anderson has studied how human memory works. He has used computers to model our cognitive architecture and has proposed a theory, called ACT*, that attempts to give a general explanation for skill learning and problem solving in all domains. According to ACT*, we have a long-term memory for facts—a declarative memory—which has an associative structure. We also have a long-term store of procedural knowledge organized as a set of production rules—If-Then rules like those in Siegler's balance-scale rules. Interaction between these memory structures and the outside world occurs in working memory.

On Anderson's theory, all knowledge starts out as factual knowledge stored in declarative memory, where we can manipulate it only by using weak, domain-independent methods such as means-end analysis or hill climbing. Learning takes place when we build new production rules from the contents of declarative memory. When we use knowledge repeatedly in solving problems, our cognitive architecture builds new, domain-specific production rules. We transform factual knowledge into If-Then rules—into condition-action pairs.

ACT* posits two mechanisms for building production rules: *proceduralization* and *composition.*

Proceduralization eliminates the need to search declarative memory for a specific fact by building the fact into a production. This allows us to use the fact directly whenever the condition associated with it becomes active in working memory. For example, a general rule might be

IF the goal is to perform an operation on a number and there is a calculator function that performs this operation
THEN apply the calculator function to the number.

This rule is general because it states a link between possible mathematical operations and possible calculator functions, without specifying either. To apply the rule, we have to specify an operation and then search long-term memory to see if there is a calculator function to perform the operation. After proceduralization, the general rule gives way to a set of more specific rules such as

IF the goal is to find the square root of x
THEN enter x into the calculator and press the button marked √.

The new production creates a mental link between a specific operation (finding the square root) and the appropriate button on the calculator. We no longer have to try to remember whether there is such a button.

Composition combines rules we use repeatedly in sequence into a single rule that gives the same overall result. This can speed up our problem solving. For example, suppose you repeatedly have to find the final prices of items after you get your customary 20 percent discount and pay the mandatory 8 percent sales tax. You might start out with two rules:

IF the goal is to find the price after a 20 percent discount
THEN multiply the price by .80.
IF the goal is to find the price including the sales tax
THEN multiply the price by 1.08.

After repeated use, composition collapses these two rules into one:

IF the goal is to find the price after the 20 percent discount but with the 8 percent sales tax
THEN multiply the price by .864.

Anderson contends that we can explain most skill learning by showing how learning mechanisms like these build new condition-action pairs.

In his research, Anderson observed that students at all grade levels had difficulty absorbing and using verbal instruction. Reading and listening to lectures might put facts into declarative memory, but once there the facts aren't always easy to use. As we have seen several times, facts can remain inert in problem-solving situations. According to ACT*, we organize facts into new production rules— we link facts to conditions of use—only when we use the facts repeatedly to solve problems.

Anderson and his colleagues also knew that children learn better with private tutors. Generally, children who are tutored reach the same level of achievement 4 times faster than children taught in classrooms (Anderson, Boyle, and Yost 1985). Often, tutoring helps the weakest students most and has little effect on the most able.

With his background in computing, Anderson conceptualized the tutoring interaction as one in which an expert-like set of production rules interacts with, develops, and corrects a student's initial, buggy model of factual knowledge. A computerized tutor built on ACT★ principles might improve a student's performance as effectively as a human tutor, Anderson reasoned, and a successful tutor might also provide data to support ACT★. At worst, building a tutor would result in an explicit cognitive model of expertise in a particular field, or domain, that might give a precise, detailed description of educational objectives in that domain.

The Sorry State of Geometry

Anderson chose geometry as the target domain. Though some educators question the value of geometry at all, it is often the only experience students get in constructing proofs, a notion central to higher math and logic. Also, for many students it is their first and only exposure to the rigor and precision of scientific thinking. It can serve as an example of what careful, critical thinking in other domains might be like.

However, what is elegant and essential to mathematicians and scientists—constructing proofs and thinking critically—is alien and unpleasant to most high school sophomores. If students understand geometry—if it is taught meaningfully—geometry is also useful. When taught poorly, geometry is as meaningless for high school students as multi-digit subtraction and word problems are for younger children.

As it is traditionally taught, constructing geometry proofs is a highly ritualized task. Figure 4.6 shows a typical, moderately difficult problem and its proof in the standard two-column format. The rules of the geometry game appear to be simple, at least as they are formulated for students. What you do in geometry is prove statements such as "M is the midpoint of EF." Using the "givens" and other geometrical facts, students have to create a chain of inferences from the givens to the conclusion and give a reason for each link in

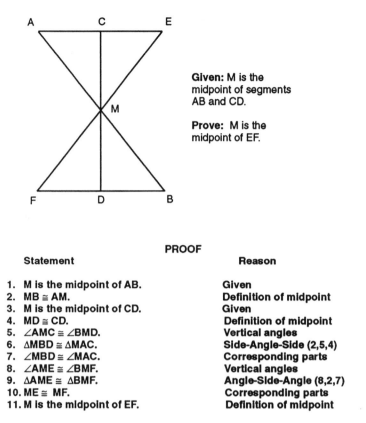

Given: M is the
midpoint of segments
AB and CD.

Prove: M is the
midpoint of EF.

PROOF

Statement	Reason
1. M is the midpoint of AB.	Given
2. MB ≅ AM.	Definition of midpoint
3. M is the midpoint of CD.	Given
4. MD ≅ CD.	Definition of midpoint
5. ∠AMC ≅ ∠BMD.	Vertical angles
6. ∆MBD ≅ ∆MAC.	Side-Angle-Side (2,5,4)
7. ∠MBD ≅ ∠MAC.	Corresponding parts
8. ∠AME ≅ ∠BMF.	Vertical angles
9. ∆AME ≅ ∆BMF.	Angle-Side-Angle (8,2,7)
10. ME ≅ MF.	Corresponding parts
11. M is the midpoint of EF.	Definition of midpoint

Figure 4.6
A geometry proof in the standard two-column format.

the chain. Reasons can be givens, definitions ("If M is the midpoint of AB, then AM = MB"), postulates ("For a line, L, and a point P not on L, only one line can be drawn through P parallel to L"), or theorems proved previously (e.g. the theorem of alternate interior angles). Students write statements in the left column and reasons in the right column; they generate two lists.

GPTutor breaks from this ritual. It has three components: an expert model, a tutor, and an interface.

The Expert Model

A geometry tutor built on ACT★ principles would have to teach students to do proofs like the one above. It would have to contain an expert model in which, as ACT* requires, geometric knowledge is encoded as a set of productions. Anderson and his colleagues performed a task analysis to identify the geometric knowledge experts had and how they used it. By 1983 they had codified a set of 200 production rules that were adequate to solve all the problems in the first four chapters of a standard high school geometry text—the material typically covered in one semester.

In the rules, the conditions refer to features of the diagram, givens, established inferences, and goals; the actions state the allowed inference. A typical rule might be

IF the goal is to prove that $\triangle XYZ$ and $\triangle UYW$ are congruent and XYW and ZYU are intersecting lines
THEN infer that $\angle XYZ = \angle UYW$ because of vertical angles.

This rule was used twice in the proof shown in figure 4.6. For example, it states the goal of proving line 6, and it justifies the inference at line 5, where X = A, Y = M, Z = C, W = B, and U = D.

The 200 rules are an expert model for constructing geometry proofs. Each rule represents a packet of knowledge which a student must have and which can be taught via a tutor-student interaction. The computer-generated proofs in which the rules were used were just like those that capable human subjects constructed. Where the computer proofs deviated from ideal human performance, they did so in ways in which competent humans might deviate from one another.

Once the knowledge was in the computer, the tutor could capitalize on the computer's speed and memory. For each problem in the curriculum, the computer "expert" could generate and store a solution file of *all* the most common (although not necessarily obvious) proofs. This file of possible proofs provided a standard with which to evaluate students' performance and correct their buggy rules.

The Tutor

The computerized tutor component contains information on how to teach students, including both strategies and error messages. The tutor compares a student's reasoning with possible paths in the expert model's solution file. When an error occurs, the tutor immediately gives remedial feedback. If the student makes a logical error that violates one of the rules of geometry, a window containing an error message appears and tells the student what he or she did wrong. The student can enter a different answer or ask for help (either a review of a previously learned rule or, if the student asks, a hint or strategic help). The tutor gives strategic help automatically whenever the student makes two logical errors in a row. Persistent logical errors result in GPTutor's giving strategic help to the point of completing the proof for the student. If a student does not make logical errors, he can explore any path through the problem space he desires until he makes correct but inappropriate inferences, makes multiple mistakes, or asks for help; the tutor will then give explicit hints to get the student back on a solution path.

The Interface

Students interact with GPTutor using a monitor, a keyboard, and a mouse. Initially, GPTutor displays the problem diagram at the top left of the monitor, the conclusion at top center, and the givens at the bottom (figure 4.7, upper panel). Students apply operators by pointing to statements on the screen with a cursor and by typing information on the screen; they can link statements on the screen whenever they can give an appropriate reason for doing so.

Unlike the two-column format, the way GPTutor displays information on the computer screen helps students see the purpose and structure of geometry proofs. On GPTutor, a proof is a path across the monitor from the givens to the goal where there is a geometrical justification for each step. Students see that to construct this path they have to generate new knowledge by applying geometrical operators (definitions, postulates, and theorems) to existing knowledge states. Thus, the GPTutor display lets the students visualize the problem space for geometry proofs. From among all the possible paths that the geometrical operators can generate, starting from the givens, the students have to find a path that leads to the goal. The display format also makes clear what geometrical operators do: they take premises as raw material, or conditions, and produce an output, or action, that is a new piece of knowledge. What students learn in geometry aren't facts for memorization, but rules and procedures with which to infer new knowledge.

This format, unlike the standard two-column format, also represents what experts really do in the proof process. In traditional

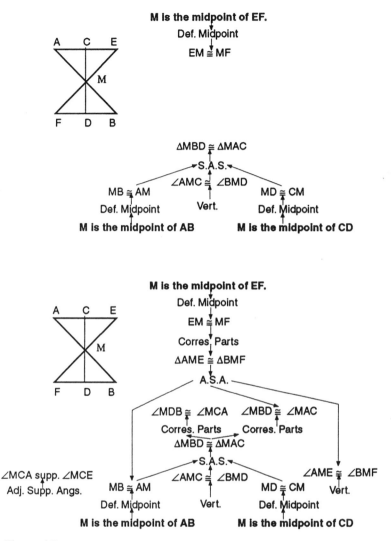

Figure 4.7
This is how the proof in figure 4.6 appears in the GPTutor format. The initial
screen (upper panel) includes the problem diagram, the givens (boldface type at
bottom of screen), and the statement to be proved (boldface type at top of
screen). This panel shows how the screen might look early in the proof. The
student has reasoned backward (downward-pointing arrows) from the goal to
the statement that segments EM and MF are congruent, and has reasoned
forward (upward-pointing arrows) from the givens to the statement that triangles MBD and MAC are congruent. The lower panel shows the additional
forward and backward reasoning leading to the completed proof. (From Anderson et al. 1985, p. 5. Used with authors' permission.)

instruction, high school students often get the impression that the geometry game requires steady forward progress from givens to conclusion. Actually, experts often construct proofs by reasoning both forward from the givens and backward from the eventual conclusion. Arrows pointing up on the GPTutor screen represent forward reasoning; arrows pointing down represent backward reasoning. The geometry proof game demands that you construct a path, but it doesn't have to be a one-way street. Students are relieved to learn this. Reasoning both forward and backward isn't cheating; it's an essential part of the game.

The upper panel of figure 4.7 shows how the student might work forward from givens to the congruence of triangles MBD and MAC (all arrows up) and backward from the conclusion to the statement that segments EM and MF are congruent (all arrows down). At this point the student's problem is to find a way to connect these two intermediate results. The student uses one more forward and one more backward inference to make the connection.

The lower panel shows the complete proof and illustrates another feature that can be lost in typical geometry instruction. Even good problem solvers commonly embark on blind paths and generate information that is not used in the final solution. The inference about the relation between angles MCA and MCE at the lower left is not used in the proof; neither is the inference about the congruence of angles MDB and MCA. Also, a number of paths starting from initial inferences merge as the proof inches up the screen. A proof is more like an inverted tree than a list.

These features of how proofs look on the screen may contribute significantly to GPTutor's success. We have seen that students think of postulates, definitions, and theorems as facts, when they are really operators that generate new knowledge. We have seen, too, that the traditional two-column proof format doesn't really capture the way in which an expert constructs a proof. Because so little of the actual expert process is apparent in the conventional learning and problem-solving environment, an enigmatic aura surrounds the learning of geometry (Koedinger 1991). GPTutor reflects more accurately the cognitive processes involved in constructing proofs and thus can help make geometry less enigmatic and more meaningful to students.

GPTutor results in knowledge acquisition in the context of problem solving, just as Jasper does. The GPTutor curriculum introduces one new concept at a time and instruction proceeds at the student's own pace. This allows the student to work on relevant problems until the concept is mastered—that is, until the student has built the new production rules he or she needs.

GPTutor in the Classroom

By 1985, GPTutor was ready for testing. Toward the end of the developmental stage, Anderson and his colleagues taught three students with their computerized tutor. One student came for remedial work after failing tenth grade geometry; two were eighth-graders with no background in geometry. All three learned geometry successfully, were able to solve problems more complex than those usually given in the classroom, and claimed to like geometry at the end of their tutoring.

The real test occurred during academic years 1985–86 and 1986–87 in a Pittsburgh public high school. Janet Schofield, a psychologist who worked on the evaluation, called the school "Whitmore High" to maintain the confidentiality of the students and teachers in the study; she looked in particular at the social impact of GPTutor in the classroom.

Whitmore is a typical urban high school. It has 1300 students, 55 percent of whom are black, 40 percent white, and 5 percent other (mostly Asian). The faculty is 80 percent white and 55 percent male. Two teachers used GPTutor in classrooms with small groups of students for one semester of geometry instruction in each of the two evaluation years. The first year was primarily a shakedown year— time needed to adapt a prototype to the classroom. During the second year, controlled experiments measured GPTutor's effectiveness.

The GPTutor classes spent 30 percent of their class time doing proofs on the machines (Wertheimer 1990). In one semester, students did over 200 proofs. The control group, taught traditionally, did the same proofs at the blackboard, as "seat work," or as homework. At semester's end, the evaluators compared the GPTutor and traditional classes using an eight-problem test. Students did the proofs in the standard two-column format. The GPTutor students averaged 79 percent on the post-test (according to their teacher, very good for a group that usually performed poorly)—and a standard deviation higher than the students in the traditional classes. In terms of grades, one standard deviation translates into a one-letter-grade difference (e.g., C's become B's).

GPTutor, like human tutors, helped weak students the most. The greatest improvement occurred in two groups that generally cause teachers the most difficulty: low-achieving bright students who might be bored with the traditional classroom, and students of average ability and below who lack confidence in their math skills. GPTutor also increased students' concentration, their attention, and their enthusiasm for a previously distasteful subject.

Schofield's social-psychological research revealed other, unintended benefits of GPTutor. At Whitmore, as at many schools, computers were available but were rarely used to teach academic subjects. Often teachers and administrators have no rationale for using computers to teach (Schofield and Verban 1988). GPTutor provided a rationale. Anderson and his colleagues could explain to teachers that constant monitoring and guidance of student problem solving, comparison of ideal and buggy models, and the possibility of individualized, immediate feedback facilitate learning in ways impossible in a traditional classroom. The teachers now had several good reasons to use computers for teaching.

In the classroom, GPTutor affected both students' and teachers' behavior. The tutor's learning-while-solving design resulted in a shift from lecture and group instruction to problem solving and individual instruction. When lecturing, teachers often call disproportionately on the brighter students; this saves time and saves less able students from embarrassment in front of their peers. The drawback, from a cognitive perspective, is that the more able students give answers before the slower students can completely solve the problems—not an ideal situation if knowledge is best acquired during problem solving.

With GPTutor, the slower students received more attention than the brighter ones. Schofield estimated that slower students received 4 to 5 times more attention than in a traditional classroom. Students could work at their own pace, so the teacher could assist the less able learners while not slowing down the others. Even though the less able received more attention, it was not a source of embarrassment. Errors were made between student and computer, and the teacher gave help privately. Most of the time, the class did not know who the teacher was helping or why.

GPTutor changed the teacher's role in the classroom from that of a purveyor of truths to that of a supportive collaborator. This shift was apparent to the students. As one said, "He doesn't teach us any more. He just helps us." Teachers became less likely to initiate interactions with students; often, they didn't have time. Teachers were too busy responding to students' requests for help. This gave the students more control over the learning situation. The teachers' help complemented and individualized the computer-generated feedback. Rather than becoming impersonal, as some might fear, learning with the computers became more highly personalized because the teacher could assume a helping role.

GPTutor affected grading and evaluation. Because it allows self-paced instruction, grading everyone to the same standard for the semester, on the basis of homework, quizzes, and tests, didn't seem right to the teachers, who began (some of them reluctantly) to consider effort as a factor in determining grades. Oddly, GPTutor also raised difficulties in the evaluation of teachers. The GPTutor classes ran so differently from traditional classes that the chairman of the math department did not know how to rate the teachers.

Students increased their effort and spent more time on task. GPTutor classes always started promptly. Some students would begin working before the bell sounded and would continue until the bell signaled the end of the period—behavior rarely seen in the traditional classes, where students spent the first 5 to 10 minutes socializing. Much to everyone's surprise, the GPTutor resulted in a high level of competition among the students, even though learning was supposed to be self-paced. Students competed to see how quickly they could work through the curriculum. Interchanges like this occurred: "Val, what problem are you on?" "53." "Damn, we're only on 42."

The students worked hard because they enjoyed it more. Seeing a similarity between computer games and GPTutor, they worked playfully but productively at geometry. Working on the tutor also created a sense of personal challenge, which many students enjoyed. Students were uninhibited in expressing their frustration and anger to the machines, something they couldn't do to a teacher. One student reported, "It's fun, it makes you want to learn something!"

From Theory to Practice to Theory

Anderson and his colleagues feel they can improve on their underground classic. They think that a tutor built around a refined expert model might be able to improve a given student's performance two standard deviations, or two letter grades, above what that student might achieve in a traditional classroom.

In the test of GPTutor at Whitmore, the computers recorded all of the work done on them. When analyzing those data, the researchers noticed interesting differences between stronger and weaker students. Strong students spent more time at the outset planning a proof. These students developed a global plan before they touched the keyboard, but once they had started they completed the proofs quickly. Weak students used the given information to begin making inferences immediately without developing a strategic plan. Although GPTutor uses a different proof format than the standard one, it still works inference by inference, using local information. In contrast, the student experts planned strategically and used larger chunks of knowledge in their proofs (Koedinger and Anderson 1990).

Ken Koedinger, one of Anderson's postdoctoral fellows, is using these insights to build a second-generation tutor, ANGLE (Koedinger and Anderson 1993). According to Koedinger, the classroom data led to more "good old-fashioned cognitive research: analyzing verbal protocols of good solvers, characterizing problem spaces, doing task analyses, and writing a computer simulation to match the verbal protocols." This research resulted in a new expert model for ANGLE, a model that utilizes global knowledge and exploits the visual information found in problem diagrams.

Initial tests of ANGLE in a laboratory study were promising. ANGLE matched GPTutor's one-letter-grade improvement after only 1.5 man-years of development, versus GPTutor's 10 man-years. It is still hoped that a two-grade improvement is possible.

Why does GPTutor remain an underground classic while Jasper is much more widely disseminated? Part of the answer is that GPTutor did not benefit from anything comparable to Joe Wyatt's efforts to link research, corporations, and schools around the Jasper project. Differences between the instructional interventions themselves, though, are also part of the explanation.

Jasper requires one VCR per classroom of 20 to 25 students. With GPTutor, ideally, each student should have a computer; at worst, each should share a terminal with one other student. Although the cost of computers continues to drop, one VCR is much less expensive than 10 to 12 Macintosh SEs, the least expensive machine that can run GPTutor. Furthermore, educators unanimously endorse the importance of word problems, but there is less agreement on the educational importance of Euclidean geometry.

Most significant, teachers are more comfortable with Jasper, and schools can accommodate it more easily. Teachers are more familiar and comfortable with VCRs than they are with artificial intelligence programs. Teachers also have more control over Jasper. Jasper now can provide only a few week's instruction per year; teachers integrate it into their regular, traditional curriculum. Children become highly engaged in the adventures, but the teachers still control the details of the curriculum and the classroom discussion. GPTutor, in contrast, provides a complete curriculum and puts the teacher in the untraditional role of coach and private counselor. This, as Schofield's research showed, has some benefits, but not every teacher is comfortable in this passive, coaching role.

Finally, teachers control the pace of Jasper instruction, whereas GPTutor is self-paced. School structure and traditions can't easily accommodate self-paced instruction. Self-paced instruction does not fit easily into the traditional school year or day. What do you do for students who need more time than five class periods a week to master a computerized curriculum? A student can't use GPTutor in study hall or at home unless the school or the parents invest in a computer. What do you do with students who can progress through a semester of geometry in six weeks? Educationally this would be highly desirable, but it would bring with it practical problems many schools are loath to address. This raises an important question for school restructuring: If we wanted to use computer-based, self-paced instruction, how would we have to reorganize our schools? Someday, and it may be soon, we might want an answer to this question.

Anderson, Koedinger, and their colleagues are well aware of the obstacles to widespread use of intelligent computerized instruction in our schools. They believe that eventually these obstacles will fall. For now, they point out that GPTutor has considerable educational value even if the computer program itself is not used in classrooms. On their view, the computerized tutor itself is not what is most important educationally; what matters is the cognitive model that drives the tutor. Koedinger observes that the GPTutor and ANGLE expert models have powerful implications for curriculum organization, invention of new proof formats, and testing. These are benefits in themselves, as Anderson recognized in 1980.

Cognitive models of expert performance, for any task in any domain, make the requisite knowledge and skills explicit. As compendia of what experts know and do, the models themselves can inform educational change now, even if computer tutors are never built. "It is these models we must get to educators," Anderson reminds us.

5
Science: Inside the Black Box

Try answering the following four physics problems. To solve them you need no mathematics, but you do have to understand some basic physical principles. A hint, in case you haven't worked at physics in a while, is that the problems require using Newton's First and Second Laws of Motion. The First Law says that if no unbalanced force acts on a body, the body moves uniformly in a straight line. The Second Law says that if an unbalanced force acts on a body, then the force equals the product of the body's mass and its acceleration. The answers are given in note 1.

Problem 1. A coin is tossed in the air and follows the path shown in panel A of figure 5.1. In which panel, B or C, do the arrows correctly show the forces acting on the coin on the upward (a) and downward (b) parts of its trajectory?

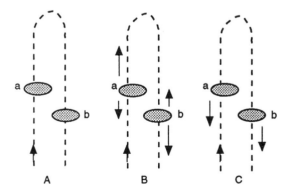

Figure 5.1
(From Clement 1982. Used with permission of the author and the *American Journal of Physics*.)

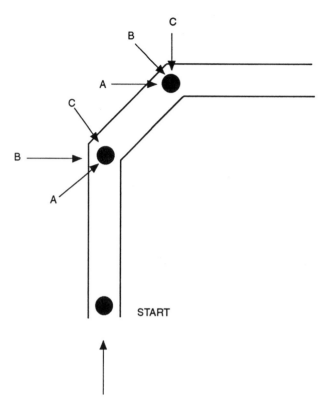

Figure 5.2
(From White and Horwitz 1987. Used with permission of Barbara Y. White.)

Problem 2. Suppose you are trying to get a hockey puck to travel along the track shown in figure 5.2. At the beginning, somebody hits it in the direction shown.

(i) In which direction, A, B, or C, does somebody hit it so that the puck makes the first turn?

(ii) In which direction, A, B, or C, does somebody hit it so that the puck makes the second turn?

Problem 3. Under normal atmospheric conditions, an object is placed on a scale and the scale reads 10 pounds (figure 5.3). If the scale and the object were placed under a glass dome and all the air were removed from under the dome, what would the scale read?

Problem 4. An object weighing 1 kilogram in normal air takes 1 second to fall a distance d (figure 5.4). How long will it take an

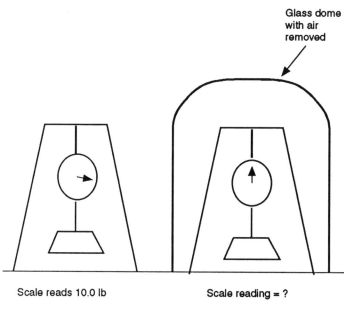

Scale reads 10.0 lb   Scale reading = ?

Figure 5.3
(From Jim Minstrell's diagnostic quiz. Used with his permission.)

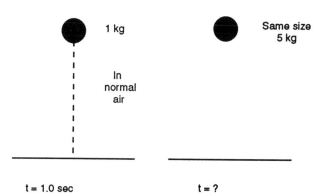

t = 1.0 sec   t = ?

Figure 5.4
(From Jim Minstrell's diagnostic quiz. Used with his permission.)

object the same size but weighing 5 kilograms to fall the same distance?

If you didn't answer all the questions correctly, don't feel bad. Most people get them wrong. By chapter's end you will understand these problems and why we tend to make the mistakes we do. These problems appear simple, but they are classic examples from cognitive science and science education of how naive theories or misconceptions dominate everyday reasoning about physical objects. Science educators also know that these misconceptions are hard to change with traditional science instruction.

John Clement (1982) was one of the first to study how we reason about the coin problem. He found that what leads us to choose B rather than C is the misconception that flipping a coin gives it an *impetus*. On the upward path, we reason, the impetus gradually diminishes, until it becomes less than the force of gravity and the coin falls. According to Newton, however, once we toss the coin it would continue on a straight-line path indefinitely unless an unbalanced force acts on it. The only force acting on it is gravity. Gravity causes the coin to slow down until it reaches the top of its trajectory, and then to speed up as it falls back to the ground.

Clement found that only 12 percent of students in a first-year engineering course, all high school physics graduates, answered the coin problem correctly. Worse, 72 percent of these students still gave the wrong answer after their first semester of college physics, as did 70 percent after *two* semesters!

Engineering students who persevere through two semesters of college physics are among the most successful science students in our schools. Yet, after all this formal instruction, their naive conceptions of force and motion remained in place. They couldn't apply Newton's Laws to simple problems, though they could all, no doubt, recite the laws and write equations for them.

The coin problem is not an isolated case, and physics isn't the only science where misconceptions occur. Cognitive scientists and science educators have examples of misconceptions from the physical and biological sciences at all grade levels—misconceptions that persist through years of science instruction.

Cognitive research suggests how science instruction might be improved to correct these misconceptions. It also suggests what must be done to teach science as a high-order skill. The National Assessments show that most students can recall simple science facts, but that serious deficiencies occur at the higher levels of science proficiency. Students are weak in applying the facts they know, interpreting data, evaluating experimental design, and using specialized scientific knowledge to draw conclusions. They are poor at reasoning scientifically, which is to say they don't really understand science. Most of the examples in this chapter are from physics, but the results, insights, and conclusions generalize to other school sciences.

Inside the Black Box

A favorite metaphor among scientists is the *black box*. A black box is a process or phenomenon such that scientists know what goes in and what comes out, but are ignorant of what happens in between. Scientists find black boxes intellectually intolerable; they are obsessed with finding out what goes on inside them. Fred Reif, a physicist and a pioneer in applying cognitive science to improve science instruction, wonders why scientists don't bring the same obsession to teaching science. "While we make great efforts in physics to understand the mechanisms that underlie observed phenomena," he writes, "we are often content to consider scientists and students as 'black boxes' whose internal intellectual functioning can be left largely unexamined in spite of its importance for teaching" (Reif 1986, p. 48). Reif doesn't expect physicists to become psychologists, but he feels that science teachers could and should exploit what cognitive science has discovered about how their students think and learn.

The cognitive revolution showed that we can make sense of what goes on inside the mental black box. We can begin to understand the mental processes involved in learning and doing science.

Effective science instruction has to be sensitive to how long-term memory works. All learning depends on prior knowledge. Learners actively construct understanding by relating current experience, including classroom instruction, to preexisting schemas stored in long-term memory. Just as children spontaneously develop informal math knowledge from infancy, they also spontaneously construct scientific schemas—little theories about how the physical world works. Unlike preschoolers' informal knowledge of numbers, which is largely consistent with formal school theories, much of their informal, self-acquired science knowledge is inconsistent with formal science. Math education has to build on students' informal math conceptions. Effective science instruction has to start from student's informal science conceptions, build on those informal ideas that are consistent with formal science, and correct or eliminate the others. The glimpse cognitive research gives us into the black box can guide science instruction. Researchers have documented scores of scientific misconceptions, and in some cases have traced their development in children. We know much about novice-expert differences in scientific problem solving, especially in physics. We know how differences in what people know and how they organize their knowledge influence their problem solving. Understanding students' informal, naive ideas gives us a starting point for science instruction, and expert performance gives us an educational goal.

Misconceptions and Cognitive Development

The development of sophisticated experimental methods has helped developmental psychologists discover how much children, even infants, know about the physical world. Infants can't speak or even move well; but they can look, and they do so voraciously. Psychologists exploit this trait in a method they call *preferential looking*. The idea is simple. If you show an infant two objects or displays and the infant consistently prefers to look at one rather than the other, then you can infer that the infant notices some difference between the two objects or displays.

Psychologists sometimes elaborate on preferential looking by conducting *habituation* experiments. They show an infant a display until the infant begins to lose interest in looking at it. They then show the infant a test display. If the infant remains bored with the test display, it apparently sees no difference between the two displays; if the infant looks longer at the test display, it must see some differences.

Elizabeth Spelke, a developmental psychologist, studies how infants perceive objects. In one series of experiments, she showed 4-month-old infants a display like the first one in figure 5.5, until they began to lose interest in it (Spelke 1990). She then tested the infants with two displays: one showing a single moving rod and the other showing a fragmented moving rod. On average, infants looked twice as long at the fragmented as at the single rod. They found the fragmented rod more interesting; they saw it as different from the habituation display. Spelke reasoned that the infants had created a

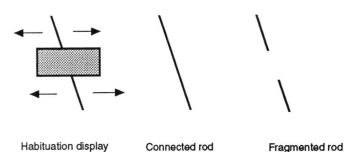

Habituation display   Connected rod   Fragmented rod

Figure 5.5
(From Spelke 1990, p. 34. Used with permission of Ablex Press.)

representation of a single connected rod during habituation. Although they were not able to see such a rod in the habituation display, they inferred that there was a single rod, so the fragmented rod in the test display surprised and interested them. Spelke found the same effect whether the rod in the habituation display moved left-right, up-down, or forward-back. If the rod did not move in the habituation display, children looked equally at the connected and fragmented rods in the test condition. Apparently, 4-month-old infants have no difficulty recognizing a partly hidden, moving object as a single object rather than as two separate ones.

Older infants, from 6 to 8 months old, have sophisticated understanding of how *hidden* stationary and moving objects behave. Renée Baillargeon (1986) used the habituation and preferred-looking techniques to study how infants perceive and understand events that involve moving objects. In the habituation event, the infant sat in front of a display that had a small screen placed to the right of an incline plane. The experimenter raised the screen to show the infant that nothing was behind it and then lowered the screen. At this point, a toy car rolled down the incline plane, disappeared behind the screen, reappeared to the right of the screen, and exited the display. After habituation, Baillargeon showed the infants two test events: a possible event and an impossible event. In the possible event she placed a box at the back of the display, behind the tracks the car rolled on. In the impossible event, she placed the box on top of the tracks so that it blocked the car's path. In both test events, the car rolled behind the screen, reappeared at the right, and rolled out of the display. The second event is "impossible" because a car can't roll through an obstructing box and reappear.

Baillargeon reasoned as follows: If the infants understood that (1) the box continues to exist in its same location when the screen hides it, (2) the car continues to exist and follows the same trajectory when hidden, and (3) the car can't roll through space occupied by the box, they should see the impossible event as genuinely surprising and look longer at it. If the infants lacked any one of these three beliefs, they should not see the event as impossible and should look equally at the possible and impossible test events.

When tested, the infants preferred to look at the impossible event! Baillargeon thus concluded that by the age of 6 to 8 months infants have all three beliefs. They have schemas that enable them to encode, or represent, both stationary (the box) and moving (the car) objects as permanently existing, even when hidden from sight. Moreover, infants appear to use these representations to reason about simple collision events involving objects they can't see. They realize that a hidden solid object (the car) can't move through space occupied by another hidden solid object (the box). The infants have a theory. Thus, Baillargeon writes, "the general problem for research becomes that of examining infants' naive 'theories' about the rules that underlie the displacement of objects, specifying the nature and range of their causal reasoning abilities" (1986, p. 40).

Parents and siblings don't teach infants these theories; infants acquire these schemas by observing the world around them. Spelke argues that this schema-building process gets started because there are information-processing principles hard-wired into the brain. The principles organize infants' initial experiences and call their attention to relevant features of physical objects. Spelke thinks that four principles are enough to get the process started: (1) that objects move as wholes on continuous paths (object cohesion), (2) that objects do not penetrate one another (boundedness), (3) that objects do not change shape as they move (rigidity), and (4) that objects move separately unless they come into contact (no action at a distance). On this view, the concept *physical object* is not something children learn, but an innate organizing concept that structures human experience. Humans come into the world wired to organize experience in terms of rigid objects that move along continuous paths and that interact by bumping into one another.

More important, Spelke observes, the same four principles—cohesion, boundedness, rigidity, and no action at a distance govern everyday, naive physics reasoning. This Spelke sees as a source of

Learning tools:

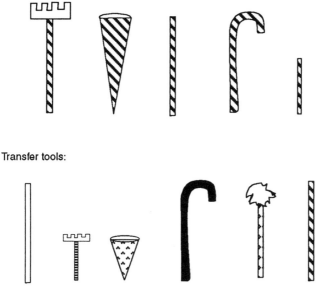

Transfer tools:

Figure 5.6
(From Brown 1990, p. 116. Used with permission of Ablex Press.)

both misconceptions and conceptions in naive physics. "It is possible," she writes, "that the principles by which infants perceive objects come to be deeply embedded in human thinking" (1990, p.54). If this is so, science instruction sometimes has to change how and where we apply these deeply embedded principles.

Between 17 and 36 months, children begin to understand what *causes* objects to move or be moved. Ann Brown (1990) has studied how young children learn to use tools and how they transfer this learning to novel situations. In one experiment, a child sits by its mother in a seat that prevents the child from reaching beyond arm's length. The experimenter presents a moving toy just outside the child's reach and gives the child a set of "tools" (figure 5.6). The experimenter puts the toy in motion and asks the child to get it. If the child doesn't use the tools spontaneously to get the toy, the mother picks the appropriate tool (here the rake or the hook) and shows the child how to use it. When the child can solve the problem three times in a row without help, the experimenter gives the child a set of "transfer tools," among which is at least one tool (here, the black hook) which the child could use to get the toy. Young children take less than 30 seconds to choose the right tool from the transfer set. If there is a correct choice in the transfer set, the children seldom make a mistake. The children couldn't be tricked into choosing a tool identical in color to the learning tool but too short or lacking an efficient pulling head. No child ever selected a nonrigid tool. If a child used the hook in the learning set, the child would not choose a hook from the transfer set if the hook was too short; the child would choose the rake instead. In this experiment, children did not choose tools on the basis of surface features, such as color or shape; they chose on the basis of relevant causal features, including rigidity, length, and effective pulling head. Children as young as 18 months had deep representations of how the tools might cause an object to move.

Between 3 and 10 years, there is a surge in children's scientific understanding. They develop schemas and naive theories not just about physics and motion, but also about biology and psychology (Carey 1985). One example, pertinent to physical science, is how during these years children develop an understanding of matter and material objects. Carol Smith, Susan Carey, and Marianne Wiser (1985) showed how this theory emerges as children construct distinct concepts of size, weight, and density.

Most adults understand that all material objects are made of matter, that only material objects have weight, and that not everything is a material object. If two objects are made from the same material, adults know that the larger object will weigh more. Adults know that shadows and holes are not material objects and know there are different kinds of matter that differ in density (weight per unit volume). Having the concept of density allows adults to understand why a smaller object made out of one kind of matter can be heavier than a larger one made of a different material. We adults have a theory about material objects that is so ingrained that we seldom think about it.

Children acquire this theory gradually, developing distinct concepts (schemas) for size, weight, and density. Smith, Carey, and Wiser traced how these concepts emerge between ages 3 and 10. In a series of careful experiments, they had children sort objects by size, weight, and density and then explain why they sorted the objects as they did. The idea behind these experiments is simple. Suppose we have a basketball, a bowling ball, and a steel ball bearing 2 inches in diameter. Sorting the objects by size from largest to smallest would give basketball, bowling ball, ball bearing. Sorting by weight would give bowling ball, ball bearing, basketball. Sorting by density would give ball bearing, bowling ball, basketball. Using many more objects—cylinders of different sizes and made of different materials— Smith, Carey, and Wiser explored in detail children's sorting patterns and their reasoning about size, weight, and density. Using these data, they determined whether the children had these concepts and how the children understood them.

Jean Piaget argued, on the basis of his experiments, that children between the ages 3 and 6 do not have distinct concepts of size and weight. Using their sorting tasks, Smith and her collaborators found that children as young as 3 years can sort objects correctly by either size or weight.

The density concept, "heavy for size," emerges only gradually. Children 4 to 5 years old, when asked to sort objects according to "heavy for size," sort by weight only and show no knowledge of density. By age 6, about one-third of the children Smith, Carey, and Wiser studied made correct density judgments. Nine-year-olds sorted objects correctly by density 75 percent of the time. For most of the older children, size, weight, and density were distinct concepts.

Once children have differentiated these concepts, they have a naive theory of material objects very much like an adult's. Most 10-year-olds understand that weight is an essential property of material objects. They will say that any material object, no matter how small, weighs something and that a styrofoam ball weighs something, though they can't feel its weight. They also can distinguish between the object and the material from which the object is made. If you ask them to describe what happens if a wooden table were to be put through a grinder, they say you would no longer have a table, but you would still have wood. The 10-year-olds' theory of matter is not entirely correct, however. They believe that matter is homogeneous and continuous. They will say, for example, that no matter how small you cut a piece of aluminum you will always have aluminum. This is a sophisticated theory, but it is distinctly at odds with the correct atomic theory of matter. The atomic theory tells us that matter is discontinuous, and that atoms place a lower limit on how small we can divide matter and still have the same material.

Developmental research tells us that by the age of 10 to 12 children have acquired considerable informal knowledge about how the physical world works, although often their schemas and concepts are fragmentary, poorly integrated, and inconsistently applied. In this way, children's and even adults' informal knowledge is rather unscientific, even where correct. Whereas formal science seeks highly integrated theories that have broad scope (Newton's three laws, Maxwell's four equations), many of us muddle through with fragmentary, parochial concepts and schemas.

Andrea diSessa (1982) and Barbara White (1988), among others, have studied how school children think about forces and motion, using problems similar to those in the quiz above and analyzing children's think-aloud protocols. Sixth graders' answers and explanations are not very different from those given by high school, college, and adult naive physicists.

Answers to the coin problem show that sixth-graders believe that a force gives an impetus to an object and that the impetus diminishes gradually until the object stops. Responses to the hockey-puck problem show that sixth-graders (like most adults) believe that an object moves in the direction in which it was last pushed. White found that children are not at all clear about what happens when a force acts on a moving object, like the puck, that already has a velocity. Among White's sixth-graders some argued that the new velocity would override the initial velocity (causing the object to move in the direction of the second force), some that the two velocities would fight for control and one would win (this would use energy, so the object would move more slowly after the second impulse), and some that the two velocities would take turns (the object would go in one direction for a while, then in the other). Children may know a lot about the physical world, but they don't understand Newton's Second Law, nor do they understand how multiple forces combine to give an object a single velocity. Many adults and high school science students don't understand these things either.

The Jumping-Off Point

By watching the world around them, children develop rather sophisticated proto-scientific concepts and schemas. This has several consequences for how we think about and design science instruction for children.

In science, as in math, children often have a lot more knowledge than we think. Serious science instruction need not wait until junior high school. Children's knowledge about material objects and what causes them to move are rudimentary scientific theories. The challenge, as in early math instruction, is to understand children's theories and concepts and build effective instruction on them—instruction that helps students map their informal understanding of how the world works onto the formal scientific theories they encounter in school.

Developmental research on scientific understanding has another worrisome parallel with math learning. The results reviewed above summarize what we know about the typical developmental trajectory. However, not all children follow this standard developmental path. Some findings suggest that children who have difficulty with school science may not have developed informally the schemas they need to understand school science instruction.

Smith, Carey, and Wiser's (1985) work on how children develop an informal theory of matter provides an example. In one of their experiments, they worked with fifth-graders at a private day school in Cambridge, Massachusetts. Among these students, about 50 percent fully distinguished weight from density and believed that continually dividing a piece of aluminum resulted in ever smaller pieces of aluminum. Three-quarters of these fifth-graders thought that a styrofoam ball weighs something and that repeatedly dividing it would result in pieces that still had weight. Two-thirds of the children could correctly order objects by density.

Carol Smith decided to take the experiments out of the laboratory and into classrooms. She and her colleagues developed a computer-based curriculum to teach the theory of matter to middle school students (Smith 1990). Smith tested the curriculum in an inner-city public school. The results of a pretest given to assess what the children knew before they used her curriculum surprised her. On the pretest, the public school seventh-graders (again from low-socioeconomic-status families) did poorly in comparison with the original group of private school fifth-graders. Only 20 percent thought a piece of styrofoam had weight, and only 44 percent thought dividing the styrofoam would result in pieces that still had weight. Only 3 percent of the seventh-graders could correctly order objects by density. The low-SES seventh-graders had not developed the understanding of material objects found among the more privileged fifth-graders.

Smith's six-week curriculum was intended to teach the concepts and representations fundamental to the theory of matter to the seventh-graders. The research team worked closely with a highly motivated classroom teacher who was on the verge of admitting he couldn't get his students to understand density. The new curriculum replaced the regular science class. The research team and the teacher first taught the concepts of volume and mass, and then introduced density. Computer software modeled the key concepts for the students, using a series of increasingly more sophisticated visual representations (Grosslight and Snir 1989). At the most sophisticated, quantitative level, the software made volume, mass, and density "countable" for the students. A grid of squares laid over the rectangular objects let students count squares to find volumes. Small black "weight dots" inside the rectangle symbolized the object's weight; the students could count those. Density is mass per unit volume. The students could find this property and see how it related to volume and mass by counting the number of weight dots within each square of the volume grid. This is a transparent visual representation of weight per unit volume.

The students used these visual models of volume, mass, and density to answer questions, perform experiments, and play games. The games tested skill at identifying and manipulating the size, weight, and density variables. The program might present an object and challenge the student to create a second object that had half the volume of the first one but the same weight. Throughout the curriculum the software complemented, but did not replace, exploration and experimentation with real objects.

The curriculum presented these concepts in far greater depth and duration than the usual curriculum, but the teacher and the researcher would argue that the investment was worth it. After instruction, 67 percent of the seventh graders thought that the piece of styrofoam had weight, 80 percent believed cutting the styrofoam into smaller and smaller pieces resulted in pieces that still weighed something, and 25 percent could correctly sort objects by density. This is a vast improvement over the students' pretest performance, and it shows a level of understanding approaching that found in the original middle-class experimental group.

Smith's work tells us that not all children develop the robust, naive theories that most school science instruction assumes. Robbie Case and Sharon Griffin (see chapter 4) found a similar problem in math learning: Not all children arrive at school with a robust understanding of the number line. It seems that in our society some children, a disproportionate number of them from low-income families, have not had the experiences that develop the conceptual prerequisites for what we are trying to teach in school. If our science and math curricula assume that all students have these robust, naive conceptual prerequisites, then children lacking them will start at a serious disadvantage.

One goal for elementary science instruction might be to ensure that all children have the schemas and representations they need to benefit from formal science instruction. The challenges would be the same as in early math: Identify children who do not have the requisite informal theory, teach it to them, then help these children make the transition from their informal theories to formal school science.

Early instruction in physical science might concentrate on the theory of matter and on notions basic to naive physics. Carey (1985) has identified a similar set of concepts central to children's understanding of the biological sciences. Based on their experiences in the lab and in classrooms, Carey, Smith, and Wiser urge schools to organize science instruction around age-appropriate experiments and experiences. Children learn science better through activities than through lectures, because activities allow them to acquire knowledge while using it to solve problems. Compelling problems and activities provide vivid fixed points around which conceptual change can occur.

Carey gives this example: "For children who believe small objects, like a grain of rice, weigh nothing, it is an amazing experience to see that adding grains of rice one at a time to one side of a balance scale eventually tips the scale. If each of the grains alone weighs nothing, how can this happen?" This is a dramatic event for first-graders. It is an anomaly that challenges their naive theories. Appropriate instruction around the dramatic event can help children evaluate, revise, and reorganize their schemas. Dramatic demonstrations coupled with good instruction can be equally effective in helping high school students learn physics, as we will see below.

Expert vs. Novice Physicists

Problem-Solving Behavior

As the results from the above quiz suggest, traditional science instruction doesn't always engage and transform our naive theories. Even where we know scientific facts, we often lack the high-order proficiencies we need to understand experiments and reason about problems. Careful study of expert-novice differences in solving physics problems yields insights into why and where traditional instruction fails. It also suggests how to make it better.

Dorothy and Herb Simon (1978) were among the first to analyze expert-novice differences in physics. Around the same time, Jill Larkin and Fred Reif (1979) began similar research. The solve-aloud protocols collected by the Simons and by Larkin and Reif revealed the obvious differences: Novices took longer to solve a problem than experts and made more mistakes. But the protocols also revealed profound novice-expert differences in each major aspect of problem solving—initial representations, use of operators to generate or infer new knowledge, and methods for choosing among possible operators.

Jill Larkin and Ruth Chabay (1989) used the problem in figure 5.7 to illustrate these differences. An idealized protocol based on a novice's attempt to solve the problem might look as follows, with the left column recording what the novice says and the right column recording the equations the novice writes:

I have to find μ. What equation do I know with μ in it? Well, $f = \mu N$.	$f = \mu N$ (i)
In that equation N is the normal force. Normal force in these problems is usually weight, and the problem says the weight is 50 pounds. So $f = \mu \times 50$.	$N = 50$ $f = \mu \times 50$ (ii)
Now, if I can find f, I can solve for μ. f is a force, and the problem says we have a force of 10 pounds. So I can substitute this and get $10 = \mu \times 50$.	$f = 10$ $10 = \mu \times 50$ (ii)
So, now I have an equation where the only unknown is μ, which is the answer, and I can use algebra to solve for μ.	$\mu = \frac{1}{5}$ (iii)

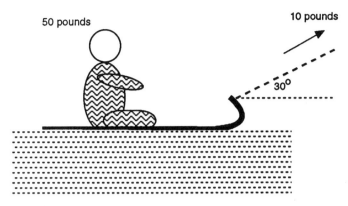

Figure 5.7
A girl pulls a sled at constant speed along a horizontal surface, using a rope making an angle of 30° with the snow surface. The sled carries her little brother, and the sled and the brother together weigh 50 pounds. If the girl is pulling with a force of magnitude 10 pounds, what is the coefficient of friction, μ, between the sled runners and the snow surface? (From Larkin and Chabay 1989, p. 153. Used with permission of Association for Supervision and Curriculum Development and authors.)

The protocol suggests that the novice bases his initial representation on reading the problem and looking at the picture. The novice realizes that the goal is to find the value of μ, the coefficient of friction. He searches the textbook or his long-term memory to find an equation containing μ and writes it down. His initial problem representation leads him to use three operators, or inference rules, to move from the initial representation to new knowledge states: use any algebraic or arithmetic operation ((iii) in the protocol), use any physics equation taken from the textbook ((i) in the protocol), and substitute values stated in the problem or values calculated for variables in the textbook equation ((ii) in the protocol). The novice chooses which of these operators to apply by using a backward reasoning strategy. He starts from the desired unknown and tries to work backward to information given in the problem. This backward reasoning is similar to what is done in geometry proofs, where one sometimes works backward from the statement to be proved to the givens. Here the novice tries to reason backward to infer new knowledge that would give him numerical values for all the unknowns in the equation except μ. When he has numerical values for all the

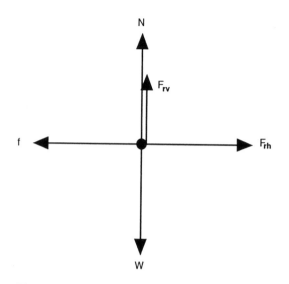

Figure 5.8
The expert's diagram showing all the forces acting in the sled problem. (From Larkin and Chabay 1989, p. 157. Used with permission of Association for Supervision and Curriculum Development and authors.)

variables except μ, he solves for μ using algebra (and gets the wrong answer).

An expert's idealized protocol looks very different. As the expert begins to think aloud, she draws a diagram (figure 5.8) showing all the forces and how they interact in the problem. What she says and writes in the balance of her protocol refers back to the diagram:

Okay, the boy-sled system moves at constant speed. So, there is no net force on the system. This means I can separately add up the horizontal and vertical components of the force on the system and make them balance, adding to zero. $\Sigma F = 0$

Horizontally, there is a force from the rope, F_{rh}, and there is friction, f. They balance. $F_{rh} = f$

Vertically, there is the downward force of the boy-sled, W, a force up from the rope because it is pulling at an angle of 30 degrees, F_{rv}, and the normal force, N, exerted by the snow on the sled. They all balance and add to zero. $N + F_{rv} = W$

f depends on the normal force and the coefficient of friction.

$$f = \mu N$$

So, we can combine all these equations and solve for μ in terms of F_r and W.

$$\mu = F_{rh}/(W - F_{rv}).$$

The expert's initial representation leads her to speak immediately of the "boy-sled system," an object not mentioned explicitly in the problem. She also notes that the sled's speed is constant, a key clue for a physicist. The expert's operators are also different from the novice's. She appeals to statements such as the following: (1) The net force on the systems is zero. (2) The total force can be decomposed into its horizontal and vertical components. (3) Values for balanced forces can appear in statements of equality. Finally, notice that the novice's *first* equation, $f = \mu N$, is almost the expert's *last* one. The expert introduces it only when she can solve it using information and quantities she has already derived from the problem statement.

In contrast to the novice, the expert reasons forward from information in the problem to the solution, a value for μ. After representing the problem using scientific concepts (force, boy-sled system) and drawing the diagram, the expert applies operators to information stated in the problem (the givens) to generate new knowledge. When she has inferred all she can, or all she needs, she introduces the textbook equation and solves it using the information she has generated.

The representations, operators, and methods used by experts and novices are very different. Different initial representations lead to different choices of operators. As a result, experts and novices work in very different problem spaces, and their different problem spaces prompt them to use different methods. Experts reason forward from givens to goal; novices reason backward from goal to givens. The expert's thinking starts from a qualitative understanding of physical principles, and her reasoning invokes these principles. The novice's thinking involves mostly formal equations, symbol manipulation, and algebra applied to textbook equations.

Other research, to which we will now turn, shows that these expert-novice differences in problem-solving behavior derive from differences in the content and the organization of the respective schemas that guide novices' and experts' initial problem representations. Differences in behavior arise from differences inside the black boxes.

Schemas

Michelene Chi, Bob Glaser, and Ernest Rees (1982) reasoned that if schemas determine initial representations and if initial representations guide solution methods, then schemas should guide how people decide which problems are similar and which are different. They asked eight experts (physics Ph.D. candidates) and eight novices (undergraduates who had taken one semester of college physics) to sort 24 standard textbook problems into categories based on how they would solve them.

Both experts and novices formed between eight and nine categories and took around 40 seconds to decide in which category a problem belonged. But experts and novices formed very different categories. For example, novices sorted all incline-plane problems into one category and all spring problems into another. The experts saw things differently; they grouped some incline-plane problems with some spring problems. When asked why, the experts pointed out that the same laws of physics could be used to solve both the incline-plane and the spring problems they had grouped together.

Finding similar differences in how their subjects formed and justified other categories, Chi, Glaser, and Rees concluded that the novices sorted problems by surface features, such as objects mentioned in the problem (e.g., incline plane), key words in the problem that have special meanings in physics (e.g., coefficient of friction), or the physical interaction of objects in the problem diagram (e.g., blocks on incline planes). Novices categorize problems using features they can take directly and literally from the problem statement. The features they use would be obvious to anyone reading the problem. In contrast, they concluded, the experts formed and justified their categories according to physical principles and laws (e.g., conservation of energy, Newton's Second Law). They grouped problems by the laws they would use to solve the problems. These are *deep features*—similarities only an experienced physicist would notice or know about. Only a physicist thinking in terms of conservation of energy would see an incline-plane problem and a spring problem as belonging to the same category. Experts in a domain see that domain at a deeper, more abstract level than novices. Expert physicists tend

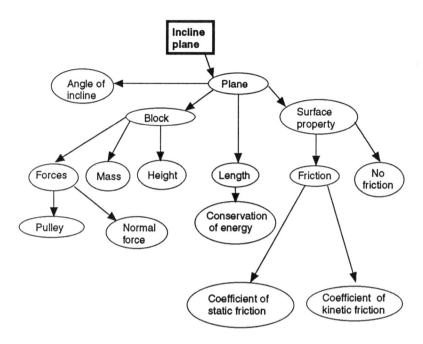

Figure 5.9
Network representation of novice's incline-plane schema, containing primarily
surface features of the incline plane. (From Chi, Glaser, and Rees 1982, p. 58.
Used with permission of Lawrence Erlbaum Associates.)

to see the world as systems governed by physical laws, not as collections of physical objects.

Chi and her colleagues then charted how the experts' and novices' schemas differed in content and organization. They took 20
concepts (including *incline plane, center of mass, friction,* and *conservation
of energy*) that experts and novices had used to demarcate categories
in the sorting study. The investigators presented these 20 concepts
one by one to both novices and experts. Each subject had 3 minutes
to say everything he or she could think of about each concept. If
concepts are parts of schemas in long-term memory and if long-term
memory has an associative structure, then the order in which subjects
mention concepts in their elaborations should reveal the links among
concepts in their schemas.

Figures 5.9 and 5.10 illustrate typical novice and expert incline
plane schemas. The novice has an extensive schema, but it contains
primarily surface features, such as angle of incline, length, height,

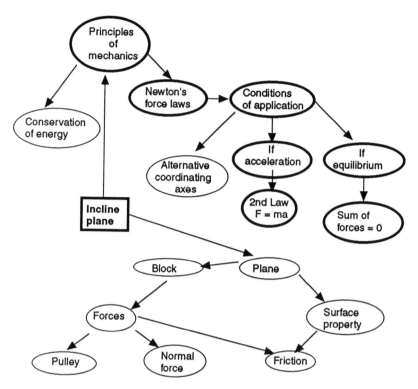

Figure 5.10
The expert's schema immediately connects the notion of an incline plane with
the laws of physics and the conditions under which laws are applicable. (From
Chi, Glaser, and Rees 1982, p. 58. Used with permission of Lawrence Erlbaum
Associates.)

and whether there is a block resting on the plane. At the end of the
elaboration, the novice mentions conservation of energy and associates it with the length and height of the incline plane. In contrast,
the expert begins by mentioning the laws of physics that apply to
incline plane problems: Newton's Laws and the conservation of energy. The expert then elaborates the conditions under which Newton's Laws are applicable: If there is acceleration, use $F = ma$
(Newton's Second Law); if there is there is no acceleration, there is
equilibrium and the forces in the problem sum to zero. Only then
does the expert bother to mention surface features. The laws of
physics and when to use them are central to the expert's schema;
surface features are peripheral.

Schemas and Problem Solving

The differences between novice and expert schemas translate into the observed differences in problem-solving behavior. Expert schemas result in deep representations; experts categorize problems in terms of features not obvious from the problem statement. On the sled problem, the expert immediately mentions the "boy-sled system" and "no net force"—terms mentioned nowhere in the problem. The expert's initial problem representation contains things only a physicist would see. Physicists see collections of objects as *systems* and interactions among systems as *forces*.

Representing, or encoding, situations at this level of abstraction allows the expert to see dissimilar everyday situations, such as incline planes and springs, as physically the same. Most important, the initial parts of the expert's incline-plane schema are principles she uses to reason toward a solution. According to Larkin (1985, p. 148), "Two problems with very different naive representations can have identical scientific representations. Thus, if one has the knowledge to solve one of them in its scientific representation, the other problem becomes trivial."

The expert's initial representation in terms of systems and forces motivates the operators she uses. *System* and *force* are concepts that occur in the laws of mechanics. The laws say how these concepts interrelate, making the laws immediately applicable, once the solver encodes problems in these terms. In reasoning about the sled problem, after mentioning systems and forces the expert notes "constant speed," a condition mentioned in Chi's schema. This tells the expert that she is dealing with a case of equilibrium, which implies that the forces in the problem sum to zero—a fact she can use to develop an efficient solution strategy. The expert knows that forces can be broken down into separate horizontal and vertical components and that these components all have to add up to zero. From this point, the expert proceeds to fill other slots in her schema using information stated in the problem or derived from the problem. She uses the information to work gradually forward toward a value for the unknown coefficient of friction.

The novice includes only surface features in his schema and mentions only surface features in his reasoning. He mentions things like "weight" and "normal force." He begins writing equations and substituting values into them right away. His superficial initial representation leads directly to textbook equations—equations he knows must be relevant. He writes an equation containing an unknown for the coefficient of friction. Once he has written this equation, he can use his knowledge of algebra and symbol manipulation to create a chain of inferences back to information stated in the problem. With luck he can create a chain in which the only remaining unknown is μ and he can solve for it.

Larkin and Chabay (1989) claim there are three kinds of knowledge and representations involved in scientific reasoning: *everyday knowledge* (naive schemas), *scientific reasoning knowledge* (expert schemas), and *formal equations* (mathematical versions of expert schemas). The first two kinds of knowledge are qualitative; only the formal equations are mathematical and quantitative. The expert has all three kinds of representations, but the novice has only the first and the third. Unfortunately for the novice, there is no overlap or obvious connection between naive schemas and formal textbook equations. There is no direct translation from the language of naive schemas to the language of formal physics equations.

So what is a novice to do? He has naive representations, and is learning formal equations in class, but he lacks a crucial intermediate piece. Without that piece, the novice has little idea how, why, or in what order to use equations in problem solving. Lacking domain-specific physics knowledge that would allow him to use strong methods to guide application of equations, he relies on weak methods instead.

The novice's backward method is an instance of the weak method of means–end analysis that was described in chapter 3. The novice writes an equation containing the desired unknown, identifies major differences between that equation and the goal state (here a specific value for μ), and picks algebraic or arithmetic operators to reduce one or more of those differences until he can solve for the unknown.

Using means–end analysis is not a moral or cognitive failing; it is a clever strategy to exploit what you know in general when you don't know much in particular. Expert physicists use means–end analysis when working on unfamiliar problems, or on the frontier of research, where they don't know which laws or schemas to apply. Experts, however, unlike novices, use means–end analysis to choose among abstract physical laws and principles. Novices apply the method to equations—to strings of symbols. It allows them to use general knowledge of how equations work, and how equations should look, to solve problems for which they lack specific physics knowledge. The novice knows algebra, assumes that the equations he has just read about in the textbook are relevant to the problem, and puts this limited knowledge to use in solving the problem. What is surprising is that so many students can be academically successful using this method.

Some students do spontaneously connect the equations with more expert schemas. Others realize that their naive schemas will not work in physics class, so they ignore their everyday knowledge, rely on means-end analysis to manipulate equations, pass the course, and go on to college physics where they do more of same. Physics courses do not require that students learn physics.

As in math, physics instruction fails to impart understanding because it does not always make explicit connections between equations and the underlying conceptual structures. The lack of connection shows in students' poor performance on problems like those in our opening quiz. One cannot solve such problems using means-end analysis on equations. These problems demand qualitative reasoning based on an understanding of physical laws. They require expert-like schemas that many students don't have. Those who don't have the expert schemas tend to fall back on naive schemas and give incorrect answers.

For many students—even students in the second semester of a college engineering curriculum—physics instruction leaves naive schemas intact and fails to impart the experts' qualitative representations. Students need the qualitative understanding contained in the expert schemas to build initial representations of physics problems. With the right representations the problems become easier to solve. An obvious solution, as with the balance scale and the number line, is to design science instruction to teach the expert representations explicitly. To do this, instruction must first engage and then change the students' naive representations.

ThinkerTools: Physics in Middle School

Barbara White, a cognitive psychologist, and Paul Horwitz, a physicist, developed a physics curriculum called ThinkerTools to engage and then change students' naive representations (Horwitz 1988; White

1988; White and Horwitz 1988; White, in press). ThinkerTools combines the cognitivists' glimpses inside the black box with the power of computer technology to teach Newton's Laws to sixth-graders.

In this case, the glimpses inside the black box came from detailed studies of how children solve force and motion problems like those in our quiz. As was mentioned above, researchers, including diSessa and White, have shown that by sixth grade children answer the quiz questions much as adults do. Children, like adults, have an impetus theory of motion, believe that an object moves in the direction in which it was last pushed, and do not understand how forces act on a moving object to change its velocity. Children do, however, have a correct intuition about what happens when a force acts on a stationary object: They know that when they kick a ball they give it a speed and a direction. The cognitive research provided White and Horwitz with a description of children's naive representations.

On the computer side, ThinkerTools is what science educators call a *microworld* or a *discovery world*. Microworlds, unlike much educational software, are not computerized page-turners or space-age drill and practice devices. Microworlds are computer models or simulations of phenomena found in the physical world—what the expert physicists call *systems*. A computer can be programmed to do almost anything. It can simulate how objects behave in our Newtonian world of mid-size objects, in a world like ours but with no friction, or in a world like ours but with no gravity. Microworlds allow students to see what simpler worlds would be like, to manipulate simulated objects in those worlds, and to design experiments to discover which laws best describe the worlds.

When cognitive research guides the design of microworlds, the learning objectives can be based on students' prior knowledge—both correct and oversimplified—and on what is conceptually difficult. Microworlds can be constructed that begin with the students' initial understandings but that gradually lead them to more expert understandings, schemas, and representations. Microworlds offer the additional advantage, from a cognitive perspective, of active learning. Students learn by designing and running experiments in the worlds, not by reading, watching demonstrations, and solving textbook problems. The results are impressive. Sixth-graders taught with ThinkerTools have a more expert understanding of Newton's Laws than do high school physics students.

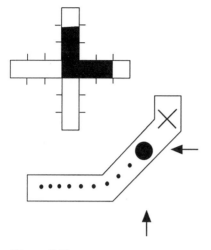

Figure 5.11
A screen display from a ThinkerTools microworld. Here the student is attempting to maneuver the dot to hit the target (X). (From White 1988. Used with author's permission.)

Designing ThinkerTools

In developing ThinkerTools, White and Horwitz's challenge was to use students' correct intuition that when you kick a ball you change its speed and direction as the starting point for a series of microworlds that would gradually transform naive schemas into expert ones. The microworlds had to help students incorporate features of the computer model into their mental models and schemas of physical situations. Internalizing the microworld's features should help students construct more powerful, expert-like initial representations and improve their problem-solving skills in physics.

To ease the cognitive demands on students, White and Horwitz designed their four microworlds to be as simple as possible. Each world models only the ideas and processes that, according to cognitive analysis, are crucial for understanding the target phenomena. ThinkerTools does not depict balls, coins, and hockey pucks. It uses a dot that moves when an unbalanced force acts on it. Using a joystick, students can apply forces to the dot as short bursts, or impulses, and so control the dot's speed and direction. Multiple visual representations show how impulses affect the dot (figure 5.11). Besides changing speed and direction when a force is applied, the dot leaves a wake of small blips showing its path and position at fixed time intervals. Where the blips are evenly spaced, the dot has constant velocity; where their spacing changes, the dot has accelerated or decelerated. Students can see what happens to the wake as they apply impulses.

In addition, there are multiple illustrations of the dot's horizontal and vertical velocity components. Arrows at the bottom and right edges of the screen continually point at the dot. As the dot moves, the arrow at the bottom moves horizontally and the arrow at the right moves vertically, showing how the velocity components change. A two-dimensional "thermometer"—White and Horwitz call it a *datacross*—gives a more abstract picture of the dot's velocity components. The horizontal mercury level represents the horizonal velocity component and the vertical level gives the up-down component.

The dot is more abstract than the world of everyday objects, but its behavior models that of everyday objects. This helps students connect the microworlds to intuitive, everyday features of our world. The microworlds also explicitly represent abstract notions, such as velocity and velocity component, yet, they are considerably less abstract than the formal mathematical equations that express Newton's Laws. The microworlds are at a level of abstraction midway between everyday experience and the formal laws of physics. They can help students make the transition from naive to more expert schemas.

Each of the four microworlds is designed to allow students to see qualitatively how forces cause objects to move.

Motion in One Direction

The first world lacks friction and gravity. Students can apply impulses to make the dot go right or left, but not up or down. Students explore this world by solving simple problems, such as applying impulses to make the dot hit a target at a specified speed. They see that if the impulse is applied in the direction in which the dot is moving it adds one unit to the dot's speed, and that if applied in the opposite direction it subtracts one unit from the dot's speed. All this is perfectly reasonable to a child who has kicked a ball and who knows basic arithmetic. World 1 reinforces the child's correct intuition that applying a force causes an object to change speed and can cause an object to stop or reverse direction. Because there is no

friction or gravity, children also see that once a force has acted on
an object the object continues on its path at uniform speed. Thus,
they see a simple example of Newton's First Law.

Motion in Two Dimensions
The second microworld allows students to apply both up-down and
left-right impulses. Students explore this world by manipulating the
dot to make shapes and by navigating the dot around obstacles. They
notice that what they learned in world 1 about horizontal motion
also applies in the vertical direction. They also learn, because they
can see it on the datacross, that applying an upward or a downward
impulse doesn't affect the dot's horizontal velocity component. They
learn that the horizontal and vertical components are *independent* and
that a force in any arbitrary direction can be *decomposed* into horizontal
and vertical components. (The importance of understanding how
forces decompose into independent components was apparent in the
expert's solution to the sled problem.)

The final problems in world 2 have students make the dot hit a
target by setting appropriate values on the datacross and then releas-
ing the dot. This gets the students to predict the dot's speed and
direction by combining values of horizontal and vertical velocity
components. They can see how independent forces combine into a
single resultant force.

These are important insights. The lessons of world 2 correct
misconceptions that can dominate reasoning about the hockey puck
problem. After the children have tried to maneuver the dot around
a few corners in the microworld, they see that a moving object does
not always go in the direction in which it was last pushed. A horizontal force applied to an object moving vertically does not result in
horizontal motion, but in an "in-between path." This is what happens
to the hockey puck. In that problem, the velocity that results from
the initial hit would be represented on the datacross as shown at
lower left in figure 5.12. If the student has mastered the game of
setting the datacross to make the dot move to hit a target, he sees
that he would need to set the datacross as the second one shown in
the figure; that is a horizontal component like B is needed to make
the first turn. Making the second turn requires that the datacross's
vertical component be zero and that only a horizontal force remain,
as shown at lower right in the figure. To achieve this, one applies
force C to cancel the initial vertical component.

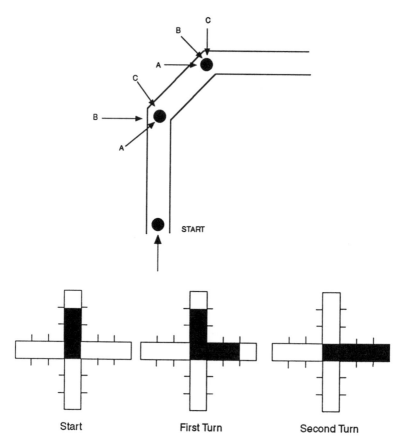

Figure 5.12
The hockey puck problem on ThinkerTools.

Continuous Forces and Gravity

The third world is a one-dimensional world, but a world in which students can apply impulses at varying rates. Students can repeatedly double the frequency at which they apply impulses, but as the frequency of the impulses increases the magnitude of the impulse decreases. This lets students apply very small impulses in rapid succession. With this device, they can understand a continuous force, like gravity, as a limiting case of many tiny impulses applied in very rapid succession. They realize that what they learned in world 1 about discrete forces also applies to reasoning about continuous forces.

This world allows a dramatic demonstration of what happens in the coin problem (figure 5.13). If a force gives the dot a large vertical velocity, the datacross will show a large amount of mercury on its vertical arm. Gravity, the only force now acting, gradually reduces this vertical velocity until the datacross' mercury level falls to zero as the coin reaches the top of its path. Then, as the coin falls, the mercury fills the "negative" bottom half of the vertical arm. This shows that the coin does not fall to earth because it gradually loses its impetus and gravity takes over; rather, once the coin is tossed, gravity is the only force acting on it.

Analyzing Trajectories

The fourth microworld adds gravity from world 3 to the two-dimensional world 2. Students learn that when objects move vertically they accelerate because of the continuous force of gravity. They learn that when objects move horizontally (if there is no friction) they have constant velocity. In this world, students can analyze and solve problems about thrown balls and pushed objects and so make numerous connections between the microworld and everyday experiences.

Thus, ThinkerTools begins with a microworld in which students can readily apply their prior correct knowledge about how objects move. Each subsequent world adds new principles and competencies based on mastery and understanding of the preceding worlds. The progression of the microworlds is based on what children know and what they have difficulty learning. The microworlds take into account students' likely prior knowledge, their ignorance of how forces combine, and the difficulty of understanding continuous forces and then provide a learning path to help students negotiate these obstacles.

The Theory of Instruction: Using the Microworlds

Cognitive research also guides the use of ThinkerTools in the classroom. The research-based instructional assumptions underlying the ThinkerTools curriculum are similar to those that motivate the adventures of Jasper Woodbury: that learning should be anchored in everyday experience, that active problem solving is preferable to rote mastery of facts, transfer is more likely if learning occurs in contexts

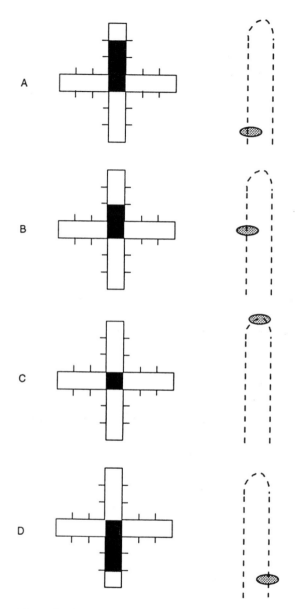

Figure 5.13
The coin problem on ThinkerTools.

similar to those in which the knowledge should be used, and that instruction should involve shared, group discussion that makes reasoning explicit and overt. To meet these goals, ThinkerTools teachers use *each* microworld in four instructional phases: motivation, model evolution, formalization, and transfer.

The motivation phase piques the students' interest by asking them to predict how everyday objects might behave. Students might be asked what happens if someone blows on a ball that is resting on an almost frictionless surface. Once it is in motion, what happens if someone blows on it a second time? Answers vary: the ball goes twice as fast, a little bit faster, or the same speed but farther. In this discussion, the children use their naive conceptions and misconceptions to explain their answers. The teacher answers questions but does not say who is right or wrong. The children want to learn more because they realize they can't all be right. Using real-world objects as a source for physics puzzles motivates the students to create links between their daily world and the microworlds they will begin to explore. Discussing the predictions makes students comfortable with sharing their reasoning and is a first step toward making their reasoning overt.

In the next phase, model evolution, children work in pairs to solve problems and conduct experiments in the microworld. The exercises help students discover the laws governing that particular world. The teacher provides enough initial structure and background information, so that most students can discover the laws. The curriculum is careful not to let students get lost or sidetracked in the microworlds. This phase exploits the benefits of active, collaborative problem solving, and is a form of guided discovery learning. The emphasis is on learning and using knowledge to solve problems, not on the rote mastery of facts.

In the formalization phase, children get to the core of the scientific method and scientific reasoning. Working in groups of three or four, the children test a small set of laws that might govern the microworld. Their task is to run experiments to find out which laws are correct. For each law they judge incorrect, they must show the class a microworld situation where the law is false. To do this, the children have to understand how experimental data can falsify a general law. The students are then told that they can keep just one of the correct laws. Which one would they pick, and why? This leads to a metaconceptual and methodological discussion: What makes one scientific law better than another: simplicity? precision? generality? Students learn there is more to a good theory or law than just accounting for the data. This is a sophisticated idea for sixth-graders, but one that is crucial for understanding science. This phase creates a shared learning context in which students use their understanding to explain and justify their reasoning. Their scientific reasoning becomes public and overt which requires them to monitor their thinking and thereby develop metacognitive skills.

In the final instructional phase for each microworld, transfer, the children apply their best microworld laws to real-world situations. The first real-world application is the predictive question the teacher asked in the motivation phase (e.g., how would the law they chose as best account for the motion of the ball on the nearly frictionless surface?). The teacher asks why some of the original answers and intuitions were incorrect. She asks students to go to the microworld and add factors, such as friction, that might account for the faulty intuitions. When they add these new factors does the dot behave differently? How does it behave? Finally, the students attempt to apply the microworld laws to a variety of real-world situations and experiments—carts on tables, balls dropped from various heights, and the like. This creates links from the microworld back to the real world, helps the students see how their microworld knowledge transfers to actual situations, and reinforces the idea that the laws learned in the microworld are useful in predicting and controlling events in the everyday environment.

As the children work through the microworlds, they build powerful schemas that capture much of Newtonian mechanics. But ThinkerTools teaches more than the subject matter of physics; it also teaches how to generate scientific knowledge and how to reason scientifically. The four-phase instructional process contains within it key features of the scientific method: Ask questions, perform experiments, formulate laws, see how the laws generalize, and where necessary revise the laws. ThinkerTools helps students learn about experimental design and see how data relate to experiments. It has them use scientific facts and principles to draw inferences. These are among the high-level proficiencies that, according to the NAEP, are lacking in many students. ThinkerTools allows students to develop a high-level concept of what it is they are trying to learn and do in science class. They aren't learning facts, they are trying to discover a set of laws that explain the world in which they live.

ThinkerTools in the Schools

White and Horwitz tested ThinkerTools at a middle school in a Boston suburb. They compared sixth-graders who had used their curriculum against a group of matched sixth-graders who had completed a unit on inventions in the normal science curriculum and against a group of high school physics students in the same district who had just completed a 2½-month study of Newtonian mechanics. Two regular classroom teachers taught the ThinkerTools curriculum every school day for 45 minutes over 2 months, after which the ThinkerTools students, the comparison students, and the high school students were given a test to assess their understanding of Newtonian mechanics. The test consisted of 17 items researchers use to study misconceptions in physics—items much like those in the quiz above.

Not surprisingly, the ThinkerTools students did much better than the other sixth-graders. The average test score for the ThinkerTools students was 11.2 out of 17, versus 7.6 for the other sixth-graders. The ThinkerTools students also did significantly better than the high school students who had studied Newton's laws in a traditional curriculum. For example, 63 percent and 46 percent of the ThinkerTools students answered the two parts of the hockey puck problem correctly, versus 20 percent and 10 percent of the high school students.

The ThinkerTools teachers, neither of whom had previously studied or taught physics or used computers in the classroom, both felt they handled the curriculum successfully. One teacher had attended two one-week training workshops; the other attended only one. They were fascinated by how ThinkerTools allowed them to watch the students' thinking and learning develop—to get inside the black boxes. One teacher said, "It is neat to watch. It's funny, five years ago I could never have envisioned doing something like this. And, I can see five years down the road that this is the way that things are going to be as far as I'm concerned." (White 1988, p. 73)

The most encouraging result was that one of the school districts that had participated in the study adopted ThinkerTools as a permanent part of its sixth-grade science curriculum. White is currently at work upgrading and expanding the curriculum. She and her colleagues at Berkeley are exploring how they can use ThinkerTools in teacher training programs. They hope that the curriculum will help middle school science teachers learn physics and help them apply the lessons learned from cognitive research to all their science teaching.

High School Physics from a Cognitive Perspective

Microworlds promise an exciting new method for teaching science. For those who fear that the teacher's "five years from now" might stretch to 10 or 20 before complete microworld curricula are available or affordable, there is more good news. Microworlds are not essential for effective science instruction. What is necessary is a new approach to classroom teaching, a change in how teacher and students interact. One of the best places to see this new approach is in Jim Minstrell's physics classes at Mercer Island High School. (See Minstrell 1989; Minstrell 1984; Minstrell and Stimpson 1990.)

Mercer Island is an upper-middle-class suburb of Seattle. The high school serves just over 1000 students in four grades. Jim Minstrell has been teaching there since 1962. He holds bachelor's, master's, and doctoral degrees from the Universities of Washington and Pennsylvania, and during his career he has worked on several national programs to improve high school physics instruction. Although deeply committed to educational research, he prefers the classroom to a university department or a school of education. "I have one of the best laboratories in the world right here," he observes. He adopted what he calls "a cognitive orientation to teaching" for practical, not theoretical, reasons. The cognitive approach addresses a fundamental classroom problem that confronts science teachers: Students' preconceptions influence how they understand classroom material.

In the early 1970s, after a decade of outstanding teaching (as measured both by students' test scores and by supervisors' evaluations), Minstrell became concerned about his effectiveness. His students couldn't transfer their formal book and lecture learning to the physics of everyday situations, and they showed little understanding of basic physical concepts, such as force, motion, and gravity. At first he thought, following Piaget's theory, that his students lacked logical, or formal operational, skills. However, when he tested this hypothesis, he found otherwise.

Minstrell describes a task of Piaget's in which students are given two clay balls of equal size. Students agree that the two balls weigh the same. But if one ball is then flattened into a pancake, many students will then say that the pancake weighs more than the ball. They reason that the pancake weighs more because it has a larger upper surface on which air can press down. This is not a logical error but a conceptual one. Students believe that air pressure contributes to an object's weight.

"Students were bringing content ideas to the situation, ideas that were greatly affecting their performance on questions that were supposed to be testing their reasoning," Minstrell recalls.

Minstrell became actively involved in research on students' misconceptions, and he tried to apply the research in his classroom. First he expanded his classroom agenda. A teacher's primary goals are to control the students and to provide explanations that allow the students to solve textbook problems. A third goal, in the current climate of accountability, is to prepare the students to pass standardized tests of low-level skills. Minstrell maintains the first two goals, minimizes the third, and adds two goals of his own, based on cognitive research: to establish explicit instructional targets for understanding and to help the students actively reconstruct their knowledge to reach that understanding.

Minstrell attempts to diagnose students' misconceptions and to remedy them by instruction. Most teachers aren't trained to recognize and fix misconceptions. How does Minstrell do it?

Facets

Minstrell assumes from the first day of school that his students have some knowledge of physics and that they have adequate reasoning ability. Unlike expert scientists who want to explain phenomena with a minimum of assumptions and laws, students are not driven by a desire for conceptual economy. Their knowledge works well enough in daily life, but it is fragmentary and local. Minstrell calls pieces of knowledge that are used in physics reasoning *facets*. Facets are schemas and parts of schemas that are used to reason about the physical world.

Students typically choose and apply facets on the basis of the most striking *surface* features of a problem. They derive their naive facets from everyday experience. Such facets are useful in particular situations; however, they are most likely false in general, and for the most part they are only loosely interrelated. Thus, students can quickly fall into contradictions. Two facets Minstrell typically finds students using when reasoning about objects are (1) that larger objects exert more force than smaller objects and (2) that only moving objects exert force. The first facet explains why the smart money was on Goliath, not David; the second explains why a football can "force" its way through a window. But how do you explain what happens when you throw a ball against the side of a building? The first facet suggests that the wall must exert a larger force on the ball than the ball does on the wall, but the second facet says that only the ball can exert a force, not the wall. So how is it that the ball bounces off the wall? As Minstrell sees it, the trick is to identify the students' correct intuitions—their facets that are consistent with formal science—and then build on these. As Minstrell says, "Some facets are anchors for instruction; others are targets for change."

Benchmark Lessons: What Are Your Ideas Right Now?

At the outset, Minstrell's students are not different from other high school juniors and seniors. Early in each course unit he administers a diagnostic test to assess qualitative, not quantitative, physical reasoning.

Between 50 percent and 75 percent of the students believe that when a heavy object and a light object are dropped or thrown horizontally, the heavier one hits the ground first. As many as half believe that when two moving objects are at the same position they are traveling at the same speed; yet they all know that to pass a car on the highway the overtaking car must be going faster, even when the two cars are side by side. Nearly half believe that air pressure affects an object's weight. Almost all believe that a constant, unbalanced force causes constant velocity. The results of the diagnostic tests give Minstrell a profile of which facets are prevalent, which ones might be anchors, and which ones are targets for change.

Minstrell organizes his course into units, such as measurement, kinematics, gravity, and electromagnetism. Some lessons, usually presented early in a unit, are particularly important in helping students change their reasoning. Minstrell calls these *benchmark lessons.*

In a benchmark lesson, the teacher and the students dissect their qualitative reasoning about vivid, everyday physics problems into facets. They become aware of the limitations of each facet, and they identify which facets are useful for understanding a particular phenomenon. They then explore how appropriate facets can be combined into powerful explanations that can be used to solve other problems.

The benchmark lesson on gravity begins 6 weeks into the course. By this time Minstrell has established a rapport with his class. He has created an environment conducive to developing understanding, a climate where questioning and respect for diverse opinions prevail, a climate where the process of scientific reasoning can be made explicit and self-conscious. Even veteran teachers marvel at how uninhibited Minstrell's students are in expressing ideas, suggesting hypotheses, and arguing positions.

Minstrell explains to the students that the unit will begin with a three-problem diagnostic quiz, and that their answers will be the subject of discussion for the next two days. He reassures them that the quiz is not intended to embarrass them or show how little they know. He wants to find out what they already know, and he wants them to be aware of what they already know. (Problems 3 and 4 in the quiz above are taken from Minstrell's quiz.)

As the students work, Minstrell moves among them and observes their answers and explanations. After 15 minutes he collects the quizzes and goes to the board at the front of the classroom. He reports that on the first question, the scale problem, he saw several answers, and he writes them on the board: 15–20 pounds, a little over 10 pounds, exactly 10 pounds, a little less than 10 pounds, and about 0 pounds. "Now let's hold off on attacking these answers. Rather, let's defend one or more of them," he suggests.

Ethan explains why he thinks the object in the vacuum weighs nothing: "I felt it was zero, because when you're in space you float. It would be related to that." Minstrell helps fill in the argument: "When you're in space things seem weightless. Space is essentially an airless environment, so the object would weigh nothing."

A few students argue that the object weighs the same in the vacuum as in air. One says that when air is present the air above and the air below the scale balance out; some air pushes down and some pushes up, with no net effect. Chris, baseball cap on the back of his head and arms crossed, offers: "Ten pounds. The vacuum inside only has a relation to air pressure, not a relation to mass."

Two students argue that the object in a vacuum weighs slightly more than 10 pounds, because under normal conditions air helps hold up the scale. When you remove the air, the object will weigh more because there is no air supporting the scale.

The most popular student response is that the scale would read slightly less than 10 pounds. These arguments invoke facets involving density and buoyancy. John presents the rationale: "It's gonna be a little less than 10. You remember Bob Beamon. He set a world record in the long jump at the Mexico City Olympics. He jumped really far there because there is less air and it is lighter and so everything weighs less."

In the class period devoted to discussion, over half the students offer explanations for one of the answers. Minstrell is strictly a facilitator, offering no facts, opinions, or arguments himself. He then encourages students to present counterarguments. When the counterarguments and the responses have run their course, Minstrell signals the start of the next lesson segment: "Sounds like there's some pretty good arguments here across the spectrum. So what do we do?" The students urge him to run an experiment. He says, "Luckily, I happen to have a scale, a bell jar, and a vacuum pump here."

Minstrell calls two students to the front to help conduct the crucial experiment. Such demonstrations are dramatic and exciting for the students and allow them to see which prediction is correct. Research also suggests that such experiences have an important cognitive role in inducing conceptual change. They provide an initial experience that places naive and expert theories in conflict. As the students try to resolve the conflict, the dramatic demonstration serves as an organizing structure in long-term memory (an anchor) around which schemas can be changed and reorganized (Hunt 1993).

The first student reports that the object on the scale weighs 1.2 newtons under normal circumstances. Minstrell starts the vacuum pump, and the students watch the gauge as the pressure drops inside the bell jar. The pump stops when the pressure gauge reads nearly zero.

"Did the weight go to zero?" Minstrell asks. Somewhat amazed, the students respond that the weight stayed the same. Minstrell suggests that they see what happens when the air rushes back into the jar. He opens the valve and the air whistles in. A student exclaims, "Air or no air in there, there's not much difference either way!"

Minstrell asks "What does this tell us about gravity and air pressure?" "Air pressure doesn't affect weight," the students respond. They have started to correct a major misconception. Other experiences in the unit and throughout the course reinforce this benchmark discovery that air pressure and gravity are distinct physical phenomena.

Don't Feel Dumb!

A few days later, Minstrell and the class analyze their reasoning about the time it would take a 1-kilogram and a 5-kilogram object to fall the same distance (problem 4 above). They run the crucial experiment—a miniature replay of Galileo's apocryphal experiment at Pisa. After both balls hit the floor simultaneously, Minstrell returns to the board where he had written the quiz answers. "Some of you were probably feeling pretty dumb with these kinds of answers. Don't feel dumb," he counsels. "Let's see what's valuable about each of these answers, because each one is valuable. Why would you think that heavier things fall faster?"

A student suggests that heavy things (such as barbells) are harder to pull up, so it seems they would fall back to the ground more quickly too. "Right," Minstrell says. "When you lift something heavy, that sucker is heavy. Gravity is really pulling down. 'Aha,' you think, 'big effect there.' A useful rule of daily life is the more of X, the more of Z."

Why would anyone think a heavier object falls more slowly? A student argues that heavier objects are harder to push horizontally than light ones, and that because they are harder to push, one moves them more slowly; thus, when a heavier object is dropped, it must fall more slowly. Minstrell reinforces what is correct about this intuition. He points out that the first argument uses the facet of direct proportional reasoning and the second argument the facet of indirect proportional reasoning. Minstrell and the class will revisit these facets when they grapple with Newton's Second Law, $F = ma$ (i.e., when a force acts on an object the acceleration is directly proportional to the force and inversely proportional to the object's mass).

Minstrell concludes: "So, there are some good rationales behind these answers. Part of what I'm saying is that the rationales you have—the physics you've cooked up in the past 16 to 19 years of living—are valuable. But they are valuable only in certain contexts." The trick to becoming a competent qualitative physicist is knowing when to use which facet. It's not just a matter of having the pieces of knowledge; what counts is knowing when to use them—linking *conditions* of applicability to cognitive *actions*.

The unit on gravity continues with students doing experiments in the classroom and around the school building. It ends with seven problems, all taken from standard high school texts, which allow the students to assess their mastery of the unit's central facets and concepts.

Throughout the unit, Minstrell has not lectured, expounded or "taught" in the traditional sense. He has identified students' initial intuitions, made their reasoning explicit by eliciting and debating their positions, provided vivid benchmark experiences to help trigger conceptual change, and encouraged them to reason about these views and experiences. He has taught physics from a cognitive perspective.

Does It Work? Why?

In 1986 Minstrell initiated a collaboration with Earl Hunt, a cognitive psychologist at the University of Washington, to assess and refine his classroom method. Hunt, a "basic" cognitive scientist who has developed an interest in an applied science of learning, describes himself as the "wet blanket" of the project. "I'm the professional skeptic who must be convinced that it is the cognitive approach and not just Minstrell that accounts for the effects," he says.

A comparison of students' scores on pretests and posttests makes it clear that Minstrell's method works. The students learn physics. But why does it work?

One concern is whether the method's success depends entirely on Jim Minstrell's pedagogical talents. This was the first issue Hunt and Minstrell investigated. Could someone other than Minstrell use the method successfully?

Minstrell trained Virginia Stimpson and Dorothy Simpson, two math teachers at Mercer Island High who had never taught physics, to use his method. At Mercer Island, as at most high schools, which students end up in which physics sections is due more to scheduling than to student choice or teacher selection. Thus, students of varying abilities are likely to end up in each section. This allowed Minstrell and Hunt to make reliable comparisons between the performances of Minstrell's students and the performances of Stimpson's and Simpson's. Gini's and Dottie's students did at least as well as Jim's, so the effect (at least at Mercer Island High) is not due to Minstrell himself.

Is Minstrell's method better than other instructional methods currently in use? Minstrell himself has shown at Mercer Island High that his method is superior to traditional methods. His students have fewer misconceptions at course's end than do students taught traditionally. For example, on the pretest 3 percent of Minstrell's students showed correct understanding of both Newton's First and Second Laws. When he used the traditional methods and curriculum, Minstrell observed that after instruction 36 percent understood the First Law and 62 percent the Second Law. When he used his cognitive approach, 95 percent of the students ended up with a correct understanding of the First Law and 81 percent with a correct understanding of the Second Law (Minstrell 1984).

Minstrell and Hunt compared Mercer Island students with students at a neighboring, comparable high school that Hunt calls "Twin Peaks." The physics instructor there also uses a conceptual, qualitative approach in his course. Performance on standardized math tests is the best predictor of high school physics performance. On this measure, Mercer Island and Twin Peaks students were not significantly different. So, in physics one would expect similar outcomes at the two schools. However, on the same final exam in mechanics, taken after 3 months of studying that topic, the Mercer Island students scored about 20 percent higher than the Twin Peaks students across the entire range of math scores. "This is an important result," skeptic Hunt emphasizes, "because it shows that the method does not selectively appeal to brighter students as measured by math achievement."

For good measure, Minstrell and Hunt also compared Mercer Island students with students in a "nationally known experimental, physics teaching, research and development program." The Mercer Island students consistently outperformed the other experimental group on all topics tested. Hunt adds: "We regard these data as particularly important because the questions we used in this comparison were developed by the other experimental group."

These results have allayed some of Hunt's initial skepticism, but Hunt and Minstrell realize that much remains to be done. The success of Minstrell's theory-based curriculum vindicates the cognitive approach, but for Hunt success raises further theoretical questions. He has begun a research program back in his laboratory to refine the theory underlying Minstrell's method. Why are benchmark lessons so important? How does transfer occur? How do students develop deep representations and make appropriate generalizations? Minstrell's classroom is a good laboratory, but a teacher who is responsible for seeing that his students learn physics is limited in the experiments he can conduct. No doubt, in a few years results from

Hunt's basic research will feed back into Minstrell's applied research at Mercer Island High.

The next challenge for Minstrell and Hunt will be to test the method elsewhere. What will happen when teachers who are not under the innovators' direct supervision try to use the method? Instructional materials, including videotapes of benchmark lessons for each unit, will soon be ready for dissemination. The next step will be to assemble an implementation network (if possible, one like that for Jasper) and conduct applied research in a variety of classroom situations.

Teaching for Understanding

Jim Minstrell's students end up with a better understanding of physics, in part, because they learn more expert, qualitative representations and how to reason with them. There is a price to pay for this deeper understanding. As Earl Hunt points out, "From a traditional perspective one might argue that Minstrell's classes fail, because often students don't get through the standard curriculum. Last year, they did not complete electricity, and atomic physics and waves were barely mentioned." Hunt thinks that changes in curricular time and course coverage will be crucial in making science instruction more effective. Hunt is quick to add that in other countries curricula sometimes allow two to three years to teach what we cram into one.

The applied work of Smith, White, Horwitz, Minstrell, and others shows that we can teach qualitative representations in such a way as to make a significant impact on students' scientific understanding. All who have attempted to teach for understanding, though, emphasize that teaching the desired representations takes time. Minstrell spends over a week developing Newton's laws, not one or two days as in most traditional courses. ThinkerTools spends 8 weeks on four microworlds. Smith's weight and density curriculum takes 6 weeks to teach concepts usually covered in a day or two. Reflecting on his classroom experiences, Minstrell (1989, p. 147) advises: "We must provide the time students need for mental restructuring. Hurrying on to the next lesson or the next topic does not allow for sufficient reflection on the implications of the present lesson."

Results from cognitive research indicate that if we want more students to understand science the instruction should start early in school, and that throughout the curriculum instruction should build on students' correct intuitions and prior understanding. We should try to teach experts' qualitative representations to students, and along with this content we should teach students how to reason scientifically. Better science instruction along these lines may require a "less is more" (or at least a "longer is better") approach to the science curriculum.

6

Reading: Seeing the Big Picture

Charles is in the seventh grade. He has an IQ of 70 and reads at the third-grade level. He has had several years of remedial reading instruction in a public school, but seems to make little progress. Charles has sufficient decoding skills to read aloud, but has almost no comprehension of what he reads. He is representative of many students who will fail—students whom our educational system can't reach.

Teachers report that they often see students who are unable to comprehend written language. What is odd is that these children can tell stories and have no trouble understanding spoken language. Sometimes they can even read aloud, but still have difficulty understanding what they have read. Obviously, standard reading instruction has failed these students in a fundamental way.

On the first day of a new remedial reading program, the teacher asked Charles to read a short passage about reptiles. To see if he understood the passage, the teacher asked him to formulate a question based on the passage, a question that might appear on a test. Although he tried, he couldn't think of a question and gave up. He had not understood and retained enough of what he had just read to frame a question about it.

After 15 days in the new remedial program, the teacher and Charles repeated this exercise. After Charles had read a passage about antarctic research, he immediately offered the question "Why do scientists come to the South Pole to study?" By this time he also had raised his comprehension scores on the reading passages from 40 to 75 percent, an average performance level for a seventh-grader. On comprehension tests given in his regular classroom, he improved from the 25th to the 78th percentile in social science and from the 5th to the 69th percentile in science. At the end of the 20-day program he had gained 20 months on standardized reading comprehension tests, and he maintained this improvement long after his remedial instruction ended.

Charles was the beneficiary of *reciprocal teaching,* a method that applies results of cognitive research to reading instruction.

Students like Charles puzzle teachers in part because teachers are skilled readers. It is hard for a skilled reader to understand how there can be such students at all. For teachers and other skilled readers, reading is effortless. Most of us can easily read 300 words per minute, five words every second. Given how reading appears or feels to us experts, we can't imagine what it is like for Charles. If we read a sentence like this one aloud (or even silently), we can't help but understand it, just as we can't help but understand any sentence of our language we say aloud. Charles is saying sentences of his language aloud, why can't he understand them, as we do?

The answer is that we bring more skills to the task than Charles, and as expert readers we are hardly aware of it. To understand spoken language requires language-comprehension skills. To understand written language—to read—requires decoding (word-recognition) skills *plus* language-comprehension skills. There is more to reading than being able to say the words aloud or being able to say them silently to oneself—there is more to it than decoding. Expert readers automatically and simultaneously apply both sets of skills in reading. Charles, on the other hand, has decoding skills, but either he lacks language-comprehension skills or he is unable to apply them while he reads.

To help students such as Charles, we have to look beyond how reading feels to us and beyond the teaching of isolated subskills—even important ones, such as decoding. As one educator told me, "We have to see reading in the big picture." Reciprocal teaching is an example of how children can benefit if we take this larger view. It helps children apply their language-comprehension skills to written language.

Cognitive Models of Skilled Reading

Reading, although effortless for most of us, is a complex and demanding cognitive task. To teach reading effectively—to understand and remedy the difficulties Charles has—we have to appreciate its complexity. As Marcel Just and Patricia Carpenter (1987, p. 3) observe, "What we sometimes fail to appreciate is that skilled reading is an intellectual feat no less complex than chess playing." What is surprising is that so many people learn to execute this daunting intellectual feat. If we want to understand how to teach reading more effectively, we must understand what makes it so daunting.

Cognitive psychologists have developed models of skilled reading that spell out the task's complexity. These models can help us see reading in the big picture and understand why it can be difficult (Just and Carpenter 1987; Rayner and Pollatsek 1989). Like other cognitive models, they describe in some detail reading's component skills; more important, however, they also describe how those skills interact to result in fluent reading. Although reading is much more complicated than solving balance-scale problems, scientists' knowledge of it is sufficiently detailed that they can write production-system programs that simulate skilled reading.

When they study reading, cognitive scientists have a unique source of data for developing and testing their models: eye movements. Contrary to how it seems to us, when we read our eyes don't move smoothly and continuously across the page; rather, they pause on a word, quickly jump to another, and then pause again. Psychologists call the pauses *fixations* and the jumps *saccades*. Sometimes our eyes jump backward rather than forward in the text. Researchers call the backward jumps *regressions*. Reading is like a very fast slide show, with approximately four slides per second and with an occasional backtrack to a previously viewed slide. Our mental processing integrates the slides into what appears to be a smooth, continuous motion picture.

Psychologists use a computer-controlled device called an *eye tracker* to make precise measurements of eye movements. By measuring the reflection of a beam of infrared light (invisible to humans) off a subject's cornea, the tracker can compute precisely and continuously where the subject is fixating, how long each fixation lasts, and the direction and speed of saccades. Figure 6.1 shows some eye-movement data Just and Carpenter collected from a college student who was reading an article on flywheels.

Using eye trackers, psychologists have discovered that for skilled readers an average fixation lasts 250 milliseconds (msec), or a quarter of a second. Skilled readers fixate around 80 percent of content words (nouns, verbs, and modifiers) and around 40 percent of function words (articles, conjunctions, and propositions). Fixa-

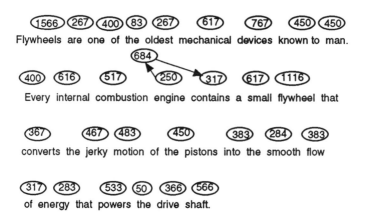

Figure 6.1
A college student's pattern of eye movements while reading an article on fly-wheels. The numbers over the fixated words indicate how many milliseconds the reader fixated on that word. This reader had one regression, on the word "engine". (From Just and Carpenter 1980, p. 330. Copyright 1980 American Psychological Association. Reprinted with permission.)

tions consume 90 to 95 percent of reading time. A saccade takes 15 to 20 msec. Most saccades are forward (left to right when reading English), but 10 to 15 percent of saccades are regressions to previously fixated material. These experiments have also shown that we take in information from the text only during fixations; we take in no new information during a saccade (Just and Carpenter 1987).

Psychologists exploit this quirk of our visual system to test hypotheses about what controls and regulates eye movements in reading. A saccade takes at least 15 msec, but the display on the eye tracker's computer screen can be changed in only 5 msec. If the experimenter alters the text in the display during a saccade, the subject is oblivious to the change. Thus, psychologists can change the display during a saccade—change the number of letters visible around the fixation point, control how long the fixated material is visible, change spellings and words, alter grammatical construc-tions—and see how any such change affects subjects' eye movements, reading speed, and comprehension. If researchers design these ma-nipulations cleverly, on the basis of task analysis of the reading process, they can discover how cognitive processes at various lev-els—perceptual, word, sentence, text—contribute to skilled reading.

In reading research, eye movements give researchers a "window on the mind."

Looking through this window, researchers have developed models like the one sketched in figure 6.2. Reading, for the cognitive scientist, is another kind of problem solving. The problem's initial state is the printed marks on a page. The goal is to construct a meaning from the marks and store the meaning in long-term memory for later use. The problem-solving operators are the skills and knowledge we have to transform the marks into meanings. These operators include knowledge about word forms, word meanings, grammatical rules, topics, and literary forms. All this knowledge is stored in long-term memory. The information processing occurs in working memory, where these operators get their input and leave their output. To read fluently, we have to represent and process massive amounts of information rapidly and at a variety of levels— visual, lexical, grammatical, conceptual, and metacognitive. Reading places huge demands on working memory's limited capacity.

The flow chart at the left of figure 6.2 shows the processes triggered on each eye fixation. On each fixation, a reader processes the new information at the visual, lexical, grammatical, conceptual, and textual levels and stores an interpretation of the text up to that point in long-term memory. The process stops when there is no more text to process. Skilled readers, being metacognitively aware, monitor the processing to be sure that their interpretation is consistent and that they are comprehending the text.

One Loop Through the Cycle

A closer look at the various processes and subprocesses shown in the flow chart in figure 6.2 will help us appreciate why, in the big picture, skilled reading is an intellectual feat on a par with expertise in chess.

Starting at the bottom, the reader fixates new material, which serves as input for the word-recognition process. Word recognition consist of two subprocesses: *initial encoding* and *lexical access*. In initial encoding the reader encodes the string of printed letters into a visual representation. Next, in lexical access, the reader matches the visual representation with word patterns stored in a part of long-term memory called the *lexicon*. The lexicon is the reader's mental dictionary, containing information that associates word forms with their possible meanings and their grammatical parts of speech in the read-

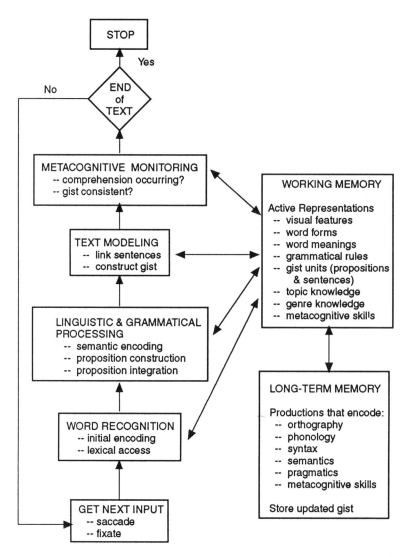

Figure 6.2
A sketch of a cognitive model for skilled reading. A skilled reader relies on knowledge stored in long-term memory to construct meaning from text and is able to control numerous representations that must be active in working memory. The flow chart on the left indicates the representations and levels of processing involved during each fixation. An average fixation lasts 250 msec.

er's language. In lexical access, the reader checks to see if the visual representation matches a word form in his or her language. If a match is found, word recognition ends. Word recognition is a visual or perceptual skill, and it is the *only* process in the model that is unique to reading. We use all the other processes—linguistic and grammatical processing, text modeling, and metacognitive monitoring—for both reading and speech comprehension.

A fundamental skill for understanding language is knowing what words *mean*. The end result of word recognition is that the reader associates a letter string with an *entry* in the lexicon. Like a word in a dictionary, a single letter string in the lexicon may have several different meanings associated with it. If the meaning of a word is ambiguous, the reader must choose from among possible meanings the one best suited to the current context. Researchers call this process of choosing a meaning *semantic encoding*.

In the case of simple, well-written sentences in which the reader knows the meanings of the words, semantic encoding is an effortless, unconscious process. When ambiguities arise, skilled readers realize something is amiss and their eye movements change to find information that might resolve the ambiguity. Here is a striking, although contrived, example: "Tomorrow was the annual, one-day fishing contest and fisherman would invade the place. Some of the best bass guitarists in the country would come to this spot." (Beck and Carpenter 1986, p. 1099) After reading the first sentence, a reader assumes that the text is about fishing. This assumption influences subsequent semantic encoding. Eye movements proceed smoothly forward to "bass", which the reader semantically encodes as a kind of fish. Trouble starts when the reader fixates "guitarists". The original encoding of "bass" as a species of fish doesn't make sense as a modifier for "guitarists". The reader's interpretation is no longer consistent. Eye movements slow and the pattern of saccades changes as the reader searches for information with which to resolve the inconsistency—information that results in the re-encoding of the letter string "bass" in its musical meaning.

Once the appropriate meanings (including the grammatical parts of speech) of individual words are available, the reader can begin to combine them into longer meaning units. Here the reader uses grammatical knowledge to construct *propositions* or clauses. Propositions are simple meaning structures that attribute a state or an action (usually named by a verb) to an agent or an object (usually named by a noun). One simple written sentence can contain many propositions. "John hit the red ball" contains at least four propositions: John exists; a ball exists; the ball is red; John hit it. Once the reader has constructed these propositions, he or she then *integrates* them into even larger meaning units: sentences. For skilled readers who are reading well-written texts, proposition construction and integration is again largely effortless.

We become aware of processing at this level only when a text is poorly written or grammatically ambiguous—for example, "The conductor stood before the audience left the concert hall" (Just and Carpenter 1987, p. 146). The problem with this trick sentence is that "before" can be either a preposition or a conjunction. When processing this sentence, a reader generally assumes that "before" is a preposition and that he is processing a single grammatical sentence. When "left"—a second verb—appears, the reader realizes that there are two grammatical sentences to process and reinterprets "before" as a conjunction linking the two sentences. The grammatical ambiguity makes proposition integration difficult.

In the next process, *text modeling,* a reader integrates and links the information contained in individual sentences to build a mental representation of the whole text. The result of text modeling—the end product of reading comprehension—is a mental representation of the text's general meaning, or its *gist,* which the reader stores in long-term memory. As a reader takes in new information from the page, he continually modifies and updates the text model and stores the gist.

Up to this point the reading process depends primarily on information encoded in the text. Text modeling is different. It depends not only on information encoded on the page but also on the reader's stored background knowledge about the text's topic. Imagine that a Harvard classics professor and a farmer with only a high school education both read an article on crop rotation.[1] Who would read it faster? Who would understand it better? Who would remember more of it? The professor would fare poorly in this comparison, not because he is a poor reader, but because he lacks the background knowledge that helps the farmer construct the gist. Chapter 2 of Hirsch's *Cultural Literacy* (1987) spells out in some detail the importance of background knowledge in reading comprehension.

We need background knowledge in reading for at least two reasons.

First, background knowledge helps us make inferential links among the sentences that are written on the page. For example, consider these sentences: "The radio suddenly started playing. The noise frightened the infant." (Just and Carpenter 1987, p. 252) Based on what we know about radios, noise, and babies, we infer that "the noise" refers to the radio playing and infer that the radio was playing sufficiently loud to startle the baby. The two sentences say neither of these things explicitly. We make the inferences—we derive information that goes beyond what is literally on the page—by using our general knowledge about the world in an attempt to link the two sentences into a meaningful story. We make dozens of such inferences every time we read a paragraph. Without background knowledge to warrant these inferences, reading comprehension would be impossible.

Second, we need background knowledge to construct and retain a text's gist. Given how our long-term memory works (chapter 2), to understand and remember what we read we have to relate the new information to schemas already in long-term memory. When appropriate background knowledge isn't active or available, we can remember very little of what we read. Try the following experiment, originally performed by John Bransford and Marcia Johnson (1972). Read this passage once, close the book, and write down as much as you can remember:

The procedure is actually quite simple. First you arrange things into different groups. Of course, one pile may be sufficient depending on how much there is to do. If you have to go somewhere else, due to lack of facilities that is the next step, otherwise you are pretty well set. It is important not to overdo things. That is, it is better to do a few things at once than too many.

Despite knowing all the words in this grammatically adequate text, you probably understood it poorly, if at all, and could recall very little about the passage. Getting the gist was so hard that you probably read the passage slowly, using long fixations and many regressions. However, if I had given you the same passage with the title "Washing Clothes" you would have read the passage more quickly and remembered it better. The title would have activated your clothes-washing schema, and you would have used that schema as background knowledge to construct a text model that would have aided your comprehension and enhanced your retention.

Besides background knowledge about topics, skilled readers also have background knowledge about literary forms and genres. Different literary forms and genres present different kinds of comprehension problems and require different strategies and assumptions. We read Beatrix Potter's *Peter Rabbit* with a different set of background assumptions than we bring to Charles Darwin's *Origin of Species*. (For example, we would be very surprised if the animals spoke in the second work.) When we read the front page of the *New York Times* we expect the language used there to be, for the most part, literal. In contrast, when we read poetry we expect language to be used figuratively.

For the adept, when things are going well, reading is highly automatic and requires little conscious mental effort. Skilled readers spend a lot of time on automatic pilot, and that is why reading appears to be so effortless most of the time. However, when ambiguities arise or when the gist becomes muddled or inconsistent, skilled readers *know* that their comprehension is failing and can take steps to identify and solve the problem. As was discussed in chapter 3, skilled readers monitor the comprehension process. They apply metacognitive skills to their reading. They know to ask the following self-critical questions: Is my comprehension strategy working? How am I doing? Does my gist make sense?

Some children develop these metacognitive skills on their own, but some don't. Remember, too, that it is metacognitive skills that often distinguish strong from weak learners. Some students (such as Charles, mentioned at the start of this chapter) lack these metacognitive skills, or cannot apply them to reading comprehension. Rarely does reading instruction explicitly teach these skills to students.

Cognitive Models and Reading Instruction

The previous section described the main processes that occur on one pass through the flow chart in figure 6.2. The purpose of that extended (and at times abstract) discussion was to illustrate and reinforce the notion that reading is a complex, multi-level process. Yet that discussion oversimplified the reading process in at least two ways.

First, timing and speed were not mentioned. Research tells us that fluent readers initiate a new cycle through the flow chart, on average, four times per second. In 250 msec, readers take in new information and do all the processing necessary at various levels—visual, linguistic, textual, and metacognitive—to integrate the new information into the gist they are constructing. This is a remarkable cognitive achievement.

Second, the above description was strictly "bottom-up," describing how the processes work in sequence from word recognition through metacognitive monitoring. Research also shows that reading is not a serial, bottom-up process from printed page to gist. There are also top-down influences, with processes at the higher levels influencing those lower down. One of the most robust examples of this is called the *word-superiority effect*. Obviously, to recognize words we have to recognize their constituent letters. However, when experimenters briefly present subjects with stimuli such as "lint" and "tinl" and then ask them whether an i or an e occurred at the second position in a stimulus, the subjects choose the correct letter more often if it appeared as part of a word than if it was part of a nonword. That is, subjects see a letter in a word better than they see the same letter in a nonword. Psychologists interpret this as showing that higher-level word knowledge facilitates lower-level letter perception. Knowledge of word forms exerts a top-down influence on letter perception. We don't necessarily process information at the letter level and only then process it at the word level. There is interaction between the processing at these two levels.

We saw a second example of a top-down effect and interaction in the "bass" example. There, text modeling of the first sentence generated an assumption that the passage was about fishing. This assumption exerted a top-down influence on semantic encoding, so that the reader initially assigned an incorrect meaning to "bass".

Researchers have found such interactions among nearly all the processing levels in the cognitive model. This has implications for reading instruction. Reading is complex because various levels of information processing are needed, because the processing must be executed rapidly, and because the processes are highly interactive. The skills sketched in the model must work together, sometimes nearly simultaneously, for the reader to construct meaning from text. If children are to use these skills together and interactively, they should learn them together and learn to use them interactively. The models tell us, then, that teaching the component skills in bottom-up fashion, in isolation, and one after another may not be effective. Appreciating this aspect of reading's complexity amounts to seeing reading in the big picture and can help us teach reading better. Principles derived from the cognitive models can also help us design better texts to help children both learn to read and read to learn.

Explaining the Whys

Isabel Beck, of the Learning Research and Development Center, is a former classroom teacher turned educational researcher. While following her husband's military and academic career wanderings, she taught in the Pittsburgh, San Diego, and Durham public schools. In Europe, she worked at US Army bases, teaching typing to paratroopers and preparing non-commissioned officers for their exams on the finer points of foxholes and barbed wire.

When Beck and her husband returned to Pittsburgh, she took time off to have two children and then earned a master's degree in education. She decided to go to law school, but to fill the time until her legal studies were to begin she answered an LRDC advertisement to be a research assistant on a reading project for a year.

"What first got my attention was that here were people, cognitive psychologists, who had *not* taught kids to read, yet they were able to describe accurately phenomena that I had observed in the course of teaching reading, but phenomena they had not experienced first hand," Beck recalls. "How could they know? I didn't understand how they could be as smart about reading and learning as I was when they didn't have the experiences I had."

More surprising, Beck realized that their explanations for the phenomena were sometimes better than hers: "I had viewed myself as a good teacher, and as I look back I still think I was, but I could have been better. While I couldn't have worked harder or gone any more extra miles, I could have understood the whys of what I was doing. Cognitive psychology explains the whys, and I became convinced that if practitioners understood the whys their teaching would be enhanced." She declined her acceptance into law school and remained at the LRDC to study word recognition, vocabulary learning, and reading comprehension. She completed her Ph.D. and now works to explain the whys to teachers in ways that are relevant to their classroom experiences.

Word Recognition: Accuracy Plus Speed

Beck remembers one particular incident that contributed to her con-
version from a would-be lawyer to an educational psychologist. As
a teacher she had noticed that in the primary grades weak readers
did not do flash-card drills involving words with the same "confidence" as better readers. They could read most of the words correctly, but they were more hesitant. Beck would tell them "You're
doing fine, have more confidence," but her encouragement had little
effect. Then one day she went to an LRDC colloquium, given by
Charles Perfetti, on the automaticity of low-level cognitive processes.
The colloquium occurred at a time when researchers were beginning
to apply cognitive science to reading. They knew that reading demands the coordination and the almost instantaneous interaction of
visual, linguistic, and higher comprehension skills. They also knew
that limits on working memory could be circumvented if some of
the skills were automatic. A cognitive process is *automatic* if we are
unaware that the process is taking place, if it occurs outside our
conscious control, and if it requires minimal working-memory capacity. Automatic processes are fast, accurate, and nearly effortless.

Automaticity is an important cognitive phenomenon that enables us to learn and execute tasks that might otherwise be impossible. Automatic processing, like chunking, helps us conserve our
limited working-memory capacity. We can overlearn a cognitive skill
to the point where it becomes almost like a reflex—automatic. When
this happens we no longer think about executing the skill, we just
do it. Such a skill takes little, if any, working-memory capacity.
Automaticity allows us to execute some overlearned skills in parallel
with other tasks that do demand conscious effort. We can perform
the automatic skill while simultaneously using working memory to
do something else. Motor skills are familiar examples of automatic
processes. When we learn golf or tennis, we go through a period of
talking ourselves through every stroke. After much practice, the
strokes become automatic; this frees our cognitive resources to think,
or worry, about the finer (tactical and strategic) points of the game.

What Beck learned at the colloquium was that for skilled readers
word recognition is an automatic process. "The light bulb went on.
What I had mistaken as lack of confidence was lack of automaticity,"
she recounts. Though her students had all been fairly *accurate* on

word drills, her poor readers had been *slow* on them. For those students, word recognition was not automatic.

How can psychologists show that word recognition is automatic? How can they prove that a process occurs if their experimental subjects are entirely unaware of it, as the definition of automaticity says? If a word appears on a computer screen for only 20 msec, a skilled reader can't see the word and if asked whether a word appeared, can only guess. Yet after only 20 msec word recognition has occurred. How do psychologists know?

Like other long-term memory structures, the lexicon—the mental dictionary—has an associative node-link structure, in which the nodes are meaning features and the links are meaning relations. The schema for general animal knowledge (figure 2.4 above) illustrates how part of the lexicon might be organized. In such an associative memory structure, if we access one word we also activate nearby related words in the associative network. If after flashing "robin" for 20 msec the experimenter waits 500 msec and then asks the reader to decide whether two other letter strings (say, "canary" and "truck") are words, the reader identifies "canary" as a word much more quickly than "truck". The reader can do this because the invisible letter string "robin" activated the related "canary" but not the distant "truck" in the lexicon. Apparently, in 20 msec the reader unconsciously looked up the meaning of "robin" in the lexicon. That is to say, lexical access occurred. If lexical access is the *final* step in word recognition, then word recognition occurred even though the reader was unaware of it.

A phenomenon called the Stroop effect shows that word recognition is like a reflex; it occurs outside our conscious control. If we are shown the color name "red" printed in green ink and asked to name the color of the ink, our reaction time is much longer than the time we take to say "green" when shown a green color patch. Even with practice, our reaction times on this task improve only slightly if at all. The problem is that the letter string "red" activates the meaning of that word in the lexicon and interferes with naming the color of the ink. No matter how hard we try, the meaning of "red" interferes with the name of the color, green. If you try the task, you can feel the interference. Hence, word recognition occurs even when we try hard to suppress it.

Although it is difficult to prove that word recognition takes *no* working-memory capacity, data suggest that it takes very little. Using an eye tracker, Keith Rayner and his colleagues had subjects read text in an experiment where the portion of text fixated appeared for only 50 msec after the start of the fixation; words were visible for, at most, 50 msec of a 250-msec fixation (Rayner et al. 1981; Rayner and Pollatsek 1981). Under these conditions subjects' reading speeds decreased only slightly, and their pattern of eye movements was no different than under normal reading conditions. The visual information readers take from the page in the first 50 msec of a fixation is enough to allow normal reading. If we assume that processing *time* is proportional to processing *demands,* then word recognition places little demand on working memory capacity—at most, only 20 percent (50/250 msec) of the processing demands.

Thus, for skilled readers, word recognition satisfies all three criteria for being an automatic process.

Automaticity and the Great Debate

How important is automaticity—both speed and accuracy—of word recognition in learning to read? How does automaticity of word recognition contribute to the development of other reading skills? In the early 1980s an LRDC research group including Alan Lesgold, Lauren Resnick, Kathleen Hammond, and Mary Curtis was studying these questions. (See Lesgold et al. 1985.)

The research team wanted to find out the order in which children acquire various reading skills. Everyone accepted that improved word recognition is associated with improved reading, but does better word recognition *cause* better reading or does word recognition develop simultaneously with other reading skills? If improved word recognition causes other reading skills to improve, the improvement in word recognition should precede improvement on the other skills. If so, word-recognition ability in the early grades should predict later reading-comprehension scores.

The research team studied children in grades 1–4 over a four-year period to assess the development of their skills. The researchers measured both accuracy and speed of word recognition by having the children pronounce words as quickly as possible when the words appeared one by one on a computer screen. They found that a first-grader's accuracy and speed on this task was an excellent predictor of the child's reading-comprehension scores in fourth grade. They also found that word-recognition *speed* was a much better predictor of later reading comprehension than accuracy alone. In short, they found that early automaticity of word recognition—speed plus accuracy—precedes, predicts, and so most likely causes subsequent improvement in other reading skills. Beck's students who had appeared to lack confidence actually lacked automaticity, and so their chances of becoming expert readers were slim.

The study's findings also had implications for the "great debate" in reading instruction between advocates of phonics and whole-word instruction, a debate about the most efficient way to teach word recognition (Chall 1983; Beck 1981).

Phonics instruction assumes that the alphabetic principle is fundamental in learning to read. In alphabetic languages, such as English, readers have to associate meaningless written symbols (the letters) with equally meaningless sounds. Only after readers make the symbol-sound associations and combine the sounds do meaningful words emerge. Learning the appropriate associations between letters and sounds at the subword level, phonics advocates argue, allows children to become *productive* readers. By this they mean that children can sound out new words they have never seen before.

Whole-word instruction takes meaning and comprehension as fundamental. Its advocates argue that if the purpose of reading is to construct meaning, and if meaning first appears at the word level, then instruction should emphasize the word level. We should teach children new words in story contexts and have them use the words repeatedly in sentences and other drills until they can recognize the words independently. Emphasizing phonetic decoding at the meaningless subword level, whole-word theorists argue, can make children "word callers" rather than "word comprehenders."

The LRDC study included both phonics and whole-word classrooms. In the phonics classrooms, at the time of the study, teachers tested children on word recognition entirely on the basis of accuracy. Children could take as long as they needed to sound out individual words. In the phonics classes, about 15 percent of the children progressed through elementary instruction without developing automatic word-recognition skills. Surprisingly, about 15 percent of the children in the whole-word classes had the same problem. The two methods, as used in the early 1980s, were about equally deficient in making word recognition automatic for some children.

In both types of classroom, a sizable percentage of children were leaving the primary grades with grossly inadequate word-recognition skills and at risk for later reading problems. Cognitive theory suggests that, to comprehend a text, a reader must process information rapidly at the word, phrase, sentence, and text levels. All the processing has to occur within the limitations of working-memory capacity. If word recognition is not automatic and consumes most of the reader's cognitive capacity, then the processing resources that remain are not sufficient for the development and deployment of other comprehension skills. Children who can't recognize words automatically can get permanently stuck at the decoding level and may never realize or learn that the goal of reading is to construct meaning. In the LRDC study, a substantial percentage of both phonics and whole-word students read so slowly—50 to 70 words per minute—that they could not comprehend even the easiest material. Although the "great debate" was heated at the time, both sides were paying insufficient attention to the importance of automaticity in word recognition.

The study also showed that any differences between phonics and whole-word students were small and temporary, seldom lasting beyond the second grade. As a practical matter, due partly to the research, few classrooms today are purely phonics or purely whole-word. Official curricula may favor one method over the other, but many teachers' classroom methods are hybrid. Across all reading curricula, the contribution of cognitive research has been to underscore the importance of speed and accuracy—automaticity—in word recognition. Although not sufficient to ensure fluent reading, automaticity is a necessary early reading skill that precedes, predicts, and contributes to eventual expertise.

In short, maybe the debate was great, but the issue isn't. Many children have learned to read using phonics; many have learned using the whole-word method; most acquire low-level reading skills such as word recognition. Today, the results of the NAEP indicate that most American children achieve the low levels of reading proficiency and master decoding. At age 13, nearly 100 percent of American students have rudimentary reading skills and over 95 percent have basic reading skills (Mullis and Jenkins 1990). Thus, further debate about how to teach word recognition doesn't address the most pressing educational problem. The pressing problem is that too few children are acquiring the higher-level comprehension skills. They can decode, but they can't comprehend and use what they decode—they can't construct a gist. We have to address how to teach these high-order reading skills.

Improving Linguistic Knowledge: Rich Vocabulary Instruction

Children arrive at school with sophisticated language-comprehension skills and with a store of grammatical knowledge which they can apply to spoken language. One thing children must do to become fluent readers is build their vocabularies—expand their lexicons. Learning vocabulary is an impressive but unnoticed cognitive achievement. By some estimates, the average first-grader understands 5000 words, the average college student 50,000. Thus, between first grade and college an avid language learner may learn as many as 11 new words per day.

We memorize meanings for some words, but we learn many more by using what we already know while reading to figure out unfamiliar words from context. However, to figure out a word's meaning from context, a reader must already have sufficient vocabulary knowledge and comprehension skills to establish the context. This implies that the larger the reader's prior vocabulary, the easier it is for him to learn new words from context. There is a feedback loop between what one already knows and how easily one can learn more. The sociologist Robert K. Merton (1968) called loops such as these the Matthew Effect, after the author who might have been first to state it, Matthew the Evangelist: "For unto every one that has shall be given, and he shall have abundance: but from him that has not shall be taken away even that which he has." If the Matthew Effect applies to the learning of vocabulary, then investing in early and consistent vocabulary instruction should, like compound interest, pay long-term dividends for reading comprehension.

Although vocabulary knowledge correlates with reading comprehension, and although the teaching of vocabulary can improve performance on vocabulary tests, teaching vocabulary often fails to improve comprehension—often because vocabulary is taught without regard for the big picture. In the mid 1970s, Beck and Margaret McKeown began what was to become a long-term research collaboration by applying cognitive science to the problems of vocabulary instruction. (See Beck, Perfetti, and McKeown 1982; Beck, McKeown, and Omanson 1987.)

One common method of teaching vocabulary is the *dictionary method,* in which students memorize meanings of words and generate sample sentences using them. This method is the least successful in improving reading comprehension. It also can result in children's using sentences like "My family *erodes* a lot", intending to say the family eats out a lot (Miller and Gildea 1987). It teaches vocabulary knowledge largely in isolation from using that knowledge in reading and language comprehension.

Using cognitive principles, Beck, McKeown, and their colleagues reasoned that to affect comprehension, word knowledge must be accurate and efficient (that is, automatic), tightly woven into readers' lexicons, and taught in the context of language-comprehension activities. Maybe unsuccessful vocabulary instruction ignored automaticity, didn't build rich associations among word meanings in long-term memory, and didn't teach children how to use this knowledge.

Beck and her collaborators began work with fourth-graders in a city school, 80 percent of whom were below the fiftieth percentile in standardized reading and vocabulary scores. The research team developed an experimental vocabulary program based on four assumptions: Training in word use must be broad. Students must actively process the words. Students must practice extensively with the words. Students must have multiple exposure to the words in different contexts.

Instruction took place 30 minutes a day, five days a week. Instead of learning unrelated words one by one, each week the students worked on a group of 8 to 10 words in a single meaning family. For example, the "people family" of words included "accomplice", "virtuoso", "rival", "miser", "philanthropist", "novice", "hermit", and "tyrant". There were at least 10 exposures to each word during the week.

On the first day the students associated words and meanings, as in traditional programs. In contrast with the dictionary method, they quickly went on to play a game in which the teacher tried to elicit the words from the children by giving clues. The students had to explain their guesses—for example, to tell why "crook" might be associated with "accomplice". They also learned about the words' connotations. The teacher would say a word, like "tyrant", and the students would respond either "Yeah!" or "Boo!"

On the second day, the students made up sentences using the words and, to develop automaticity, played a game of matching words with meanings that was scored on both accuracy and speed. On the third day, they used their new knowledge to reason with the words. They constructed contexts or situations around the words and thought about questions such as "Would an accomplice be more likely to squeal to the police in return for not having to go to jail, rob a bank by himself, or enjoy baby-sitting?" More speed and accuracy drills took up the fourth day's session. The students also explored meaning relations among the words to learn that words are not mutually exclusive: "Could an accomplice be a novice? Would a hermit be a likely accomplice?" Throughout the week, the word play was explicit and public, so the entire class could benefit from each child's growing expertise. Justifying their answers also made the children self-aware about using, reasoning, and playing with words. It made the students metacognitively aware of how to use word knowledge.

On the fifth day, the students took a multiple-choice vocabulary test. Those students in the experimental curriculum increased their vocabulary accuracy from around 30 percent to 95 percent correct on weekly vocabulary quizzes. They scored around 80 percent when retested 3 weeks later. The experimental group also increased their speed in retrieving word meanings from long-term memory. They could associate a word with its semantic category (for example, "hermit" with the category "person") half a second to a full second faster than students in a comparison group who received traditional vocabulary instruction. Students who received the new curriculum improved from the 35th to the 44th percentile on the vocabulary subtest of the Iowa Test of Basic Skills, and on the reading-comprehension subtest students in the experimental group improved from the 37th to the 45th percentile. Students in the comparison group showed no significant improvement over their pre-instruction performance. Students in the new program also improved on making inferences about the meanings of unfamiliar words in contexts that did not give obvious clues. For example, they became much better at answering questions such as this: "When Father heard that Lisa had ripped up the letter from Steve, Father *commended* her for it. What did Father think of Steve?" This suggests that the new method also improved students' ability to figure out word meanings from context.

Rich instruction, as Beck, McKeown, and their colleagues called their method, was a vocabulary method that improved reading comprehension. It worked in part because it embedded vocabulary instruction in the larger context of language comprehension. How could a teacher use this method in an actual classroom? Classroom time is a limited commodity, and rich instruction takes a lot of it. Beck, a former classroom teacher, has an answer: "Teachers have to be clever about which words they target for rich instruction."

Common words ("dog", "mother", "red", "ball") require no instruction at all. Students can best learn low-frequency, context-specific words ("nebula", "sonata", "estuary", "gene") through subject-matter instruction. But, Beck points out, there is a vast middle class of moderately high-frequency, general-use words—"retort", "ponder", "delve", "dearth"—that should be targets for rich instruction. Beck estimates that there are around 7000 such "middle-class" word families. She also suggests that teachers concentrate on the middle-class words that are crucial for understanding a particular story and whose word families are applicable to other pieces of literature and to situations in daily life (Beck et al. 1987). If children can learn 400 of these words per year between grades 3 and 9, they will have learned 40 percent of these middle-tier words—a significant expansion in vocabulary knowledge. This is a conservative estimate; if the Matthew Effect operates, then the learning of new words will accelerate as children gradually add more words to their lexicons.

Rich instruction is finding its way into classrooms. In 1983, Beck and McKeown published an article in *The Reading Teacher* describing the method and its rationale. The article invited teachers to write in for sample vocabulary lessons. The authors received thousands of requests, and are still receiving them. About 50 teachers sent second letters commenting on the method and materials after they had used them. One follow-up letter was from Dot Ashmore, who teaches grades 4 and 5 at the Trinity School in Atlanta. She wrote back saying how the program had rekindled her interest in words. She included some of hew own lessons and a letter she had sent to parents explaining this new approach based on ideas from "some researchers." She wrote:

The researchers hypothesize that words truly "belong" to us when we know them in a way that goes beyond simple association between definition and word. With each encounter, the word can take on a new connotation, a new flexibility. . . . We hope we are providing the students many chances to encounter words that they might normally let pass over their heads. With some of these words, they will be building new connections between words. With other words, all we can expect is some beginning idea of general meaning. . . . As we try to stimulate thinking about different word relationships, we have been getting some unexpected thinking. . . . One of the pleasant surprises is that children are excited to run across one of our words.

Beck and her co-workers took delight in how Ms. Ashmore's letter captured the essence of their work. The letter is evidence that they had succeeded in explaining why rich instruction works in a way that touched the classroom.

Background Knowledge in Learning to Read

The "washing clothes" example showed us that readers need background knowledge that is not literally on the printed page. This knowledge, stored as schemas in long-term memory, helps readers make inferences and connections that are implied but not explicitly stated in the text and makes text modeling possible. Background knowledge allows readers to apply common sense about the larger world in constructing a text's meaning.

The Matthew Effect also applies to background knowledge: The more background knowledge a reader has, the easier it is for him or her to get more of it by reading. Although schemas can't be directly taught (they have to be constructed by the reader-learner), we can make schema construction easier by ensuring that any relevant background knowledge the reader has is active during reading. We can help young readers with this if our instruction and our reading materials are sensitive to what they may already know.

How sensitive to children's prior knowledge are the reading programs used in schools? The importance of background knowledge, once pointed out, seems almost too obvious for reading programs to ignore. Most school reading programs attempt to address the importance of background knowledge in the preparatory discussions and pre-reading activities suggested in the teacher's manual. The materials and techniques are based largely on intuitive, common-sense notions, but they are not always attuned to what most children know or to the central story ideas they are trying to teach.

Beck and her colleagues attacked this problem in the late 1970s. (See Beck et al. 1979.) They analyzed commonly used reading curricula from a cognitive perspective and found three major deficiencies. First, the texts often used ideas unfamiliar to the children. To counter objections that reading texts lacked content, publishers started to include literature in grade-school reading books. This provided an opportunity to expand and elaborate on children's preexisting schemas; however, the literature required specialized background knowledge beyond second- and third-graders' daily experience. Oddly, instead of expanding pre-reading activities to cope with the more difficult content, the reading programs reduced pre-reading activities. Second, in the remaining pre-reading activities, the concepts chosen for discussion—concepts intended to activate relevant background knowledge—were often peripheral to the story's gist. Third, the strategies, exercises, and comprehension questions in the teachers' manuals paid too little attention to central story concepts.

At this point, the researchers wondered what would happen to comprehension if reading lessons contained relevant background knowledge and emphasized central story content. What would happen if reading lessons were revised on the basis of cognitive principles? Beck, Omanson, and McKeown (1982) analyzed teacher's materials in two widely used reading series and then redesigned prestory preparation, pre-silent-reading preparation, story illustrations, and post-reading questions. Their hypothesis was that focusing on central story content, as derived from expert readers' gists, would improve reading comprehension.

First, they defined central story content systematically by appealing to how expert readers construct and integrate propositions and how they use these propositions in text modeling to develop a gist. The researchers divided every sentence in each story into clauses, each clause standing for a single proposition (proposition construction). Next, they analyzed how these propositions interrelated temporally and causally within the story structure (proposition integration). Once they had the propositional model, they asked expert readers to identify central story units. They defined central story units as units depicting basic, unanalyzable events that either introduce a main character or form a sequence of connected events leading from the story's start to its finish. The central story units correspond to the representations expert readers store in long-term memory as the story's gist. Beck calls these central units and the structure linking them a *story map.*

The research team used the story map to rewrite the pre-story preparation in a way that emphasized the central story schema. In the Arachne myth, for example, Arachne agrees that if Athena beats her in a spinning contest, then Arachne will never spin again. The myth's central schema is the notion of a bargain or an agreement. Pre-silent-reading preparation based on the story map would reactivate or prime relevant knowledge the children should already have stored about this central concept. For example, whereas the standard preparation might ask "What happens to Arachne?", a more focused instruction might be "On this page you will find out what happens to Arachne because of her bargain with Athena." The investigators also redrew the stories' illustrations to be sure that the pictorial information did not conflict with story events in theme or content. Finally, they prepared comprehension questions on the entire story to help the children develop a more expert story map, or gist. The research team used the central story units as a source for questions. Surprisingly, they had found that only one-third of the post-reading questions in the commercially prepared materials tapped key story events.

They tested the rewritten materials on 48 third-graders in two urban schools near Pittsburgh. First, they divided the children into two groups of 24 on the basis of reading achievement scores. Within each ability group, 12 children used the revised reading lessons and 12 the standard commercial lessons. They tested the children's reading comprehension by asking them to recall what they had read (i.e., to state the gists of the stories) and by means of multiple-choice tests. The third graders who used the revised materials outperformed the children who used the standard lessons on recall of the central story content (37 percent vs. 27 percent) and scored 10 percent higher on the comprehension questions. The revised lessons were particularly helpful for less skilled readers (those who had difficulty in getting the gist and in answering comprehension questions on central story ideas).

This was a small-scale study that used only two stories, but it was a first step in showing that comprehension can be improved if the reading materials are sensitive to the importance of background knowledge. One might argue that the improvement was small; however, in view of the Matthew Effect even a 10 percent improvement in comprehension each year beginning in third grade could have substantial long-term results.

Upon completing the study, in 1982, Beck was quick to point out that larger, long-term studies were needed to identify exactly what caused the improvement. Many researchers and teachers followed this lead. In 1990 Beck said: "I think the role of background knowledge has been disseminated to the practitioner community by much work in the field, of which my own is a part. Teachers are more sensitive to it and basal readers seem to be doing a better job. The idea of the story map seems to have been incorporated into most new reading curricula. At least the boilerplate in various programs purports to develop questions based on the idea. Still, because the idea of background knowledge influencing comprehension seems *so* obvious, subtle effects of background knowledge can be missed."

Background Knowledge in Reading to Learn

Not only should children learn to read in school; they should also read to learn. Reading, after all, is an enabling skill. How effective are textbooks in helping students learn and understand subject matter? If they are not effective, why not? Beck, McKeown and their associates are currently working on this question.

They have analyzed four commercially available social studies curricula used in elementary schools. Too often, critiques of social studies curricula are superficial and largely ideological. The LRDC group wanted to dig beneath the surface content and see how students' prior knowledge interacts with social studies lessons, independent of ideological slant. They applied methods of cognitive science to get inside the curricula.

Their analyses again revealed three major deficiencies. First, the relation between content and instructional goals was not always clear. Second, there were unrealistic assumptions about the extent of children's background knowledge. Third, there was inadequate explanation of significant events and their interrelations.

Fifth-grade American history is usually students' first exposure to history as a school subject. Beck and her colleagues decided to look in detail at how the various curricula taught the American Revolution. First, they developed a story map for this historical period. Unlike a map for the Arachne myth, a map for a history lesson is built around a history schema. Myths and history lessons are different kinds of texts. History can have a story structure, but chains of historical causation link events in the structure. Events occur and have consequences. People react, and their reactions have further historical consequences. Facts are important in history, but their causal-historical interconnection is essential. That is what makes a history book different from a novel.

The story map for the Revolution contained two central ideas: the role of Britain in the American colonies and the significance of the revolutionary motto "No taxation without representation."

How did the texts treat these central ideas? Only one of the four texts studied had any extended discussion of how a distinct American identity emerged in the colonies. The texts gave static descriptions of colonial life in New England, the Central Atlantic colonies, and the South, but gave no coherent description of how a variety of European settlements in the New World came under British dominance to form the 13 original colonies. Surprisingly, the texts did not always state clearly that the 13 colonies were British possessions and that Britain was the ruling power.

On the issue of representative government, the texts mentioned the taxation motto, that Britain levied taxes, and that colonists lacked representation in Parliament. But these facts were not historically integrated to explain what representative government is and why people can value it so highly. Apparently, the texts assumed that fifth-graders have robust background knowledge about both the role of Britain in colonial life and the concept of representative government.

The problem, as Beck and McKeown found out, is that fifth-graders don't have this knowledge. She and her colleagues studied a class of fifth-graders before they took American history. They said to each student "Tell me anything you know about the American Revolution." This statement was a general, direct probe of students' knowledge—an invitation for students to unload topic knowledge from long-term memory. It was the students' chance to reveal everything they knew about the period, including the role of Britain in the colonies and the importance of representative government. In response, 60 percent of the students gave *no* information about why the Revolution occurred, 74 percent didn't mention that the war was between Britain and its colonies, and 57 percent offered no information about which side won. When directly asked what "No taxation without representation" meant, only one fifth-grader out of 35 had any idea about the concept of representative government.

When Beck and McKeown asked the same question of 37 sixth-graders who had studied American history, 60 percent gave no information about the cause of the Revolution, 57 percent didn't mention Britain as the opponent, and 40 percent gave no information on the war's outcome. Only two sixth-graders showed an understanding of representative government. The sixth-graders' performance suggested that their fifth-grade history instruction had been highly ineffective. The texts' treatment of central ideas was not sensitive to the concepts' complexities or to the children's meager pre-instruction knowledge.

Children also lack an understanding of history's causal structure, which one must have to understand a historical period and to remember and use historical information. Beck and McKeown found this deficiency when they asked students six other questions that attempted to tap their knowledge of the Revolution from different perspectives. The questions gave students different initial cues with which to begin searching their American Revolution knowledge structures: Why do Americans celebrate the Fourth of July? What is the Declaration of Independence? What were the 13 original colonies? How did the United States become a country?

If a student understood the historical relationship among the events of the Revolutionary period, one would expect considerable overlap in the answers he or she gave to the six questions, because all the events mentioned in the questions should be connected in a causal network—an American Revolution schema. A student with an adequate understanding of the period should have a memory structure like the one depicted in figure 6.3 and should use that network to give extended, elaborated answers to the questions. In that structure, the nodes in boldface represent information contained in the test questions. A student with an adequate understanding should be able to use this information as cues to enter the structure, and should be able to follow the associative links to find additional information with which to elaborate an answer.

After their American history course, the sixth-graders in this study didn't give extended, overlapping, elaborated answers. They responded with simple, literal answers to the specific questions. They didn't have rich, connected conceptual structures for the historical period. Figure 6.4 shows the network that one of the students, Tony, constructed on the basis of his fifth-grade studies. His knowledge of the period was fragmented into four "islands." For example, he made

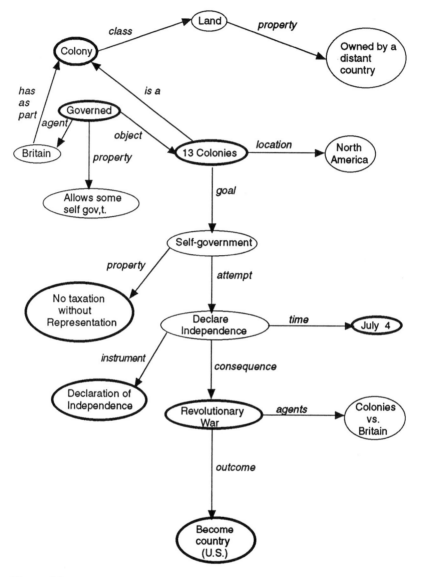

Figure 6.3
This network shows an associative knowledge structure that captures an adequate sixth-grade causal-explanatory understanding of key events in the American Revolution. The nodes are key concepts and ideas; the links are meaning relations. The boldfaced nodes represent information that appeared in McKeown and Beck's test questions. (From McKeown and Beck 1990, p. 694. Copyright 1990 American Educational Research Association. Reprinted with permission of publisher.)

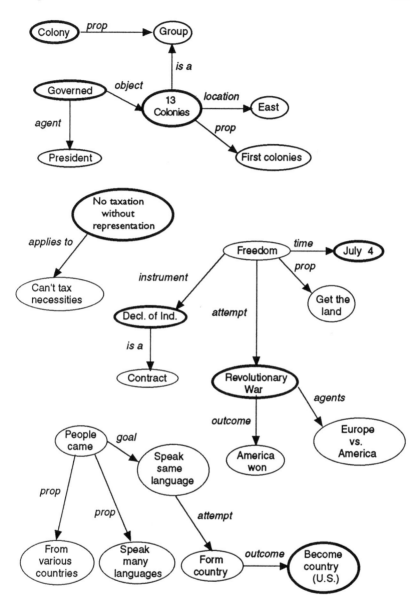

Figure 6.4
Tony's associative structure for the American Revolution, representing his understanding of the period after he had completed a fifth-grade American history course. (From McKeown and Beck 1990, p. 716. Copyright 1990 American Educational Research Association. Used with permission of publisher.)

no connection among the 13 colonies, the Revolutionary War, and the "no taxation" motto. Thus, for Tony, the question on the 13 colonies prompted comments on the first colonies and the president, but no comments on representative government, Britain, or the emergence of the United States as a new country.

Tony, and most of the other students, could recall relevant knowledge when questions were asked in one way, but not when they were asked in a different way. For example, 50 percent of the sixth-graders mentioned Britain when asked about how the United States became a country, but only 25 percent did so when asked about the Declaration of Independence, and only 11 percent when asked about the original 13 colonies. Such fractured knowledge structures, typical of novices, result in inert historical knowledge. Students might have the knowledge, but they lack the associative links they need to access the knowledge in all situations where it is relevant.

Beck and McKeown concluded that elementary school instruction isn't sufficiently explicit about history's causal structure: "As instruction is now presented in current elementary social studies textbooks, students seem to acquire bits and pieces of information. Without a focus to what is learned, these bits and pieces compete for attention, and students have no way to judge their value, role, or appropriateness for the overall topic." (McKeown and Beck 1990, p. 723)

Next, the researchers prepared revised history texts that were sensitive to background knowledge and were explicit about the causal structure of the historical period (Beck et al. 1991). They identified places in history texts where students' comprehension might fail because of lack of background knowledge, difficulty in keeping track of what terms mean, and gaps in the presentation of causal and temporal relations. They then hypothesized how expert readers might deal with these problems and revised the texts in accord with the experts' probable solutions. The result is a text that clarifies, elaborates, explains, and motivates important information. The text makes explicit how events are related historically.

For example, the first sentence in an original text read:

In 1763 Britain and the colonies ended a 7-year war with the French and Indians.

This sentence is difficult, even for an expert. It begins the lesson on the French and Indian War, a war not previously mentioned, with a statement about how it ended. The sentence is also informationally dense, mentioning Britain, colonies, French, Indians, and war. Applying the expert's gist, Beck and her colleagues turned this one sentence into seven in the revised text:

About 250 years ago, Britain and France both claimed to own some of the same land, here, in North America. The land was just west of where the 13 colonies were. In 1756, Britain and France went to war to see who would get control of this land. Because the 13 American colonies belonged to Britain, the colonies fought on the same side as Britain. Many Indians fought on the same side as France. Because we were fighting against the French and Indians, the war has come to be known as the French and Indian War. The war ended in 1763.

The revised text states explicitly some of the missing background knowledge (such as that the 13 colonies belonged to Britain) not found in the standard text, and provides more information to link ideas in the text. It gives students more information to use in their proposition construction, their proposition integration, and their text modeling.

The research team applied this method to prepare four revised lessons: "the French and Indian War," "No taxation without representation," "the Boston Tea Party," and "the Intolerable Acts." They used the original texts with fifth-graders in November as part of the regular American history class. They used the revised lessons with fourth-graders in the same school the following May.

The revised texts helped students construct richer knowledge structures for the historical period. The four revised lessons contained 124 idea units based on the expert's gist. Students using the revised material recalled 18 percent of these units, whereas students using the original texts recalled only 13.6 percent. On comprehension questions, the group using the revised lessons scored 49.1 percent; the group using the standard text scored only 29.9 percent. As with the reading lessons, the revised history materials were particularly helpful for students of lower ability. With the standard text, students in the top quartile for reading scores far outperformed students in the bottom quartile on both recalling central ideas and in answering comprehension questions. With the revised texts, the high-ability students still did better; however, the difference in performance between high- and low-ability students was smaller and was not statistically significant.

The differences in comprehension performance were not just a matter of remembering more of the text. Analysis of the students' oral answers to the six test questions allowed the researchers to assess the representations students had constructed for the various topics (Beck et al. 1991). On the "No taxation without representation" lesson, students using the revised materials were more likely to understand that the colonists' distress over taxes arose from their desire for representative government rather than from unwillingness to part with money. When quizzed with the test questions, the students showed that they had constructed more highly connected and well integrated knowledge structures. The students gave elaborated answers, and the information in the answers overlapped. Their historical knowledge was less inert, because they had moved toward constructing a causal-explanatory structure of the period's history.

National assessments have documented students' deficiencies in social science and literature knowledge. Diane Ravitch and Chester Finn (1987) discuss one such assessment in their book *What Do Our 17-Year-Olds Know?* In 1990, Richard W. Riley, a former governor of South Carolina and an NAEP board member, commenting on an assessment of civics and history knowledge, observed that most students have no more than a "Trivial Pursuit kind of familiarity" with the subject matter. Students could identify names, dates, and terms, but few knew the significance of the people or events in American history or government. Ninety-nine percent of twelfth-graders knew basic historical facts, but only 5 percent could interpret historical information (Hammack 1990). School curricula are not imparting high-order social studies skills.

The fractured pattern of information recall and the inability to grasp the significance of historical information reported in the national assessments are consistent with what Beck and her colleagues found in their small-scale studies. Their work, however, goes beyond describing *what* students don't know. Applying cognitive methods to the teaching and learning of social studies tells us *why* most students acquire only "Trivial Pursuit knowledge": Students aren't acquiring rich, complex knowledge structures, and the texts are partly at fault. The texts make unrealistic assumptions about children's background knowledge and aren't sufficiently explicit about the historical links among events, dates, and persons. Beck's work also suggests what must be done: We must revise materials and methods so that they exploit what we know about reading to learn. We have to be as concerned with *how* content is taught as we have been with *what* content is taught.

The Big Picture: Reciprocal Teaching, Metacognition, and Reading

Reciprocal teaching, the method mentioned in the introduction to this chapter, improved Charles' classroom reading comprehension by four grade levels in 20 days. This method illustrates how instruction designed on cognitive principles can help children to apply language-comprehension skills in their reading and to acquire the metacognitive strategies essential to skilled reading.

Reciprocal teaching also shows how researchers, administrators, and teachers can collaborate to apply the results of research in the classroom. Annemarie Palincsar, Ann Brown, and Kathryn Ransom—a graduate student, a professor, and a school administrator—shared the belief that cognitive research could improve classroom practice and that classroom practice can improve research.

After five years working as a special education teacher and administrator, Palincsar returned to the University of Illinois as a doctoral student. She felt her previous training in psychodiagnostics—training based on a medical model of learning disabilities—was not meeting the needs of her students. She decided to broaden her academic background and to study how sociocultural factors might influence students' experience in school.

The cognitive revolution was spreading through academic circles, but had not yet reached teacher-practitioners. Palincsar's classroom experience influenced her choice of a thesis project. In her words: "As a teacher, one of the situations I found most baffling was having children who were fairly strong decoders but had little comprehension or recall of what they had read." She was baffled by students like Charles.

At first, Palincsar was interested in how self-verbalization might be used to help children regulate their cognitive processing. Donald Meichenbaum (1985) had developed techniques based on self-verbalization to help impulsive children—children who mentally fail to stop, look, and listen—pace their actions and develop self-control. At the time, most of the work on self-verbalization had explored how it could be used to regulate social behavior. Palincsar wondered how it might be used to regulate *cognitive* behavior—specifically, how it might be used to improve reading comprehension. She wrote to Meichenbaum, who suggested that the application of his ideas to academic subjects might be strengthened by incorporating ideas from research on metacognition. He told Palincsar to discuss her idea with Ann Brown, an authority on metacognition who at that time was also at Illinois.

At their initial meeting, Palincsar showed Brown a design for the pilot study that was to evolve into reciprocal teaching. Brown offered her a quarter-time research appointment to do the study. When it proved successful (Brown and Palincsar 1982), Brown gave Palincsar a full-time research assistantship and supervised her thesis research.

Palincsar and Brown developed reciprocal teaching from the pilot study on a sound theoretical basis. (See Brown and Palincsar 1987.) They analyzed the task's demands, developed a theory of task performance based on expert–novice studies, and formulated a theory of instruction that might improve task performance. This is the same sequence Bob Siegler followed with the balance-scale task. A major difference, of course, is that reading comprehension presents a more complex problem than the balance scale.

From their analysis and a review of previous research, Palincsar and Brown (1984) identified six functions that most researchers agreed were essential to expert reading comprehension: The competent reader *understands* that the goal in reading is to construct meaning, *activates* relevant background knowledge, *allocates* attention or cognitive resources to concentrate on major content ideas, *evaluates* the constructed meaning (the gist) for internal consistency and compatibility with prior knowledge and common sense, *draws* and *tests* inferences (including interpretations, predictions, and conclusions), and *monitors* all the above to see if comprehension is occurring.

Palincsar and Brown then identified four simple strategies that would together tap all six functions needed for comprehension: *summarizing, questioning, clarifying,* and *predicting.* They explained the relation between the four strategies and the six functions as follows (Palincsar and Brown 1986): Summarizing a passage requires that the reader recall and state the gist he or she has constructed. Thus, a reader who can summarize has activated background knowledge to integrate information appearing in the text, allocated attention to the main points, and evaluated the gist for consistency. Formulating a question about a text likewise depends on the gist and the functions needed for summarizing, but with the additional demand that the reader monitor the gist to pick out important points. When clarifying, a reader must allocate attention to difficult points and engage in critical evaluation of the gist. Making predictions involves drawing and testing inferences on the basis of what is in the text together with activated background knowledge. A reader who self-consciously uses all four strategies would certainly appreciate that the goal of reading is to construct meaning.

Expert-novice studies supported the hypothesized connection between comprehension functions and strategies. After completing a comprehension task, expert readers reported that they spent a lot of time summarizing, questioning, clarifying, and predicting. Experts' "comprehend aloud" protocols substantiated these self-reports. Poor readers did not report using the strategies and showed no evidence of using them in their comprehension protocols. As Palincsar and Brown characterize it, novices executed an "once-over, desperate, nonfocused read."

But can you teach the strategies to novices? And if you can, will it improve their comprehension? To answer this question, Palincsar and Brown designed a prototype instructional intervention to teach non-experts how to use the strategies. As with all instruction, the primary problem is transfer. How should one teach the strategies to get novices to use them spontaneously? Here Palincsar, following Brown's work, based her strategy instruction on the new synthesis discussed above in chapter 3. Successful strategy instruction must include practice on specific task-appropriate skills (the cognitive aspect), explicit instruction on how to supervise and monitor these skills (the metacognitive aspect), and explanations of why the skills work (the informed instruction aspect).

The new synthesis suggests what teachers should do to help students master strategies. First, teachers have to make the strategies overt, explicit and concrete. Teachers can best do this by modeling the strategies for the students.

Second, to avoid inert strategies, teachers should link the strategies to the contexts in which they are to be used and teach the strategies as a functioning group, not in isolation. This suggests that reading-strategy instruction should take place during reading-comprehension tasks, where the explicit goal is to construct meaning from written symbols. Teachers should teach with the big picture in mind.

Third, instruction must be informed. The students should be fully aware of why the strategies work and where they should use particular strategies. Thus, instruction should involve discussion of a text's content and students' understanding of why the strategies are useful in that situation.

Fourth, students have to realize the strategies work no matter what their current level of performance. Thus, instruction should include feedback from the teacher about the students' success relative to their individual abilities and encouragement to persist even if a student is not yet fully competent.

Finally, if students are to become spontaneous strategy users, responsibility for comprehension must be transferred from the teacher to the students gradually, but as soon as possible. This suggests that the teacher should slowly raise the demands made on the students and then fade into the background, becoming less an active modeler and more a sympathetic coach. Students should gradually take charge of their learning.

Palincsar designed reciprocal teaching to satisfy all five of these requirements. Reciprocal teaching takes the form of a dialogue. Dialogue is a language game children understand, and it is a game that allows control of a learning session to alternate between teacher and student. Most important, when engaged in dialogue students are *using* their language-comprehension skills. In reciprocal teaching, dialogue directs these skills toward reading.

The dialogue becomes a form of cooperative learning, in which teachers model the strategies for the students and then give students guided practice in applying them to a group task of constructing a text's meaning. Teacher and students take turns leading a dialogue about the portion of text they are jointly trying to understand. The dialogue includes spontaneous discussion and argument emphasizing the four strategies.

In reciprocal teaching, the teacher assigns the reading group a portion of a text and designates one student to be the leader for that segment. Initially, the teacher might be the leader. The group reads the passage silently. Then the assigned leader summarizes the passage, formulates a question that might be asked on a test, discusses and clarifies difficult points, and finally makes a prediction about what might happen next in the story. The teacher provides help and feedback tailored to the needs and abilities of the current leader. The student-listeners act as supportive critics who encourage the leader to explain and clarify the text. Each student takes a turn as leader. The group's public goal is collaborative construction of the text's meaning. The teacher provides a model of expert performance. As the students improve, the teacher fades into the background.

In the first test of reciprocal teaching, Palincsar served as the teacher and worked with one student at a time. The students were seventh-graders in a remedial reading program who had adequate decoding skills but who were at least three grades behind in reading comprehension. At first, students found it difficult to be the leader, and Palincsar had to do a lot of modeling and prompting, but gradually the students' performance improved. In the initial sessions, over half the questions students formulated were inadequate. Only 11 percent of the questions addressed main ideas, and only 11 percent of the summaries captured the gist of the passage. After ten tutoring sessions, however, students could generate reasonably sophisticated questions and summaries. By the end of training, 96 percent of the students' questions were appropriate, 64 percent of the questions addressed main ideas, and 60 percent of their summaries captured the gists of the passages.

Students' reading comprehension improved along with their performance in reciprocal teaching. On daily comprehension tests, scores improved from 10 percent to 85 percent correct and stayed at this level for at least 6 months after reciprocal teaching ended. Back in the classroom, reciprocal-teaching students improved their performance on other reading tasks from the seventh percentile before reciprocal teaching to the fiftieth percentile after. Palincsar repeated the study working with two children simultaneously and obtained the same results. (Charles, mentioned above, was one of the students in this second study.)

Palincsar and Brown wanted to know if reciprocal teaching was the most efficient way to achieve these gains before they asked teachers to try it in classrooms. Reciprocal teaching demands a great deal of the teacher's time and requires intensive interaction with small groups of students. Both are valuable classroom commodities. Could the same results be achieved more efficiently by a different method? Reciprocal teaching turned out to be superior to all the alternatives tested (Brown and Palincsar 1987, 1989). In all the comparison studies, reciprocal teaching improved remedial seventh-graders' performance on comprehension tests from less than 40 percent before instruction to between 70 and 80 percent after instruction, a level typically achieved by average seventh-graders. The best of the alternative methods—explicit strategy instruction, where the teacher demonstrated and discussed each strategy and the students then completed worksheets on the strategies—raised scores from around 40 percent to between 55 and 60 percent (Brown and Palincsar 1987). These studies showed that the intense and prolonged student-teacher interaction characteristic of reciprocal teaching is crucial to its success (Palincsar et al. 1988). This is the investment teachers have to make to cash in on reciprocal teaching's dividends.

Into the Classroom

Can reciprocal teaching work in a real classroom? Here Kathryn Ransom, Coordinator for Reading and Secondary Education in District 186, Springfield, Illinois, enters the story. Ransom—a former teacher—is a veteran, professional educator. She makes it clear she has seen many trends come and go, and realizes that neither she nor the schools will please all the people all the time. Nonetheless, Ransom devotes time and effort to get new things happening in the Springfield schools. She has become adept at, as she puts it, "making deals" with research groups. "We can bring in people who have exciting ideas that need to become practical, and as the researchers work with Springfield teachers they can provide staff development experiences I never could."

Springfield's District 186 serves a population of 15,000 students, from kindergarten through high school. The system is 25 to 28 percent minority. On standardized tests, classes at all grade levels score at or above grade level in all subjects. This is a solid achievement, Ransom points out, because the majority of special education children in the district receive instruction in regular classrooms. When it was time for the classroom testing of reciprocal teaching, Palincsar approached Ransom. Ransom saw the potential of reciprocal teaching and recognized in Palincsar a researcher who could make cognitive science meaningful to administrators and teachers. The researcher and the administrator struck a deal advantageous to both.

Together, they decided to approach Springfield's middle school remedial reading teachers. These teachers worked daily with children who had adequate decoding skills but no functional comprehension skills. Ransom and Palincsar collaborated to design a staff development program that would encourage the teachers to think about instructional goals and methods and that would allow the researchers to introduce reciprocal teaching and the theory behind it. The teachers first watched videos of Palincsar conducting reciprocal teaching sessions. Later the teachers took part in reciprocal teaching sessions, playing the roles of teacher and student. Next a teacher and a researcher jointly conducted a reciprocal teaching lesson. The final training consisted of three formal sessions on the method over a three-day period.

In the first classroom study of reciprocal teaching, four volunteer remedial reading teachers used the method with their classes (Palincsar et al. 1988). Class size varied from four to seven students. Before reciprocal teaching, the baseline on daily reading-assessment tests for the students was 40 percent. After 20 days of reciprocal teaching their performance rose to between 70 and 80 percent, just as in Palincsar's initial laboratory studies. Students maintained this level of performance after reciprocal teaching and also improved their performance on other classroom comprehension tasks, including science and social studies reading. Reciprocal teaching worked in the classroom! Experienced volunteer teachers, after limited training, could replicate the laboratory results in classroom settings.

Palincsar and Ransom obtained similar results in a study that used conscripted teachers, who varied greatly in experience and expertise. The students also were more diverse in their reading deficiencies than the students in the first study. Class size varied from 7 to 15, with an average size of 12. Each teacher taught one reciprocal teaching group and one control group; the latter received standard reading-skills instruction. Again, after 20 days of reciprocal instruction, scores on daily comprehension tests improved to 72 percent for the reciprocal teaching group, versus 58 percent for the control group. Thus, average classroom teachers, working in less-than-ideal circumstances and teaching groups of seven or more students, replicated the original laboratory results. As the ultimate test, the Springfield team ran an experiment in which the strongest student in a remedial group served as the teacher. In this study, the student-teachers improved their scores on comprehension tests from 72 percent to 85 percent correct. The other students in the group improved their scores from 50 percent to 70 percent correct.

Since the study ended, in 1989, reciprocal teaching has become a mainstay in the Springfield schools. It is now used in all remedial reading classes, and its methods have been incorporated in some form into all regular classroom reading programs. Even more encouraging, Springfield teachers exposed to reciprocal teaching and to the importance of strategic thinking attempt to integrate these elements into their teaching of other subjects.

One benefit of reciprocal teaching, and of similar projects in the Springfield system, has been the teachers' participation in extended applied research. This was part of Ransom's original agenda. A project running over 5 years, as reciprocal teaching did, provides a powerful way to change teachers' behavior. Most in-service training for teachers lasts only a day or two and at best can have only a minor impact on their thinking and their performance. Ransom sees collaboration in classroom research as a way for teachers and researchers to interact in a dignified, mutually beneficial way. The teachers gain meaningful in-service experience that is intellectually satisfying. Working closely with fellow teachers and other education professionals helps them overcome the isolation of seven-hour days as the only adult in the classroom. The research team also gains, as the reciprocal teaching researchers will attest. The teachers initially helped refine reciprocal teaching for classroom use, providing important insights into how to make an instructional prototype work in a school. Later, they helped identify new research questions and helped the researchers design ways to test the method's classroom effectiveness. Because of her Springfield experience, Palincsar decided that all her subsequent educational research would be done in close collaboration with classroom professionals.

Interest in reciprocal teaching continues within District 186 through instructional chaining. A network has developed in which teachers who have used reciprocal teaching conduct in-service sessions for other teachers. By the 1987–88 school year, 150 teachers in 23 buildings had taken part in these sessions. Teachers formed peer support groups so they could discuss progress and problems associated with daily use of reciprocal teaching and other strategy instruction. The remedial teachers also helped the district design new reading tests to assess students' use of comprehension strategies. The Springfield experience contributed to ongoing efforts at the state level to revamp reading instruction and to develop reading tests that can measure the skills that methods such as reciprocal teaching try to impart. Veterans of the Springfield experiment now work in other schools and with national educational organizations to improve reading instruction.

In the Springfield schools and in others that have used reciprocal teaching, teachers have a better understanding of what reading is about. As Palincsar and Brown (1986, p. 770) observe, "There was a time not long ago when successful reading was thought to be execution of a series of component subskills." To teach reading one taught the subskills, from word recognition through finding the main idea, often in isolation and in a fixed sequence. Charles and the approximately 60 percent of American 17-year-olds who fail to reach the NAEP's fourth reading proficiency level—who fail to become adept readers (Mullis and Jenkins 1990)—show the inadequacy of this approach. Reciprocal teaching works. The strategies it teaches enable students to apply their language-comprehension skills to reading so that they can read for meaning. Reading is more than decoding and more than the mastery of a series of small, isolated subskills.

7

Writing: Transforming Knowledge

Tanya is a 19-year-old black woman from the inner city. Expelled from five high schools during her senior year, she never graduated. Eventually she enrolled in a community college to prepare for a high school equivalency examination as the first step toward attending college and becoming a nurse.

While at the community college, Tanya participated in a research project on writing instruction headed by Glynda Hull, from the Center for the Study of Writing at the University of California at Berkeley, and Mike Rose, from the University of California at Los Angeles. In the course of working with Tanya, they asked her to write a summary of a magazine article in which a nurse describes her experience with an ornery patient (Hull and Rose 1989). Several paragraphs from the article that figured prominently in Tanya's summary are reproduced in figure 7.1.

On the surface Tanya's summary (figure 7.2) is a writing instructor's nightmare. Many might see it as an example of extreme illiteracy and the failure of public education. One might even think Tanya has a severe linguistic disorder or a general mental impairment. Yet when Hull and Rose asked Tanya to summarize the article orally, she performed well. She also could write acceptable narratives about her personal experiences.

Heather is a white, middle-class 10-year-old. She was a typical student in one of Marlene Scardamalia and Carl Bereiter's writing studies done at the Ontario Institute for Studies in Education (OISE) in Toronto. Asked to write an essay on whether students should be allowed to choose their subjects in school, Heather produced the following:

I think children should be able to choose what subjects they want in school.

I don't think we should have to do language, and art is a bore a lot. I don't think we should do novel study every week. I really think 4s [fourth-graders] and 3s [third-graders] should be split up for gym. I think we should do a lot of math. I don't think we should do diary. I think we should do French. (Burtis et al. 1983, p. 162)

We find Heather's essay more readable than Tanya's summary. Those of us not familiar with how 9- and 10-year-olds write might find Heather's essay stilted and immature, but it is developmentally appropriate for a 10-year-old. We also would assume that Heather's writing will improve as she matures and benefits from more school instruction.

Research on the cognition of writing done by Hull, Rose, Scardamalia, Bereiter, and others tells us that both Tanya and Heather represent serious educational challenges to our schools. Although Tanya's performance is highly inadequate, the research tells us that there is a logic to her writing and that she is engaged in problem solving. If we understand how students like Tanya represent and try to solve writing problems, we can help them. The research also tells us that Heather's writing may not benefit as much as we think from school instruction. How we currently teach and use writing in

"Oh, this is going to be a great day," I said to myself. "Just be patient, kind, and understanding. Maybe he only needs some TLC to alleviate his fears. He really seems more frightened than anything." With these thoughts, I began to care for him as skillfully as I could. (paragraph 4 of original)

My thoughts were similar but deep down I really wanted to help him. What was the right approach? (7)

The next morning there was no night special to report. She had left the case, and the report she sent to the Registry of Nurses was so descriptive that it would be almost impossible to find a replacement. My second and third days were as terrible as the first. By the fourth day, the evening nurse decided she wouldn't take the abuse any longer and also left the case. To say I felt abandoned was an understatement; even the doctor didn't have any advice. (8)

"You're right," I said. " I am getting paid for what I'm doing, but there's a difference: I have pride in my profession, and I earn my pay by giving my patients the best nursing care I possibly can. But I can give the minimum, too. I can sit here most of the day and still collect my 35 bucks at the end of the shift. If that's what you want, the choice is yours. So make up your mind fast, because I'm not taking any more of your abuse. (11)

Figure 7.1
Four paragraphs from "On Handling the Difficult Patient." (From Hull and Rose 1989. Used with permission of publisher.)

the Handling About
difficult patient

this something telling about a nurse ~~te~~ who won't to
help a patience. She was a special night nurse,
this man had a stroke and was ~~paral~~ paralis on his
left side. She Was really doing a lot for the patience
She Introduced myself she asked him How was
he feeling. remark was, XXX, can't you see 'Im in
pain?" he telling the nurse he was in so much pain.
he really didn't won't to answer her. Before
she was ready to give him his I.V. Are Anything
XXX "you're killing me, you XXX."
Oh this going to Be a great Day I said to myself
just thinking alone. I have pride in What
I Do I am going to get pad no matter what I am
still ~~am~~ going to collect my money no matter
what happen I do Believe and I no that In ~~my~~ mind.
My thoughts were similar but deep down.
What was the approach? A Registry nurse
was so descriptive. impossible for me to
find a replacement. My second and thirddays
she decided she ~~won~~ wouldn't <u>Abuse</u> any longer and
~~Aso~~ also left the case felt Abandoned was an
understatement; even this doctor In this case
she Really liked what she was doing But was getting
treated Right Respect. She had chance of getting
A another job But † Don't she wanted to But then again
She wanted to.

Figure 7.2
Tanya's summary of the article. (From Hull and Rose 1989a. Used with permission of Sage Publications.)

school—the culture of school writing—leaves many high school and college students essentially at 10-year-old Heather's writing level. If we understand how many older students represent and try to solve school writing problems, we will see that their methods and strategies are essentially the same as Heather's. One consequence of this, mentioned in chapter 1, is that only one out of five high school students can write an adequate persuasive essay.

Writing: Solving Ill-Defined Problems

We all have a sense of how difficult it is to write. We have to think of something to say, organize our thoughts, and then choose just the right words to express our ideas. We remember how we disliked writing assignments in school. As adults, many of us avoid extended writing tasks. Cognitive science tells us there is a good reason for all these memories and behaviors: Writing is a form of problem solving, and the problems it entails can be particularly difficult and demanding.

According to cognitive scientists, writing tasks force us to solve *ill-defined problems*. An ill-defined problem is one for which there is no ready-made, best initial representation and no standard solution method. We can better understand ill-defined problems by contrasting them with well-defined problems, like those we find in school science and math.

In Siegler's balance-scale study (chapter 2 above), the children saw the scale and knew that the problem was to predict how the scale would tip. The balance-scale problem is so well defined that Siegler could analyze it completely and make recommendations about which representations children should learn. Also, the law of torques and Siegler's rule IV provide a standard way to solve all balance-scale problems. In geometry problems there are diagrams, givens, and a statement to prove. Geometry problems are sufficiently well defined that GPTutor's 200 rules could generate proofs for most standard high school problems.

Writing problems are different. In contrast with balance-scale and geometry problems, the initial statement of a writing task provides surprisingly little information to guide problem solving. There are almost no givens in a writing problem. When I started this book my writing task, the initial input, was a single sentence: Write a book on how cognitive research can contribute to educational reform. Three years later, the single sentence had grown into a 500-page manuscript. The statement of the writing task itself placed only the most general constraints on what an adequate solution might be. I had to develop an initial representation of the task and use it to construct a writing plan. In my plan I had to make tentative choices about what to say, who my audience might be, and how to organize the content for that audience. My plan defined the problem I tried to solve. These initial choices guided other decisions about how to translate my plan into words on the page. I had to make choices at every level, from what my gist was to the exact words I would use to convey that gist. Then, as I wrote and read what appeared on the page, I often had to revise my plan; I had to rethink and redefine my problem in the course of writing. After many cycles of planning, writing, and redefining, I arrived at what I thought was a good solution to my problem. There are so many choices and so much latitude in making them that, as with other ill-defined problems, there is no single, best solution. If I were to give my initial writing task to 100 skilled writers, no two would write the same book. The result would be 100 equally acceptable but unique solutions. Seen in this way, solving ill-structured problems may be difficult, but it also gives us opportunities to be creative.

We also can contrast solving writing problems with solving reading problems. Usually the goal of reading comprehension is to construct a gist, a highly abstract distillation of information encoded on the written page. In constructing a gist, we throw away information—including the exact wording of what we have just read. In writing—turning a gist into words—the writer has to supply all the information that the reader needs, but eventually discards in the comprehension process. The writer has to supply information at a variety of conceptual and linguistic levels to make the abstract gist concrete on the page. Envisioning what information a reader might need and deciding what information to supply make writing the difficult task it is.

Our naive beliefs about writing, and about how to teach it, rarely recognize writing as problem solving. Traditionally, writing instruction has focused on the written product rather than on the writing process. On the traditional view, writing is a special, prestigious dialect of a language. Writing is to everyday speech what gourmet cooking is to fast food. On this view, the way to learn this special dialect is to study models of good writing, spelling, and punctuation until we can incorporate the models into our repertoire of language skills. Writing teachers should give assignments, let their students write, and then correct the written products according to the rules of the prestige dialect. On this traditional view, the writing process is simple. Good writers work in stages: they collect information, organize it, write drafts, and revise them. These are the steps in the recipe for successful writing. Teachers should give children the recipe and then judge the resulting products. This view of writing instruction was prominent in the professional educational literature as recently as the mid 1970s and is still widely held by parents and teachers.

But we all know there is more to teaching gourmet cooking than handing out recipes and doing taste tests; so, too with writing. We have to learn, practice, and orchestrate the component skills of the process, be it cooking or writing. Cognitive research gives us detailed descriptions of these component skills and how they interact. It has shown that the traditional, naive theory seriously misrepresents the nature and the difficulty of writing tasks. Writing is not like following a recipe, one step after another; it is more like being a juggler, an air traffic controller, or a short-order cook in a busy diner. A writer has to attend to many things simultaneously so that no ball, plane, or pancake hits the ground. Linda Flower and John R. Hayes, who formulated an early, influential cognitive model of writing, describe it this way: ". . . writing is the act of dealing with an excessive number of simultaneous demands or constraints. Viewed this way, a writer in the act is a thinker on a full-time cognitive overload." (Flower and Hayes 1980, p. 33)

Writing has always had special appeal for advocates of educational reform, who traditionally have seen it as a prestige dialect which the properly educated should master. In the current reform climate, some think that better writing instruction might help students develop the elusive higher-order thinking and reasoning abilities called for in *A Nation at Risk*. Although writing research has not yet *proved* that better writing skills bring with them better learning and reasoning skills, one day we might find that this is the case (Applebee 1984).

While we await definitive proof, we can still argue that writing might have a special place in the curriculum. Learning how to solve ill-defined problems that put the solver on full-time cognitive overload should have some educational benefit. Most school problems aren't ill-structured. Students can handle most school problems by recalling a fact, a formula, or a routine from long-term memory. With writing problems, because they are ill-defined, there are no facts, formulas, or all-purpose routines. Writing problems can present unique challenges to students—challenges to be exacting and creative thinkers. Furthermore, writing, unlike multiple-choice tests or word problems, is a task that people actually confront in everyday life. We might want to capitalize on the one school task that approximates the cognitive and creative demands of common real-world problems. Although we know that transfer of skills from one context to another fails more often than it succeeds, we can construct school writing tasks that are very similar to the tasks students will face when they leave school. We can facilitate transfer if in school writing we give students authentic, rather than artificial, writing tasks.

Studying the Process: A Cognitive Model of Writing

Hayes and Flower began their pathbreaking research on the cognition of writing in the mid 1970s. They set out to examine the problem solving that writers did to get from the task assignment to written text—to examine the writing process. By the early 1980s, they had formulated a detailed cognitive model of expository writing.

To develop their model, Hayes and Flower embarked on a series of expert-novice studies. The novices were college freshman; the experts were writing teachers enrolled in an advanced professional development course at Carnegie Mellon University. One writing assignment Hayes and Flower used in their research was "Write about your job for the readers of *Seventeen* magazine, 13- to 14-year-old girls." The subjects were to compose aloud into a tape recorder, verbalizing everything—even crazy ideas—that went through their minds as they worked. Transcripts of writers' protocols, like the one partially shown in figure 7.3, provided the data with which Hayes and Flower formulated and tested their model.

Their original model (figure 7.4), as a cognitive theory, describes how processes in working memory operate on input from the task environment and from the writer's long-term memory. For writing, the task environment contains things external to the writer that influence performance—the statement of the writing problem, the description of the intended audience, and any other cues or instructions (e.g., "Make believe you're a free-lance magazine writer"). As the writer produces text, it too becomes a part of the task environment that can influence subsequent thinking and writing.

The writer's long-term memory contains background knowledge about the topic, the audience, and writing schemas. Just as expert physicists have schemas for applying Newton's Laws to incline plane or spring problems (chapter 5) and as an expert reader uses different literary schemas when reading Darwin than when reading Beatrix Potter (chapter 6), skilled writers have schemas. Writing schemas are general formulas or scripts the writer can follow to solve routine writing problems. We all have schemas for writing a business letter or a thank-you note. We know there are socially shared conventions for each kind of letter. A business letter has an inside address, but a thank-you note doesn't. In a business letter the salutation often includes the addressee's full name, but a thank-you note most often uses only the first name. A business letter is formal

Episode 1 *My job for a young* -- Oh I'm to describe *my job for a young thirteen to fourteen year-old teenage female audience -- Magazine Seventeen.* -a- My immediate reaction is that it's utterly impossible. I did read Seventeen, though -- I guess I wouldn't say I read it -a- I looked at it, expecially the ads, so the idea would be to describe what I do to someone like myself when I read -- well not like myself, but adjusted for -- well twenty years later. . . . .

Episode 2 --um-- Also the mention of a free-lance writer is something I've -- I've no experience in doing and my sense is that it's a -- a formula which I'm not sure I know, so I suppose what I have to do is -a- invent what the formula might be, and -- and then try to -a- try to include --- events or occurrences or attitude or experiences in my own job that would -a- that could be -- that

Episode 3a could be conveyed in formula so let's see -- / / I suppose one would want to start by writing something that would attract the attention of the reader -- of that reader and -a- I suppose the most interesting thing about my job would be that it is highly unlikely it would seem at all interesting to someone of that age -- So I might start by saying something like -- **Can you imagine yourself spending a** day -- **Many days like this -- waking up at 4:30 a.m., making a pot of coffee . . . looking around . . . -a- my** -- looking round **your house, letting in your cats . . . -a- walking out -- out with coffee** and a book **and watching the dawn materialize** . . . I actually do this . . . although 4:30's a bit early, perhaps I should say 5:30 so it won't seen -- although I do get up at 4:30 - - watching the dawn materialize **and starting to work -- to work** by reading -- **reading the manuscript -- of a Victorian writer** . . . with a manuscript of a . . . a Victorian writer . . . a person **with a manuscript of a student** . . . .

Episode 3b . . . Um - / should I (mumble) -- the thing is about saying teachers -- the -- the teenage girl is going to think teachers like who she has, and professor I always feel is sort of pretentious and a word usually -- usually I say teacher, but I know that means . . . Its unfortunate now in society we

Episode 3c don't -- but that that isn't prestige occupation. / **Talking to other people like yourselves** -- that's whoever it may be -- other people at your job -- other -- other people like yourself -- uh a lot like yourself but -- talking to other people like yourself . . . .

Figure 7.3
Excerpts from an expert writer's protocol collected by Flower and Hayes. The italicized words are things the writer read from the task assignment. The bold-faced text is the written output the writer produced. The text in regular type is what the writer thought aloud while writing the essay. (From Flower and Hayes 1981. Used with permission of National Council of Teachers of English.)

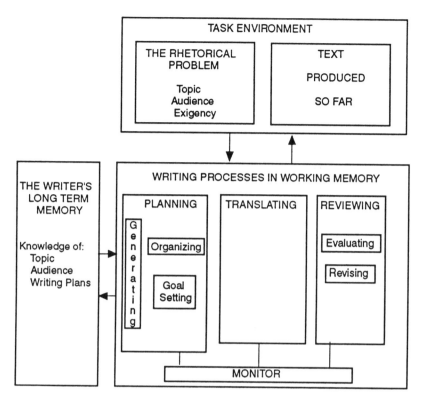

Figure 7.4
The Hayes-Flower model of expository writing shows how processes in working memory interact and use information from the task environment and from long-term memory to solve writing problems. (From Hayes and Flower 1980. Used with permission of Lawrence Erlbaum Associates.)

and often impersonal in tone, but a thank-you note is informal and personal. If we have a schema for a writing task, the schema can help us decide what to say and how to say it.

In the Hayes-Flower model, three working-memory processes interact in writing: *planning, translating,* and *reviewing.* Planning gives the writer a representation of the task and a written or mental outline for the text. Translating transforms the plan into words on the page; it handles the mechanics of writing. In reviewing, the writer compares the written product against the writing plan—what he or she intended to write. Where the text compares unfavorably to the plan, the writer makes changes in an attempt to improve the text. A master program, the *monitor,* controls and coordinates the actions of these three processes.

All the processes and subprocesses of the model work together to produce effective writing, and no one process is more important than another. To keep the discussion at a manageable length, this chapter will focus on the features of the Hayes-Flower model that most distinguish that model from the traditional view of writing—the features that can most contribute to improved writing instruction. Those features are the planning process and the monitor.

A few words about the other two processes may help justify this decision. Translating is the process that handles the mechanics of writing. In their studies, Hayes and Flower found few significant differences between expert and novice writers in the translating process, in how they handled the mechanics of writing. Also, according to the NAEP writing evaluations, most children have adequate command of writing's mechanics; current instruction does help most children master the translating process. Reviewing is a different story. Skilled writers spend much more time revising and editing their text than less skilled writers. Teaching children to revise effectively is also difficult. However, research has found that effective reviewing depends on prior effective planning. The quality of a writer's review process depends crucially on the quality of the original writing plan. It depends on the writer's seeing differences between what he or she did write and what he or she planned to write. What most distinguishes skilled from unskilled writers, and young from mature writers, is the sophistication of their planning and how they control the writing process.

Planning and Its Subprocesses

One way to handle full-time cognitive overload, especially when solving ill-structured problems, is to plan carefully. When the task is vague, the final goal is not explicit, and there is no standard solution strategy, the writer needs a plan to guide the many decisions he or she will have to make. In the Hayes-Flower model, planning involves three subprocesses: *generating content, organizing content,* and *setting goals* for the effective expression of the content.

For all of us, thinking of what to say—generating content—is the first hurdle to clear in a writing assignment. Although it seldom occurs to us, we all use a similar process to begin identifying possible content. When we write, we generate possible content by using cues from the assignment to search long-term memory. In the expert's protocol (figure 7.3), the writer uses "my job" as the initial cue to begin searching her memory for content. Using this cue, the writer starts exploring a chain of mental associations about her work life. She reads manuscripts, goes to the university, teaches a class, talks to students, and meets with her colleagues. Notice that the expert does not use everything she retrieves from memory exactly as she retrieves it. Toward the middle of episode 3 she changes "reading a manuscript of a Victorian writer"—an idea she first retrieved from memory—to "reading a manuscript of a student." When generating possible content, skilled writers check to see if what they retrieve is relevant and appropriate for the intended audience. Thus, while planning, good writers also search their memories for knowledge about the audience. For the expert, there is interaction between knowledge about the topic and knowledge about the intended audience. In episode 1 of the sample protocol, the writer envisions the audience to be much like she was 20 years earlier. She uses this audience knowledge to make decisions about content (don't talk about Victorian writers) and to identify potential problems (17-year-olds wouldn't find a professor's job interesting at all) (episode 3a). Following associative chains in long-term memory is a sure way to generate content, but the writer must keep the search under control. The trick, as this writer shows, is to follow the associations as long as they yield useful ideas, but to break the chain when the information becomes irrelevant to the task, the topic, or the audience.

Besides generating content, the skilled writer must also consider how to organize that content effectively. Good writers seldom present content in the same order in which they recall it from memory; rather, they reorganize their ideas in a way that would help their audience construct the intended gist. As an aid to eventual organization, skilled writers also search memory for writing schemas. They look for a script or a formula they might have learned to help solve familiar problems. The writer in episode 2 of the protocol tried to recall a schema for writing a popular magazine article, but she didn't have one. She realized she would have to invent an organizational structure for this task, and decided to organize her article by placing the content within the framework of her typical work day. Other writers might choose other organizational plans. Some writers might organize the article logically or conceptually. They would assume that readers have to know some basic facts about their jobs. They would present the basics, then gradually elaborate on them to give an ever more detailed description of their work.

When analyzing the protocols, Hayes and Flower observed that some of the items the writers retrieved from memory during planning were neither content ideas nor writing schemas. Skilled writers also set goals for themselves in their plans, and use these goals to evaluate the quality and the effectiveness of their texts—as guides to what might be good or desirable moves to make in solving writing problems. Goals help writers narrow their choices about what to say and how to say it. We all have beliefs about how to write so that our texts will appeal to readers. There are tricks, devices, and conventions we like to use—snappy openings, figurative language, direct quotes, avoiding the passive voice. Researchers refer to this how-to writing knowledge as *rhetorical knowledge*. We apply rhetorical knowledge to writing tasks by setting rhetorical goals when we plan. For example, in episode 3a the writer set the goal of starting her article with "something that would attract the attention of the reader." In episodes 3b and 3c she hesitated over what to call her university colleagues: "teachers" might cause her target audience to think of high school teachers, but the more accurate "professors" might sound pretentious, so she settled for "talking to other people like yourself."

The monitor, or controlling master program, is the feature of the Hayes-Flower model that most distinguishes the view of writing as a cognitive process from the traditional view. The monitor, linked to all three working-memory processes, controls how they interact. It is the mental traffic cop that decides which of the component processes gets the right of way and which should yield when there is a conflict. The monitor decides which process dominates working memory capacity at any one time and, when one process has been finished, decides what to do next. If one process interrupts another, the monitor keeps track so that the writer can return to that point after dealing with the interruption.

On the traditional theory there is no need for a monitor, because that theory describes writing as a fixed sequence of observable behaviors: A writer collects information, organizes it, writes a draft, and revises, finishing one process and then starting the next one. If this were so, the processes would never come into conflict. There would be no interruptions, and nothing to control or monitor.

Hayes and Flower found that writers rarely plan, then translate, then review. Usually planning leads to some translating, which in turn prompts more planning. Or, while reviewing, a writer might decide to draft a new paragraph to create a smoother transition between existing paragraphs. The writer's decision invokes planning, translating, and reviewing the new paragraph, possibly followed by more planning and translating, until the paragraph satisfies the writer's goals. When satisfied with it, the writer returns to reviewing at the point where he or she made the decision to write the new linking paragraph. The component processes don't occur one after another in a fixed sequence. More typically, the processes are intricately embedded one inside another.

Computer scientists call processes that have this embedded, nested structure *recursive processes.* Douglas Hofstadter, in *Gödel, Escher, Bach,* gives a simple example of a recursive process: a multi-line telephone with a hold button (Hofstadter 1980, p. 127). Suppose I am on the phone with my tennis partner and about to arrange a game for 4:30 that afternoon. My wife calls, so I put my partner on hold. My wife asks if I can pick up the children from school. Before I can answer, my boss calls; I put my wife on hold. He wants to reschedule our luncheon meeting to 4:45 p.m. I say, "Great! I'm looking forward to it." I then pop back to my wife and tell her she'll have to pick up the children. Then I return to my would-be tennis partner and tell him there is no way I can play tennis at 4:30. The hold button nests one call inside another, and the outcome of one call can influence the resolution of the previously initiated, pending calls that are on hold.

Cognitive research has shown that skilled writing, like using a multi-line phone, is a highly recursive process. We need a well-developed monitor to keep track of what writing process we were doing when we must interrupt it to execute another. The monitor keeps the complex, recursive process manageable, just like the hold feature makes multiple phone lines manageable.

Expert, Novice, and Student Writers

Using this general process model, Hayes, Flower, and other researchers were able to describe in some detail how skilled writers differ from the less skilled. Other researchers used the model to study how children's writing abilities develop.

The major difference Hayes and Flower found between expert and novice writers was in the planning process. On writing assignments such as the *Seventeen* assignment discussed above, experts wrote better articles than novices, as we would expect. We can't attribute differences between expert and novice performance on this task to differences in topic knowledge, because we can assume that each of the writers had a reasonable grasp of what he or she did for a living.

Experts and novices differ little in their ability to generate content. However, they do differ in their abilities to organize their ideas and set effective writing goals. Skilled writers have abundant rhetorical knowledge, and they use it to organize effectively and to set sophisticated goals. They are rhetorical experts who can integrate topic, audience, and linguistic knowledge to define and solve writing problems. Novices, in contrast, plan superficially. They concentrate on the topic and what they know about it; they fail to address, or even to see, other aspects of the problem, involving the audience and the communicative use of written language. They either lack rhetorical knowledge or are unable to apply it in planning solutions to writing problems. In many ways, poor writers are like people who can't solve the nine-dot problem. They represent and define the problem in such a limited way—telling what they know—that it is impossible for them to construct an effective solution.

Scardamalia, Bereiter, and their colleagues at OISE have spent more than a decade studying how children learn to write within the broader context of general cognitive development. Their research, guided by the Hayes-Flower model, has helped us understand how children progress from raw novices to more mature (but rarely expert) writers during their school years. We can describe children's maturation as writers largely in terms of their developing ability to produce more sophisticated writing plans.

When children enter school they have had extensive experience producing spoken language, but no experience with writing. The first challenge is to master and automatize the mechanics of writing—the translating process. Young children do no planning at all and have trouble generating extended content. When given an assignment, they usually start putting words on paper immediately, produce very short essays, and do no revising (Bereiter and Scardamalia 1982). Young children's writing has these features because they use their skill at generating speech to generate words to write. For a young child, being given a writing assignment is like being addressed in conversation. In conversation, we don't plan, speak at great length, or review. When spoken to we answer immediately, knowing that we can fix mistakes and misunderstandings later in the conversation. This is how young children approach writing tasks. They answer the assignment with a burst of language one conversational turn (about 18 words) long translated onto paper. They try to use the speech skills they have to solve school writing problems.

Most children solve the problem of generating extended content for writing around age 10, when they make the metacognitive discovery that the words in an assignment give clues about content. The recognition that they can use the clues to search memory's associative structure gives children a simple, effortless, and automatic procedure for generating content. They have figured out generating—one of the planning subprocesses in the Hayes-Flower model. However, because this subprocess is the only one they have mastered, they often become victims of their long-term memory. They have a process for following chains of associations through memory, but are oblivious to the constraints of audience, organization, and writing goals that help constrain the expert's search. They can follow associative chains, but don't know when to break them. For writers at this age, all and any possible content is acceptable. If asked to write on a given topic, they find it hard to think of anything about the topic they would not include in their essays. As one fourth-grader said almost incredulously to Scardamalia, "What do you mean think of something about dogs and not use it?"

Starting with 10-year-olds, researchers at OISE traced the further development of children's planning skills. To do this, they compared children's writing plans with their written texts. The essay by Heather quoted above was written for this study. Here is the plan Heather produced, which she used to write her essay on school subjects:

I don't like language and art is a bore.
I don't like novel study.
And I think 4s and 3s should be split up.
I think we should do math.
I don't think we should do diary.
I think we should do French.

Now reread Heather's essay. There is almost no difference between Heather's writing plan and her final text. Like Heather, most 10-

NOTES

-- opinion (mine)
-- responsibility of the children -- their goal in life
-- parents -- their understanding of their children
-- what will happen with what they take
-- examples
-- what rights to do they have
-- what I think about it
-- the grade (if they chose) should be 7 and up
-- school subjects should be made more interesting
-- how future will be

TEXT

I personally think that students should be able to choose which subjects they want to study in school. In grade 9 students are allowed to choose certain subjects which they want to but even then the students aren't sure. Many don't know because they don't know what they want to be when they get older. If they choose the subjects they wanted most students would of course pick easier subjects such as art, gym, music, etc. I think that this doing is partly the schools fault. If the school made math classes more interesting students would more likely pick that. Their parents should be able to discuss with the children what they should take. The parents of course have more responsibility and of course want the best for their children. Many children (if they could pick their own subjects) would paick something their parents didn't approve of if their parents were mean to them. Then the children would be ruining their own life. This would probably go around in circles. The world is a very mixed up place but it would be even worse if there wasn't any control. Control must begin with chidlren of today becuase they will be the adults of tomorrow.

Figure 7.5
A 14-year-old's writing plan. (From Burtis et al. 1983, p. 161. Used with permission of John Wiley and Sons.)

year-olds can't produce a writing plan distinct from their written text. For young children, writing is generating content and writing it down; planning is not part of their writing process.

Figure 7.5 shows a plan and a text produced by a 14-year-old. Here, the written text is distinct from the plan. The notes in the plan aren't complete sentences; they are "gist units" that the writer expands into complete thoughts in the text. The writer doesn't use all the notes from the plan in her essay, and the essay contains some material that was not in the plan. Some ideas from the plan that do appear in the essay appear in rearranged order. The fact that this writer manipulated and rearranged the notes shows that she has incorporated organizing into her planning process. Furthermore, her

1.1 I think I'd probably stay away from testing [an issue discussed at an earlier point in the protocol] because I'm not really sure; I think there should be something but I don't know enough, I'd rather stay away from it so it wouldn't weaken my **argument**.

1.2 I don't know how I'm going to put this all together without sounding so boring. Maybe an **introduction** . . . .

1.3 . . . this is just an **example**. . . . . If you state an example this is all to do with convincing too, you have to be convincing. It really isn't convincing to state a point and not back it up.

1.4 [First attempt at organization] I suppose in writing this I would say firstly that I believe students should choose and then go back to when and then why. [Second attempt at organization] After getting rid of what I think are the **disadvantages** [reasons on the contrary side] I would go on to say the **benefits** [reasons in support of position] [Final attempt at organization] I would state my **opinion**, my point of view, taking in the fact that some people would not agree with it, and taking note of this **position** I would go through the **disadvantages**, which I think obviously can be overcome. And then move on to say how . . . after those three major points are out of the way I would **conclude** by talking about the **benefits**. . . .

Figure 7.6
A mature writer's protocol explicitly mentions whole portions of text (boldface type) and considers how these rhetorical devices will help the writer meet his writing goals. (From Scardamalia and Paris 1985. Used with permission of Lawrence Erlbaum Associates.)

plan expresses a simple, general goal: The writer begins the plan with the words "Opinion (mine)." For this writer the plan has become a list of content possibilities, and its organization and the writing goals expressed influence the final written output.

In later adolescence, the separation between plan and text becomes more pronounced. Figure 7.6 is part of a mature writer's planning protocol for an essay on choosing school subjects. What most distinguishes this plan from the previous ones is that the writer explicitly mentions and considers whole portions of eventual text. The writer mentions "argument", "introduction", and "example" in the plan and reflects on how these rhetorical devices might contribute to the presentation. He is concerned with content—his reasons for and the possible reasons against letting students choose their subjects—but he thinks carefully about how to organize the content. This writer has set rhetorical goals for key parts of the text. For instance, he states that the purpose of an example is to help convince an audience. As he says, "It really isn't convincing to state a point and not back it up." This writer is using knowledge about writing and about the audience—rhetorical knowledge—to figure out how to present content most effectively.

From Cognitive Process to Cognitive Rhetoric

The Hayes-Flower model showed we could understand the cognitive process behind the written products. Maybe, researchers and educators thought, we could improve writing instruction by teaching this process.

The initial work on the cognition of writing had an almost immediate impact on school instruction. At least, it had an impact on how teachers and curriculum planners *talked* about writing. The 1980s saw a blessed rage for process—everyone claimed to be teaching writing as process. In 1983, the California Department of Education published a handbook to help teachers plan process-based curricula (Handbook 1983). However, in 1990 the NAEP writing report noted that "nearly a decade into the educational reform movement and the writing process movement . . . NAEP data indicate that students' writing instruction and their writing performance have remained relatively unchanged" (Applebee et al. 1990, p. 74).

There are at least two reasons why process instruction has had little effect on students' performance.

First, calling a curriculum "process instruction" doesn't necessarily make it so. Many of the "process curricula" embrace superficial aspects of the cognitive models but overlook the substance. As Glynda Hull observes, "Although many teachers acknowledge the importance of writing as process, rather than as product, in many cases the genuinely recursive nature of the writing process is lost or obscured in writing instruction." Planning, translating, and reviewing take the place of pre-writing, writing, and rewriting. A set of isolated processes, done one after another, replaces a set of isolated skill activities. When this is the case, instruction hasn't really changed much, and we shouldn't expect that children's writing will improve. This also shows that even if we have detailed cognitive models, it may not be obvious how to translate the research into better instruction.

Second, the early cognitive models might not have been sufficiently detailed or inclusive to guide teaching. In recent years, writing researchers, including Hayes and Flower, have been working to deepen and broaden our understanding of the writing process (Flower 1989).

To deepen our understanding of problem solving in writing, researchers are exploring how writers' initial representations of writing problems affect the quality of their final texts. How do experienced writers use their background knowledge of topic, audience, and writing schemas to construct writing plans? Flower and Higgins (1990, p. 2) call these initial representations of writing problems *task representations* and suggest that "task representations, rather than 'ability,' may be the limiting factor in student writing more often than teachers realize."

Current research is also attempting to broaden our understanding of the writing process by enlarging our conception of the writer's task environment. A writer's initial representation of a writing problem is the writer's interpretation of the task environment; the writer encodes features he or she judges important or relevant to the problem on the basis of prior knowledge and experience. In the early cognitive models, the task environment included only the statement of the writing problem and text as the writer produced it. Over the last few years, however, researchers have recognized the need to expand the task environment to include the social or cultural context in which the writing takes place. The social context (home, classroom, workplace) in which one writes or learns to write can influence how one interprets writing tasks.

Broadening the task environment in this way lets researchers integrate results and methods of cognitive science with an older tradition in the study of writing: rhetoric. Rhetoric is the study of the principles and rules that govern effective speaking and writing. If in the cognitive tradition the writer is an information processor, in the rhetorical tradition the writer is a social actor in a public arena—a social creature who attempts to influence and communicate with an audience.

Once we include the social dimension of writing, we realize that, just as we belong to many different social groups and often attempt to join new ones, we also belong to many different writing groups, or what rhetoricians call *discourse communities*. Different social groups—home, office, social club, church—have different customs, practices, and conventions that dictate acceptable behavior within them. Home, high school, college, academic disciplines, and the workplace all have different languages, conventions, genres, and expectations that govern acceptable writing. These too are part of the writer's task environment. One thing writing instruction, and education generally, should do is help students to enter new discourse communities—to join new literate subcultures.

Flower calls this deeper, wider approach to writing research *cognitive rhetoric*. It views writing problems as rhetorical problems, problems that have a social, communicative dimension. Cognitive rhetoric studies how writers think their way through rhetorical problems. Cognitive rhetoricians want to know how cognitive and social factors interact to influence writing and learning to write. This approach has interesting implications for writing in school. School itself is a social, cultural context with its own conventions, genres, and expectations. Does the prevalent school culture encourage students to think through ill-defined rhetorical problems? Maybe, in the spirit of cognitive rhetoric, we should undertake "a systematic examination of the influence of institutional settings, particularly the American public school, on cognitive processes during composing and learning to compose" (Freedman et al. 1987, p. 18).

Constructive Planning: Building Rhetorical Representations

In recent work that attempts to look more deeply into the cognition of writing, Flower and her colleagues have been analyzing the planning protocols of expert and novice writers on novel writing tasks— tasks for which it is unlikely the writers have a pre-learned schema to guide their writing. They have used the *Seventeen* magazine task to study differences in writers' initial problem representations.

Flower and Linda Carey collected think-aloud protocols from experienced and inexperienced writers up to the point where the subjects translated their first sentences onto the page. In their analyses, the researchers coded each clause of the protocols for the kind of planning statement it contained: *topic, purpose, audience,* and/or *text convention.* In the Flower-Carey scheme, topic statements are those the writer mentions as possible content for the final text. The remaining categories all refer to rhetorical features and goals.

Flower and her colleagues recognize three types of purpose statements. Some refer to what a writer chooses for the key point out of all the listed content ideas. Writers also state rhetorical purposes and goals in their plans. They might want to produce a particular effect on the audience—to "shake 'em up" or "get them to think in a different context," for example (figure 7.7, clauses 59 and 60). Sometimes writers express rhetorical goals that are more personal, such as to explore an argument or an issue. Writers also express generic purposes that consider strategic plans for organizing the text and how they might use their schema knowledge in the task. (In clause 49 of figure 7.7, the writer expresses a desire to start in a way that will put the reader into the right frame of mind.) Some planning statements mention and describe the envisioned audience (as in clauses 47 and 55, where the writer tries to anticipate how readers would respond to his topic and his text). At a more local planning level, writers mention specific text conventions they might use— rhetorical features of a text, such as introductions, summaries, conclusions, and examples, that help the writer make tactical decisions about the text and its structure (see clauses 49–51).

In the experienced writer's protocol shown in figure 7.7, rhetorical planning dominates. The initial plan contains only one topic statement. The writer considers content, but devotes most of his planning time to finding a theme, a structure, and text conventions appropriate for the intended audience. A skilled writer engages in what Flower calls *constructive planning*. Such a writer builds a unique representation and an original plan suited to the specific rhetorical situation, working between the domain of topic knowledge and that of rhetorical knowledge to develop a writing plan. The outcome of constructive planning is what Carey and Flower call a *rhetorical representation* of the writing task. It is a representation that includes all the rhetorical categories—key point, purpose, audience, text conventions—and places content within an audience-directed, rhetorical framework.

Figure 7.8 shows the protocol of a less experienced writer who also did extensive initial planning. Here, topic statements and content knowledge dominate. The writer doesn't mention a key point or purpose. His only organizational idea is to produce a two-page essay for a vaguely envisioned audience, "one with a broad range of intellect." He tries to get by using what the researchers call *knowledge-driven planning*—a more mature version of Heather's strategy of searching memory for content and putting it on the page. This planning strategy can work only if the writer's topic knowledge happens to be appropriately organized for the intended audience. A professor might be able to use knowledge-driven planning to write a superb review article for a professional journal, but the article

CLAUSE #	COMMENTS	ANALYSIS
45	All right, I'm an English Teacher	**Topic**
47	I know they are not going to be disposed to hear what I'm saying	**Audience** (draws an inference)
48	Partly for that reason and partly to put them in the right -- kind of frame of mind I want	**Purpose/Audience** (prepares reader)
49	I want to open with an implied question or a direct one	**Text convention** (develops a skeleton structure for the text)
50	and then put them in the middle of	**Text Conventions/Audience**
51	and then expand from there more generally to talk about my job more generally	**Text Conventions/Purpose**
52	and try to tie it in with their interest	**Purpose/Audience** (involves audience)
53	So one question is where to begin	**Text Conventions** (plans introduction)
54	Start in the middle of -- probably the first day of class	
55	They'd be interested	**Audience** (draws an inference; links to his goals)
56	They'd probably clue into that easily	
57	because they would identify with the first days of school	
58	and my first days are raucous affairs	
59	It would immediately shake 'em up	**Purpose/Audience** (develops specific audience goals for the introduction)
60	and get them to think in a different context.	

Figure 7.7
A skilled writer's protocol considers content for the essay, but analysis of the protocol shows extensive concern for rhetorical features and goals. (From Flower 1989b, p. 5. Used with author's permission.)

CLAUSE #	COMMENT	ANALYSIS
6	I'm going to assume I'm an engineer	**Topic** (defines subject matter)
8 .	I guess a research--a research engineer	
10	However, there's a graduate student	**Topic** (to the end of clause 22 explores aspects of job)
11	because I'm a graduate student	
12	So...really my job is going to school	
13	Let's see--I'm a graduate student	
14	and I'm an engineer	
15	and I'm a research enginerr	
16	So everything is there	
17	so maybe I should explain here that I'm a graduate student pursuing a Ph.D. in engineering	
20	I do research work	
22	I teach a course	
24	(Reads) for a thirteen to fourteen teenage audience	
25	So we have to address the fact that this girl is seventh or eigth	**Audience**
27	Okay so these are all the things going through may head relataive to engineering -- research engineering	**Topic** (reviews possible details to include)
28	These are all the things I'm supposedly doing	
29	and I'm pursuing a Ph.D.	
30	Working on a thesis	
32	My job here is wrong, the way I'm intepreting my job	
34	The way I'm interpreting my job means what I'm doing with my life at this moment in time	**Topic** (redefines topi
37	For the girl is approximately in seventh or eigth grade	
38	... the assignment has to appeal to a broad range in intellect	**Purpose** (sets general audience goals)
39	It must explain simply what I'm doing	
43	I have to generate an essay	**Purpose/Text Conventions**
44	We'll assume it's about two pages	(specifies genre and length)

Figure 7.8
A weak writer's protocol shows that his planning emphasized topic content and largely ignored rhetorical features and writing goals. (From Carey et al. 1989, p. 14. Used with authors' permission.)

would be incomprehensible to the general reader. When the writer's knowledge is inappropriately organized, the text will lack audience-directed goals and audience-sensitive organization. In knowledge-driven planning, the writer fails to adapt topic knowledge to fit the rhetorical circumstance.

In writing, as in physics, the depth of the initial representation matters. Flower and Carey's study included twelve writers, five of whom were expert writing teachers and seven of whom were college students. This sample allowed the researchers to make some generalizations about the effects of initial representations on the quality of final texts (Carey et al. 1989). When independent judges rated the quality of each writer's text, the researchers found that the writers who produced highly rated texts did significantly more initial planning than those who produced lower-rated texts. They also found that the quality of the initial planning affected the ratings. The better writers, in general, did proportionately less content planning and proportionately more rhetorical planning than the poorer ones. The writers who produced higher-rated texts included all the rhetorical categories—purpose, audience, and text conventions—in their initial plans; the less successful writers ignored some, if not most, of these planning categories. Flower and Carey concluded that successful writers build a rhetorical representation of the task and less successful writers do not.

Knowledge Telling versus Knowledge Transforming

Fifteen years' research on the cognition of writing has shown that mature, skilled writing is the result of mature, skilled planning—planning that weaves the writer's topic knowledge with his rhetorical knowledge. In terms of the initial Hayes-Flower model, this means that the generating, organizing, and goal-setting subprocesses must interact in the planning process. When this doesn't happen, the result is often evident in the text. In her early work, Flower described such text as *writer-based prose*. In her more recent work, she describes it as the result of inappropriate, knowledge-driven planning. In the simplest prose of this sort, the writer generates content from long-term memory and translates the content directly to the page. In this kind of writing, the organization of ideas in the text is the same as the organization of the ideas in the writer's long-term memory.

In the context of school writing, Scardamalia and Bereiter (1987) call this writer-based, knowledge-driven composing strategy *knowledge telling*. This is the strategy Heather used to compose her essay. She describes it as follows:

I have a whole bunch of ideas and write them down until my supply of ideas is exhausted. Then I might try to think of more ideas up to the point when you can't get any more ideas that are worth putting down on paper and then I would end it. (Scardamalia and Bereiter 1986, p. 61)

In knowledge telling, the child uses a cue from the writing assignment to locate an item in long-term memory, searches for content immediately around that item, puts that content onto the page, and then stops writing. Heather generates content, but does no further organizing or goal setting. Knowledge telling results in essays like Heather's, where each sentence makes sense but there is no organization or coherence above the sentence level. The writer could delete or rearrange sentences with no impact on the essay's quality or readability.

Knowledge telling is a clever solution to a real, everyday school problem. It allows students to complete school tasks they otherwise might find impossible: Reduce a writing assignment to a topic and tell what you know about the topic. This strategy is useful well beyond elementary school. Indeed, even college students use it to answer unexpected or unusually difficult essay exam questions. ("Was Socrates correct to think that the criminal is even more unhappy than his victim?" Whoa! I'll write down everything I know about Socrates and hope for the best.) The strategy often works, even in college.

Skilled writers aren't knowledge tellers. They generate possible content the same way novice or less skilled writers do, but they use their rhetorical knowledge to set goals and organize content before translating it into text. Scardamalia and Bereiter say that this mature planning results in *knowledge transforming*. Knowledge transforming is writing as a high-order cognitive skill. According to Scardamalia et al. (1984), the ability to see content through the filters of rhetorical knowledge is the essence of reflective, thoughtful writing. Reflective writing, because it takes the audience and the topic into account simultaneously, does not permit direct transcription of content from memory to page. The skilled writer tries to see the world as others see it. Part of the writing task, for the expert, is building bridges between what he or she knows and what others might know. Once the writer is committed to solving this problem, the text structure can't just mirror the structure of the writer's content knowledge. The writer transforms topic knowledge to meet the demands of the rhetorical situation.

Tanya Again

Cognitive rhetoric's deeper look into the planning process highlights the difference between knowledge telling and knowledge transforming. Its commitment to look more broadly at the social and cultural influences on writing can help us understand Tanya, the young women in Glynda Hull and Mike Rose's study.

Tanya's writing is not standard, and students like her need special help. Yet cognitive rhetoric's broader view lets us appreciate that in some ways Tanya's writing is more literate and sophisticated than we first think. Appreciating what students such as Tanya can do should lead us to a more positive and sympathetic view of remedial students. Hull and Rose suggest that such a view must be part of any attempt at educational reform.

Hull and Rose videotaped Tanya while she was writing. After she finished her summary, they played back the video for her and asked her to comment on what she had been thinking about while she was writing. This technique, called *stimulated recall,* results in the writer's providing something like a delayed think-aloud protocol. Hull and Rose analyzed Tanya's answers to figure out how she understood the writing task and how she had planned to execute it.

On the surface, two features characterize Tanya's text. (See figures 7.1 and 7.2.) First, she made some changes in wording from the original text: "I have pride in my profession" became "I have pride in what I do." She did copy some text verbatim, as with "Oh, this is going to be a great day I said to myself." Second, she used segments from the original text, but she used them in no obvious order and with no apparent effort to link them. For example, the "great day" sentence taken from paragraph 4 appears in the middle of the summary and immediately precedes the "pride" sentence taken from paragraph 11. This sentence, in turn, precedes material taken from paragraph 7: "What was the approach?" Typically, both of these features are assumed to be signs of poor writing. However, if we look more deeply and broadly, as Hull and Rose did, there is also evidence that Tanya set some rhetorical goals and attempted to organize her text.

Hull and Rose found that Tanya had a goal. She wanted to show them that she knew the material, but also that she was not the kind of student who would copy. Tanya used a rhetorical rule to meet this goal: Use pieces of the original text to convey knowledge, but change a few words so as not to copy. The prohibition against plagiarism was one writing rule Tanya remembered vividly from her prior, dismal educational experience.

While writing the summary, Tanya was able to consult the original article. Thus, unlike writers working on the *Seventeen* assignment, Tanya didn't have to search her long-term memory for possible content. The article itself provided more than enough content. Tanya's problem was how to choose and organize content. The first thing to notice about Tanya's summary is that she was not just copying the article or helping herself to the organization of the original article. She was evaluating possible content for relevance, although the relevance criterion is not immediately obvious. In judging relevance or importance, Tanya gave special status to sentences and ideas that were important to her and her career aspirations: "[T]he parts about the nurse are something about me . . . you see. 'I have pride', you see I can read that for me." (Hull 1989, p. 113) Tanya tested content for relevance, but she based her test on the importance of the ideas to her life, not on the importance of the ideas for her potential audience.

There is a rhetorical goal implicit in Tanya's test for relevance, although it is not the academic community's standard goal for a summary. As Flower and her colleagues observed in their study of initial planning, one possible rhetorical goal is the writer's desire to explore an issue or an idea. Tanya had a rhetorical goal of this kind in which she brought something of herself to the task.

"A fundamental social and psychological reality about discourse—oral or written—is that human beings continually appropriate each other's language to establish group membership, to grow, and to define themselves in new ways," Hull and Rose (1989) propose. Tanya had several buggy writing rules, but she was using them to try on the nurse's language and use it to express her desire to redefine her life. Rose and Hull would help a student like Tanya by letting her try on the written language of others with whom she may have some affinity. Gradually, they would make the imitation

more focused and help Tanya learn writing schemas, audience awareness, and other rhetorical skills needed in academic writing.

Although Tanya is superficially illiterate and a paradigm of failure, her summary, when viewed this way, has a history and a logic
that make it comprehensible. This insight is a starting point for
appreciating the abilities, and not just the disabilities, of remedial or
underprepared students. "We assume," Hull and Rose write (1989b,
p. 10), "that cognitive behavior is sensible and logical. And we
assume that it's rich—even when it diverges from our expectations—
and that it can be examined and closely traced and represented." On
this assumption, helping Tanya demands an understanding of what
Tanya brings to the task—her academic, social, and cultural background knowledge—and how she uses that knowledge to represent
and define writing problems. The problem Tanya defines and solves,
using her knowledge, is not necessarily the one set forth by the
teacher. Understanding how Tanya defines the writing task—understanding her initial representation of the writing problem—provides
a basis for effective instruction.

Tanya doesn't have a serious linguistic problem or a general
cognitive impairment. She lacks experience and familiarity with academic writing, and she has some specific buggy writing rules that
a teacher can fix. Hull and Rose's assumption allows us to see students like Tanya in the same way BUGGY (chapter 4 above) allowed
us to see students struggling with multi-digit subtraction. Although
it is not obvious on the surface, cognitive analysis reveals that in
writing, just as in arithmetic, students are following rules, which
may be buggy. If we can identify their buggy writing rules, we can
provide appropriate help and instruction to fix the bugs.

The applied side of the Hull-Rose project also has similarities
with BUGGY. During their research, Hull and Rose have compiled
hundreds of hours of videotape and transcripts of students writing
or interpreting literature. They are organizing the material into a
database for use in teacher training. The database contains student
cases that teachers, working in groups, can study and analyze. The
teachers' task, when working on a case, is first to understand the
literacy problem a student like Tanya might have. Then, using what
they know about cognition, metacognition, learning, and literacy,
the teachers discuss how they might address the problem in the
classroom. By this process, the teachers can begin to understand
students like Tanya and their nonstandard, though rational, repre-

sentations of literacy tasks. Such understanding is a first step toward informed, sympathetic literacy instruction.

Writing in the Culture of School

The deeper, broader view that cognitive rhetoric affords also reveals something interesting, if not disturbing, about students such as Heather. Cognitive rhetoric encourages us to look at how students' mental processing interacts with writing and with learning to write in the culture of school. From this perspective, we can begin to see that the school culture surrounding writing encourages knowledge telling, whereas few school practices foster knowledge transformation. We shouldn't assume that 10 more years of school writing will make Heather a knowledge transformer. Classroom culture plays into and reinforces the strategy of knowledge telling.

Based on years of studying how children develop writing skills, even in schools that took pride and care in writing instruction, Bereiter and Scardamalia (1986, p. 66) report that "older school-age writers have mastered knowledge telling in a number of genres. Few have shown signs of going beyond it." This doesn't mean that knowledge-telling students are lazy or are looking for an easy way out. More likely, they are just adapting their behavior to meet the demands of the tasks their teachers give them. Unfortunately, knowledge telling is a developmental dead end, suited for school tasks and little else.

School culture and the purpose of writing in that culture make knowledge telling a rational, rewarding strategy. In 1971 a major study reported that academically successful high school seniors found school writing uninteresting and purposeless (Emig 1971). High school seniors did little planning and even less revising, and described school writing as routine and mechanical.

A study of qualitative changes in the writing of British students found that the demands of school tasks themselves influenced student writing (Britton et al. 1975). The most striking change in students as they progressed through school was an increased tendency to write for the teacher as examiner. By the twelfth grade, 61 percent of the British students were writing in this mode. This also occurs in American schools, where—besides grammar—the writing skill most emphasized is routine recital of previously learned subject matter. Students learn to write for the teacher, a person who knows more about the topics than the students. The teacher tests the students' knowledge by means of written assignments. This reduces writing to recitation, or knowledge telling. Often, programs that encourage writing across the curriculum—the integration of writing into all subject domains—lead to recitation across the curriculum. The purpose of writing in school is to display what one has learned, not to express what one thinks about what one has learned (Applebee 1984, 1986).

In their experience, Bereiter and Scardamalia contend, it is hard to find school situations that are conducive to writing goals *other* than knowledge display and recitation. In fact, they write, "the conscientious teacher *conspires* to see to it that there is a congruity between the way students encode knowledge on acquisition and the retrieval requirements of course assignments and tests" (Bereiter and Scardamalia 1985, p. 67). Often, teachers expect students to recite knowledge on exams in the order in which the teacher presented it and the students encoded it. Teachers encourage this parroting when they present items on a test in the same order in which they appeared in the course or in a text, when they assign long papers on a single topic so that students have to assemble knowledge, and when they give passing marks to students who don't answer the essay questions posed. Not all these practices are necessarily bad or even replaceable, but students can use knowledge telling to satisfy all such demands.

Sometimes even writing instruction in the process tradition demands little more of students than knowledge telling. One such approach is the *natural process* mode of writing instruction. Natural process instruction attempts to increase students' writing fluency. (For a description see Hillocks 1984.) In this approach, teachers encourage free writing in a journal—something akin to brainstorming on paper—on whatever interests the student as a way to explore a subject. Students write for a peer audience and receive feedback (generally positive) from peers and from the teacher; the feedback provides a basis for revision and rewriting.

Tanya's writing instruction at the community college was in this natural process style. She wrote many narratives or stories, on topics such as "my worst experience in school," and received feedback from the teachers. Her instructors encouraged her to develop fluency and not to worry about making mistakes. This instruction, no doubt, helped Tanya, but it didn't teach her planning strategies and rhetorical skills that would have contributed to better expository and argumentative writing. Tanya needed direct, explicit instruction about how to perform academic writing tasks, such as writing a summary. Instead, she could use the knowledge-telling strategy to complete most of her writing assignments.

The writing strategies students choose are the results of their previous writing experiences that occur in school. If background knowledge shapes students' interpretations of current situations, prior school experience influences how students represent and define school writing tasks. Carey and Flower's (1989) recent studies of how college freshmen represent writing tasks supports this dismal appraisal of school writing.

In one pilot study, Carey and Flower discovered that half the students paid no attention to what school writing assignments said; they just used their standard paper-writing strategies. In a related study, when asked what their goals were in a writing assignment, 20 percent of the students said their goal was to present what they had learned, 18 percent said they were trying to cover key points, and 13 percent said their goal was to get by with minimum effort. None said anything that suggested an attempt to be creative or to develop a unique solution for a rhetorical problem. The school assignments these students had completed over the years had severely limited their ability to represent writing tasks as opportunities for originality and for imaginative adaptation of their knowledge. These were not underprepared or remedial students, but college freshman enrolled in prestigious universities. Yet, for these students knowledge telling was the strategy of choice for doing school-sponsored writing assignments. As Flower and Higgins (1990, p. 34) conclude, "the knowledge-driven planning strategy . . . appears to be a normal or default move in school writing. . . ."

As a result of school experiences, writing is for many high school students and college freshmen as meaningless and artificial as multi-digit subtraction is for many grade school students. After twelve years of schooling, students see writing as just another weird school task.

If we want students to learn how to transform knowledge, we have to involve them in authentic writing tasks. What passes for language instruction in many schools—traditional grammar, diagramming sentences, reading literature, speaking correctly, and writing for the teacher as examiner—doesn't qualify as authentic. As Hull says, "We have to present writing as a process that is not an end in itself, but that serves a larger communicative purpose. Most things kids do in the name of writing are school-bound and have no real counterpart in the world beyond the classroom." Students must write in the classroom with an understanding that writing is a complex, recursive, audience-directed process. Two experimental classroom interventions that attempt to achieve this goal are Flower's Collaborative Planning and OISE's CSILE project.

Collaborative Planning: Making Thinking Visible

Students seldom engage in constructive planning or attempt to build rhetorical representations of writing problems. Why? Does their school experience leave them without rhetorical knowledge, or do they have this knowledge only in an inert form? An answer to this question must guide instructional design.

Several studies indicate that students have rhetorical knowledge but can't spontaneously use it in their planning efforts. In the early 1980s, Scardamalia and Bereiter had some elementary teachers give their students complex, problematic final sentences for stories, such as "And so, after considering the reasons for it and against it, the duke decided to rent his castle to the vampire after all, in spite of the rumor he had heard." The students were then told to work collaboratively to create stories leading to those endings. Surprisingly, this simple intervention helped the students immensely. When given such a prompt and allowed to work in groups, they engaged in constructive planning. They developed writing plans that were distinct from their texts and which included features associated with rhetorical representations. Their discussions of the writing problem showed they worked back and forth between plan and text. They solved the problem recursively as they jointly reconsidered their plan and revised their story. With this simple external support, children could incorporate rhetorical knowledge they already possessed to choose story content and solve their writing problem (Bereiter and Scardamalia 1982). This suggests that elementary school children have rhetorical knowledge, but often in an inert form.

Flower and Carey wondered if the same might be true for their college freshmen. What would happen if, during planning, the researchers were to give the students prompts intended to encourage them to consider the rhetorical features that knowledge-driven planning ignores? (See Flower and Higgins 1990.) They devised a set of prompts to remind students about rhetorical features during planning, and presented the prompts via a fictitious computer program called the Collaborative Writer.

The researchers asked each student to pretend that the Collaborative Writer would write a paper for him or her if the student would develop a writing plan by thinking and talking aloud to the computer in response to its questions and prompts. The computer asked difficult, annoying questions. After a student formulated a plan, the computer might say "Thank you, that was a good plan, but I was always told to consider alternatives. Can you think of another way?" Or "How will you deal with the readers who disagree with you?" Even with these prompts, some of the students stuck to knowledge-driven planning. Half of them, though, showed considerable skill at constructive planning when prompted by the Collaborative Writer. These students considered their purpose, their audience, and their presentation, reaching levels of rhetorical planning usually found only among graduate students and more skilled writers. If given appropriate external support, students would give up knowledge telling and engage in constructive planning.

The researchers were surprised less by the results than by how much the freshmen enjoyed and valued the 90-minute computer sessions. The students wanted more, and several asked if their roommates could participate in the experiment. Many commented on how this kind of exercise would help them in their course work. Flower and Carey realized they had inadvertently found an instructional intervention that students valued and that might work in the classroom. They reasoned that if a fictitious computer could improve students' planning by asking preprogrammed questions, a fully interactive human respondent might encourage even more thinking and planning. Their experiment evolved into a teaching intervention they call Collaborative Planning (Flower et al. 1992).

Collaborative Planning is a process that helps students visualize all aspects of a rhetorical representation—topic, purpose, audience, and text conventions—as they plan. In this regard, it shares features with ThinkerTools, with Jim Minstrell's physics class, and with Reciprocal Teaching. The two physics curricula had students present and defend their reasoning to their classmates; this made the scientific reasoning process overt for all in the class to observe. In Reciprocal Teaching, group discussion made the normally invisible process of reading comprehension visible and explicit. Collaborative Planning does the same for writing and for planning to write. "If we wish to

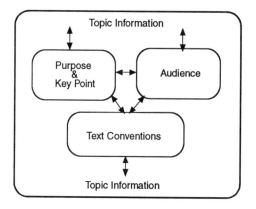

Figure 7.9
The Planner's Blackboard. (From Flower et al. 1992. Used with authors' permission.)

help people plan," Flower et al. (1992) claim, "we not only must support the complex process of constructing a plan . . . , we must also make this strategic process itself visible as a critical force in effective writing."

To provide this public, visible support, Collaborative Planning uses the metaphor of the Planner's Blackboard. The Blackboard helps the writer envision a *planning space* as a mental blackboard where he can post ideas as he plans (figure 7.9). The blackboard reminds the writer about content knowledge, rhetorical knowledge, and their interaction. In the background there is a big Topic Information board. In the foreground are three smaller boards for posting rhetorical items: Purpose and Key Point, Audience, and Text Conventions. These are the features which experienced writers consider carefully but which inexperienced writers ignore. Arrows remind the writer to integrate the contents of all four boards into his plan.

As with Reciprocal Teaching, there is an important social dimension to Collaborative Planning. Collaborative Planning builds an audience, albeit a very small one, into the planning process. It makes planning into a loosely structured social process involving two people: the writer and the supporter. The writer explains and elaborates his or her plan to the supporter; the supporter listens, asks questions, and encourages the writer to develop the plan. The student in the supporting role prompts the writer to consider rhetorical features in the writing plan and to post ideas on the appropriate mental board. Depending on the quality of the collaborative session, prompts might range from a superficial, literal appeal to the blackboard ("Who is your audience?") to more challenging demands ("I still don't see your main point" or "Is that a good example to use for your intended audience?"). Flower calls these more pressing demands for rhetorical planning *invitations to think*. Eventually the supporter and the writer switch roles.

As a social interaction, Collaborative Planning involves two would-be members of a discourse community in an attempt to develop a plan that might influence a larger audience. The social interaction allows otherwise-inert rhetorical strategies and knowledge to become active. It gives each student insights into what is normally a silent, hidden planning process, and it provides opportunities for the student to reflect on it. As Flower and Higgins (1990, p. 16) note, "In the social dynamics of collaborative planning not only the teacher but each partner models constructive planning, in the form of rhetorical, reflective thinking, for the other." The students become partners in shared problem solving, in the joint construction of meaning. The partners, through their prompts, remind each other to think about the high-level issues of purpose, audience, and goals. Their dialogue is a form of joint, public metacognition that allows them to share the burden of monitoring the planning process.

In studies, Collaborative Planning has helped college freshmen break the knowledge-telling habit. When the researchers analyzed audio tapes from Collaborative Planning sessions, they found that over 80 percent of the writers' comments referred to the rhetorical features of key point, purpose, audience, and text conventions. The supporters, in turn, issued the writers numerous invitations to think. Analysis of the final written texts showed that the writers accepted and addressed 89 percent of these invitations, most often in their introductions and conclusions. Although Flower and her colleagues realize there is much more to learn about how novice writers become experts (the learning trajectory for writing is not as straightforward as that for the balance scale), their most recent effort to turn research into instruction does appear to help students learn planning skills. Collaborative Planning aids students in making the transition from disengaged knowledge telling to writing as a high-order, knowledge-transforming act.

An added advantage of Collaborative Planning is that it is adaptable to different kinds of classrooms and different kinds of writing.

It is a research-based *framework* for teaching planning skills that teachers can creatively adapt to their classroom needs. As part of the Making Thinking Visible project, run by Flower's center at Carnegie Mellon, teacher-researchers in the Pittsburgh area are exploring how to use Collaborative Planning. One teacher is using it to help her fifth-graders improve their creative writing, another to teach her eleventh-grade English students how to use text conventions such as symbolism and foreshadowing in narrative writing.

Applications of Collaborative Planning extend beyond English classes. Len Donaldson, a tenth-grade social studies teacher, is using it to improve his students' critical thinking and problem-solving skills (Donaldson 1989). In their research papers, his students usually listed facts—for example, everything they could find out about World War II—with little purpose, focus, or audience awareness. When his students engage in Collaborative Planning, they produce more thoughtful, better-developed research papers. Donaldson feels that the process makes thinking visible to both teacher and students, and that it makes students aware of their abilities as critical thinkers, planners, and writers. He reports that this has also affected the quality of daily class discussions. In discussion, students became more open to divergent ideas and non-traditional interpretations. Donaldson thinks that Collaborative Planning helped his students develop a keen awareness of the importance of analyzing, organizing, and evaluating information, not only in school and in writing but in their daily lives as well.

CSILE on Huron Street

Huron Street Public School is several blocks from OISE and the University of Toronto campus. The students are the Commonwealth mix one often finds in Canada—children of English, Celtic, East Indian, and Caribbean backgrounds, and more recent arrivals from Eastern Europe, the Soviet Union, and Latin America. This school is the site of an experiment to improve writing and to create a learning environment in which knowledge transforming replaces knowledge telling. Here Scardamalia, Bereiter, and their OISE colleagues are testing CSILE, a Computer Supported Intentional Learning Environment.

CSILE (pronounced "Cecil"), which is based on 20 years of cognitive research, fosters strategic thinking and the development of learning skills in the course of subject-matter instruction. These skills, in turn, allow students to regulate and monitor their learning. CSILE aids students in becoming active learners who know how to learn, who can set their own learning goals, and who can apply effective metacognitive strategies to learning problems.

CSILE confronts directly the traditional classroom practices that favor knowledge telling. If school writing tasks are to result in knowledge transforming, they must have a genuine rhetorical purpose. CSILE creates a classroom culture in which the purposes of writing are to communicate with fellow students and to help writers master new ideas. "An interesting aspect of CSILE is that it attempts to teach the knowledge transforming strategy directly. Advancing knowledge is the central classroom goal," according to Scardamalia. "The interesting question is: If one makes knowledge transforming the primary educational objective, will one get better writing as a secondary result?"

This is an intriguing educational experiment because it reverses the traditional roles of writing and thinking. We typically think that producing better writers is the way to produce better thinkers and learners; CSILE reverses the cause and the effect in this assumption. Do better learning and better reasoning—after all, that is what knowledge transforming consists of—lead to better writing? The early data coming out of Huron Street School suggest that the answer is "Yes!"

On the blackboard in a fourth-and-fifth-grade CSILE classroom is the beginning of a unit on oceans. The teacher has helped the students summarize on the blackboard what they already know about oceans. The summary is not a list of isolated facts; rather, it has the form of an associative network. Written in the corner of the board, in the place where teachers write things that are never to be erased, are three questions: "What are three important things I *already know* about the topic? What do I *wonder* about? What *words* would I use to look up information about the ocean from my database?" These questions remind the students of the importance of preexisting knowledge and the importance of metacognition—reflecting on what they already know and what they would like to know—in learning. In the back of the room are eight Apple workstations, with color monitors, which are linked to a mainframe computer that supports CSILE.

CSILE is a sophisticated information-management environment. At its heart is a student-generated database into which students can enter both graphics (which they call *charts*) and text (which they call *notes*). Each student is a member of a small study group (6–8 members) and spends 30 minutes a day on a workstation composing material for the database. The material in the database relates to all aspects of the curriculum—science, math, social studies, and language. Students can generate new items for the database, retrieve items indexed by the student-authors' names or by key words, browse through the database, comment on other students' charts and texts, and submit items they have written or drawn for publication. The computer allows all student entries to be electronically linked or associated in any way the students think appropriate. With this capability, the students can create node-link, associative knowledge structures on the computer screen. At the end of a course unit, the study group meets as an editorial board to decide what material in their collective database they will publish as their group report.

CSILE encourages the students to focus on the growing body of knowledge they are building together and on what they need to know collectively. The system promotes a *community of scholarship* in the elementary classroom, restructuring the flow of information so that the students are essentially and actively involved in knowledge construction. The students are members of a knowledge-building team; the teacher is a coach, a guide, and a fellow learner.

CSILE involves students in what Glynda Hull would consider authentic writing tasks. They are writing to generate a knowledge base for the class' instruction, writing critiques of other students' entries, and editing their contributions. They are writing to communicate and transform knowledge for their classmates, not to recite it to the teacher. For these students, writing is both a cognitive and a social act.

A fully operational version of CSILE has been in daily use in two fifth-and-sixth-grade classrooms at Huron Street since autumn 1986. Positive results are starting to emerge. CSILE students perform significantly better than other students on the language portions of standardized achievement tests, although that is not the purpose of the research or the outcome measure the OISE group most values. The researchers' main interest, in these initial years, has been to see how the children compose unit reports and write notes for the communal knowledge base. Any computer-based system will encourage children to write *more,* but with CSILE they also write *better.* The researchers have found at least two ways in which the students' writing improves.

First, as students become more experienced with CSILE, they tend to use mental-state verbs and rhetorical words ("wonder", "understand", "explain", "argue", and "hypothesis") more than students in a traditional classroom. Use of the mental-state verbs suggests increased metacognitive awareness of mental processes. Their increased metacognitive awareness is also evident in the CSILE students' abilities to predict what they will learn in a new unit and to describe beforehand what they will need to learn to master a unit. Their writing indicates that they are aware of what they know, what they don't know, and what they must do to reach their learning goals. The rhetorical words are those that often refer to uses of language and to discourse elements in writing—words that usually appear in the plans of mature, expert writers.

Second, when giving handwritten answers to the question "What have I learned from doing this unit?" the CSILE students write well-constructed essays which contain some mature text conventions, whereas typically elementary students rely on straightforward knowledge telling.

Figure 7.10 compares excerpts from two "What I Learned about Primates" essays, one written by a CSILE student and the other by a non-CSILE student. The non-CSILE student's paragraph is garden-variety knowledge telling. He begins with gorillas because that's what he knows most about. The remainder of the paragraph is a series of declarative sentences about gorillas—a string of facts transcribed in the order in which they are retrieved from long-term memory and where consecutive sentences have no relation one to another. The writer could drop or rearrange the individual sentences with little impact on the paragraph's quality or coherence.

The CSILE student's paragraph has a different flavor. This student, too, "tells what she learned," but in an interesting way. She engages the reader with questions and talks about her own interests. She states her focus explicitly: There is a particular primate, Koko, she wants to talk about. The paragraph has organization above the sentence level, which gives it an overall coherence. Independent judges consistently rate CSILE students' end-of-unit summaries

Student from a traditional classroom:

I know most about gorillas so that's what I'll start with. There are different types of gorillas. For instance, the mountain gorilla has much nicer, shinier fur than the low-land gorilla. They mostly eat plantain with an occaisional snail or slug. They also have been seen to eat their own dung! They live in groups which can have anywhere from 3-8 or 9 gorillas in it. There is no particular breeding season for them. The silverback - the leader has exclusive breeding rights. The baby will sleep in the same night nest with their mother until the mother has another baby which will usually not happen until the first baby is about 4 or 5. A night nest is a big nest made of all kinds of big plants.

CSILE Student:

There is another primate which I want to talk about. I expressed great interest in learning about this one special gorilla. This gorilla's name is Koko. Have you heard about this gorilla before? Koko was taught sign language by a person named Dr. Francine Patterson. From the age of 2 and up, Dr. Patterson has lived with Koko and did everything for her. At first, when Dr. Francine Patterson got Koko, Koko was a little shy, but after the years went by, Koko got more used to her. I won't go into every detail about Koko because there is a lot to tell. I will just say what I think about Koko. I think that Koko is a warm and gentle gorilla who loves animals and people. I also want to say thank-you to Dr. Patterson who has taught Koko everything. I'm glad I did this project because I had fun doing it and I now feel that I know Koko myself.

Figure 7.10
These paragraphs from end-of-unit essays illustrate differences in writing skills and styles between a CSILE student and a student taught in a traditional classroom. (Provided by Marlene Scardamalia.)

higher than those of non–CSILE students on the quality of knowledge expressed and quality of organization and presentation.

Scardamalia feels that the best examples of knowledge transforming are found not in students' final essays but in cases where a group of students pursue a question through a series of notes and comments on CSILE. One of Scardamalia's favorite examples of a CSILE dialogue occurred in a biology unit. One student wrote a note stating that sponges have three ways of reproducing. Other students became interested in the topic and started exchanging notes and comments. Early in the exchange, one student tried to think of some reasons *why* sponges have three ways to reproduce and offered a theory:

One reason why Sponges and the animals like it (Sponge) have three ways of reproducing instead of one may be because their (the animals I am referring to) cell structure is so simple that you can get the cell structure easily by . . . losing some cells. For example I have a theory about one of the ways Sponges and related animals reproduce, when a wave detaches part of the skin from a Sponge or other animals like it (the Sponge) is like algy and grows into a full sized animal this is called Regeneration and Budding is probable like it.

Then theres Sexual and I think the female eggs are probably parts of a female which are less developed than Buds so they need the sperm of the male to speed up the process.

Another student then commended the previous author but raised another question and offered a tentative reason:

I think this is a really good answer and its different from mine. One thing is, why don't other animals have three ways of reproducing as well? Maybe because there are more of them? Well, I don't know but I still think this is a great note.

The exchange proceeded from stating a biological fact, to giving reasons for it, to wondering why other animals differ from sponges. This is an example, according to Scardamalia, of how CSILE students, in all subjects, start pushing beyond the immediate information to look for deeper explanations.

CSILE's preliminary successes arise not from technology alone, but from the use of technology to implement instruction based on cognitive research. CSILE restructures the classroom by changing the traditional roles of student and teacher, by changing student-teacher interaction in the classroom, and by changing student-student interaction. CSILE discourages knowledge telling and encourages knowledge transforming.

CSILE is still in its early stages of development, and its designers are only now beginning to configure it for use in other schools. Like John Anderson's GPTutor, CSILE faces the obstacles of institutional resistance to restructuring and the expense of computer hardware. The ultimate payoff may be years away, but already CSILE is changing our perceptions about what happens, and what can happen, in the classroom.

Scardamalia and Bereiter are optimistic about the prospects of using CSILE for school writing instruction. Often when they entered a new classroom to do research and announced that the students would have to write, the students responded with a collective groan. Apparently writing was not a highly valued activity in these classrooms. But the researchers found that if they gave students procedures and tools that allowed them to come to grips with a writing task, the students became excited about writing. They became interested in the process of writing, wanted to do it, were eager to talk about it, and strove to master it. Educationally, the trick is "finding ways to give children needed handles on the cognitive processes of composing" (Bereiter and Scardamalia 1982, p. 48). Collaborative Planning and CSILE are two such handles. We can use them to restructure the classroom culture and to help both the Tanyas and the Heathers.

8

Testing, Trying, and Teaching

If I have a student who scores in the 35th percentile on a standardized math test, what does this score tell me about what the student knows and what he or she fails to understand? What does it tell me about how to help the student? Why do some students flourish and others wither academically, even though they have comparable abilities and maybe even comparable prior academic records? What do Jim Minstrell and other skilled teachers know that allows them to teach so effectively? If we are committed to educational reform, these questions about assessment, motivation, and teaching are important. Cognitive research is starting to give us some answers.

What does the percentile score tell me? Not enough. The new cognitive learning theory—a "developmental psychology of performance changes," as Robert Glaser calls it—promises new tools we can use to measure educational achievement. "In the future," suggests Glaser (1986, p. 331), "achievement measurement will be designed to assess these performance changes." We should be able to design tests that yield fine-grained, diagnostic data about individual students' understandings and misunderstandings in subject domains; we may even be able to measure directly students' abilities to learn and to apply what they learn. If we had such data—data which current standardized tests can't give us—we could use them to diagnose a student's learning problems and then provide targeted instruction that addresses those problems.

Why do some children thrive and others wither academically? Research that combines methods and insights from social and cognitive psychology is finding that children's beliefs about intelligence affect their motivation and their success in school. Classroom practices and school culture shape students' beliefs about their mental abilities; many common practices send students the wrong message.

If we want more students to thrive, we will have to restructure classrooms and schools to create environments where children believe that, if they try, they can learn.

But the new cognitive learning theory and its many potential applications don't automatically translate into better teaching practices. Knowing how to teach from a cognitive perspective, as Jim Minstrell does, is not a trivial accomplishment. Although most of us don't think of teaching as a problem-solving task, Minstrell and other skilled teachers solve complex, ill-structured problems each time they teach a lesson. Research on teacher cognition is discovering the representations and the strategies teachers use to solve these problems. We are beginning to understand the differences between expert and novice teachers, and between effective and less effective teaching performances. We are beginning to understand what teachers have to know and how skilled teachers use this knowledge. If teacher training programs can effectively convey this knowledge, we can have many more expert teachers who teach from the cognitive perspective.

Cognition and Testing: From Correlations to Causes

Imagine that a paramedic squad has just rushed you to a hospital emergency room. You tell the attending physician you have severe chest pains, shortness of breath, and numbness in your left arm. The doctor notes these symptoms and examines you for others. He then says, "There is 70 percent chance you will be dead within 4 hours. You appear to have some general, life-threatening physical deficiency." On the basis of his clinical experiences with hundreds of other patients, the doctor may have made a highly reliable prediction. He derives his prediction from extensive knowledge about statistical correlations between symptoms and outcomes.

Now imagine that is all the doctor could say or do. Imagine that the science underlying medical practice consisted entirely of unexplained statistical relations between symptoms and outcomes. If so, doctors could give prognoses, but could make no diagnoses. Therapies and preventive measures would, at best, be based on other unexplained correlations, on common sense, or on unfounded speculation. Fortunately, biological science supports medical practice. Biology helps explain symptoms in terms of internal, unobserved bodily processes. The doctor wouldn't say you had a general physical deficiency. He'd say you had a heart attack that damaged certain coronary tissues, and that this condition should respond to specific treatment. The doctor could even suggest some preventive actions, such as changing your diet and exercising, to help you avoid future coronary events.

Many of our educational assessment tools, particularly standardized aptitude and achievement tests, rely on unexplained statistical correlations. This leaves the teacher-student relationship at the same level as the doctor-patient relationship in the above thought experiment. Our tests, which are based on many other cases we have observed and on statistical relations among them, allow us to compare and rank students by their relative academic health and to make predictions about educational outcomes. They allow us to attribute unfavorable outcomes to general intellectual deficits, but they don't help us make educational diagnoses, begin informed therapy, or prescribe preventive measures.

New cognitive theories of learning and intelligence support new approaches to student assessment. Cognitive science attempts to explain observed differences in intelligent human performance in terms of internal, mental mechanisms. Cognitive science is to education what biology is to medicine. Cognitive mechanisms underlie and cause the statistical correlations we measure with standardized tests. If we know what causes the correlations, we can make diagnoses, prescribe appropriate therapy, and identify preventive measures. We can use tests not only to measure learning but also to improve it.

The Traditional Theory of Testing

Tests, be they of intelligence, aptitude, or achievement, are devices that sample small sets of student performances. The Scholastic Aptitude Test (SAT), for example, doesn't ask about everything a student might know or everything he will study in college; it samples a student's knowledge and skills. We use this sample to rank and compare students and to make predictions about their first-year college grades. A statistical theory guides the sampling and justifies inferences from the sampled performances to the general comparisons and predictions we want to make. Much as a good doctor looks for a few reliable signs and symptoms before making a diagnosis, a good test asks a few reliable questions before making predictions and comparisons.

In designing a test, we first have to choose these few reliable questions. Items on an aptitude or achievement test should be representative of the skills and knowledge we want to assess. Experts' judgments about what students should know about a topic often guide the choice of test items. For example, the mathematics SAT includes 60 items, around 16 of which test geometry knowledge. According to the experts, these problems are sufficient to tap what students should have learned in high school geometry. The test items also have to meet a second requirement: We want to choose the smallest number of items that will yield the greatest amount of information about differences in achievement or aptitude. A test on which all students get every item correct or every item wrong would be useless; it would give no basis for comparison or ranking. Statistical analysis helps test designers choose items that are highly sensitive to differences in aptitude or achievement.

If we want to compare and rank students, then the test has to be scored against some reliable standard. Most of our tests meet this requirement by being *norm referenced* or *standardized*. When designers develop a new test, they first administer it to a norm group. The norm group's scores become the standard for scoring the test. The various scales used to report other students' scores refer back to the norm group's original performance. Sometimes tests report results as percentile scores. If a student scores in the 70th percentile, this means that his raw score—the number of questions he answered correctly—was higher than the raw scores achieved by 70 percent of the students in the norm group. (Note that if all the students in a class or a school district score above the 50th percentile, this doesn't mean they are all "above average." It means they all scored higher than 50 percent of the norm group.)

Sometimes tests report grade-equivalent scores. A grade-equivalent score of 5.0 means that the a student's test performance equaled the average performance of all fifth-graders in the norm group. It doesn't necessarily mean that the student should be in the fifth grade, or even that a fifth-grader with a score of 5.0 is performing adequately. We could make the latter inference only if we accepted the average performance of fifth-graders in the norm group as adequate fifth-grade performance. If our goal is to improve the schools, we may not want to accept that average performance is adequate performance.

All the scales and scores used to report standardized test performance are arbitrary. They depend on the absolute difficulty of the test and on the relative ability of the norm group. Ease of interpretation and convenient statistical properties influence scale choice. The test data tell us how students taking the test now compare with students in the norm group; they tell us about student symptoms *now* relative to student symptoms *then*. For some educational purposes is doesn't matter that test scores have only relative, not absolute, meaning. Relative scores are enough to let us compare and rank-order students from different schools and school systems by reference to the common standard. If you are a gatekeeper of academe—an admissions or financial aid officer—this is useful information.

Sometimes we use tests not only to compare, but to predict—to make prognoses. We want to make inferences about how a student might perform in the future. For example, an admissions officer might use the SAT to predict first-year college grades. This requires that the test designers have data not only on the norm group's raw test scores but also on their first-year college grades. Statistical analysis of these data allows us to estimate the probability that a person with a given test score, say 570 on the math SAT, will achieve a certain grade-point average in college. A test we can use in this way has what test designers call *criterion validity*. It lets us use the test score to make a prediction about the value of a criterion variable, such as college grades, that is more closely related to the actual performance that we (or an admissions officer) might want to measure.

Standardized tests are currently an entrenched feature of the American educational system, a system in which comparison and selection play a prominent role. In many ways, the SAT provides a standard that takes the place of a national curriculum. Although we should always be aware that some tests, when used for some purposes, might present unfair obstacles to some students, standardized tests based on statistical theories do permit generally valid comparisons and reliable predictions. Yet there are other inferences we would like to make about individual students—inferences about *why* students score or achieve as they do.

Suppose a reliable standardized achievement test tells us that a student ranks in the 40th percentile. This number allows us to compare the student against others and to predict his future performance, but it tells us nothing about what the student does and doesn't understand or what a teacher might do to help. The materials accompanying most achievement tests give suggestions about how students' errors might relate to deficiencies, but achievement tests are like a good game of Twenty Questions. Tests include the fewest items that will reveal the greatest differences among students. They don't yield fine-grained data about what an individual student knows. Failure on a few highly select test items isn't a sufficient basis from which to make inferences about a student's particular weaknesses. The data just aren't there to support diagnostic inferences. There may be robust statistical correlations between test performance and subsequent academic achievement, but this gives us little insight into the mechanisms underlying those correlations.

For the same reason, we shouldn't think that standardized test scores can diagnose what might be wrong with teachers, schools, or the educational system. Falling test scores suggest that something may be amiss, but the scores themselves can't tell us what the problems are or how to fix them. The same is true for the National Assessments of Educational Progress, although they are based on different statistical assumptions than the SATs. The NAEP national report cards carefully state that they only report students' performance in a way that permits valid comparisons over time; they can't offer explanations for change, or lack of it, in that performance. Nonetheless, when the reports appear there is no shortage of explanations in the media for falling or stagnant performance—too little homework, short school years, vacuous textbooks, too much television. For the most part, these explanations are speculative, derived at best from common sense and at worst from wishful thinking. Speculation, of either the common-sense or the wishful variety, is a poor basis for a program of educational reform and school restructuring.

A Cognitive Theory of Learning Assessment

Cognitive science offers a different theoretical basis for testing and evaluation, one that can provide diagnostic information to complement standardized, norm-referenced tests. Cognitive science offers a theory and methods to describe what is behind students' performances—what is causing the symptoms—within a subject domain. Cognitive theory attributes differences in performance to specific differences in mental representations and processes. Cognitive scientists might start out comparing experts and novices, but they also can, and do, describe the intervening levels of competence and how that competence develops. They offer us a developmental psychology of performance changes.

If we can develop tests to trace changes in performances, we can trace students' learning trajectories in school subjects. We can describe their progress in terms of the representations they have and the mental processes they use. This is the information we need for educational diagnosis, therapy, and prevention. To underscore this different theoretical approach to testing, cognitive scientists sometimes call the new approach *learning assessment* rather than achievement testing (Glaser, Lesgold, and Lajoie 1987, p. 48).

The cognitive theory of learning assessment is in its infancy. Widespread adoption and application will require much more work and is likely more than a few years away. Several examples from the preceding chapters illustrate the approach, how we might apply it, and how it might improve educational outcomes.

Siegler's work with the balance scale (chapter 2) can again serve as an initial example. Siegler's rule-assessment approach assumes that from early childhood rules govern some domains of human reasoning. As children develop and receive formal instruction, the rules they use gradually become more complex and sophisticated. Diagnostic tests, such as those Siegler used in his studies, can tell us which rules students are using. Siegler constructed his tests so that a student's pattern of responses to the entire set of items—errors *and* correct answers—reveals the student's rule. Siegler's rules I–IV are points on the child's trajectory toward expertise in this small domain. With the right tests, we can figure out where any child is on that trajectory. Siegler's work also showed that when we know which rule a student is using—when we make the correct diagnosis—specific instructional steps can help the student to progress more rapidly.

Similar approaches to learning assessment would work in other rule-governed subjects, such as science or mathematics. Case and Griffin extended this idea to the learning of arithmetic (chapter 4 above). Understanding the knowledge and skills needed for arithmetic in terms of the number line and operations on it led to a diagnostic test, and then to Case and Griffin's remedial curriculum.

In science instruction, students' misconceptions can impede or inhibit their learning. Jim Minstrell's practice of giving a diagnostic test at the start of the course and a diagnostic quiz at the start of each unit helps the teacher and the students identify which facets (pieces of knowledge) students bring to his physics class. The diagnoses shape Minstrell's teaching.

Minstrell and Hunt have developed a computer program, called DIAGNOSER, that combines learning assessment with instruction. DIAGNOSER is a computer-based, cognitively astute teaching assistant that poses problems like those Minstrell uses in his quizzes. Students answer the problems and give justifications for their answers. The program maps the students' responses onto a catalog of well-known facets, thus producing a diagnostic *facet profile* for each student. This is useful to the teacher, and it is a form of self-assessment for the student. Having made the diagnosis, the program refers each student to exercises and problems that reinforce correct facets and change incorrect ones. DIAGNOSER assesses students' understanding, identifies their misconceptions, and provides individualized instruction.

Intelligence and Assessment: Beyond IQ

So far we have looked at cases where the new learning theory can contribute to better measures of learning in traditional school subjects. The theory has also contributed to new views about intelligence (chapters 2 and 3). These new views are finding their way into school practices and into educators' approaches to student assessment. One example is Howard Gardner's (1983) *theory of multiple intelligences.*

Gardner's theory draws on his unusually broad research interests and on his dual academic appointments. As a Professor at Harvard's Graduate School of Education, Gardner has contributed to basic cognitive research on child development and learning. He and his colleagues have worked extensively with teachers in school settings. As a researcher at the Boston Veterans Administration Medical Center, in collaboration with neuroscientists, Gardner has observed and studied how strokes, tumors, and head injuries affect the cognitive functioning of adults. The effects can be bizarre. Some patients have normal intelligence as measured by IQ tests, but have no memory of their past personal life. Others are perfectly normal except that they are unable to do simple addition, unable to use common nouns in speech, or unable to recognize faces (including their own).

Gardner's work with brain-damaged patients suggested to him that our general notions of intelligence might be too narrow. Maybe human intelligence is not a single, unitary phenomenon; maybe we can't adequately understand or evaluate individuals using a single intelligence measure such as IQ. Gardner thinks we have at least seven distinct intelligences, or ways of knowing the world. He maintains that we have distinct linguistic, logico-mathematical, spatial, musical, bodily (using one's body to solve problems and make things), social (understanding others), and personal (understanding oneself) intelligences.

For Gardner these intelligences are domain-specific abilities, but the domains are very broad. On his theory, an intelligence has to satisfy three criteria: it has to show a clear developmental trajectory in children; it has to show up in isolated forms in selected populations, such as prodigies or autistic children; and there has to be some evidence that it is localized in specific areas or circuits of the brain.

Gardner lucidly presents the implications of his theory for educational reform in his book *The Unschooled Mind* (1991). His theory implies that students have different kinds of minds—different mixes of the seven intelligences. If so, we should expect that children will vary in how they learn, remember, and understand. Some students learn better using language skills, others using spatial information, and others using quantitative representations. "These differences," Gardner writes, "challenge an educational system that assumes that everyone can learn the same materials in the same way and that a uniform, universal measure suffices to test student learning." We should present school subjects in a variety of ways, using multiple representations that resonate with the students' multiple intelligences. We should assess intelligence and learning in a variety of ways, also.

Currently, Gardner argues, our schools emphasize linguistic and quantitative intelligence to the detriment of other ways of knowing the world. Furthermore, instruction based on the primacy of linguistic and numerical intelligence at the expense of the other intelligences unjustifiably brands some students as failures and may give too much credit for intellectual brilliance to others. Curricula designed to develop all seven intelligences should be superior to curricula that develop just two.

In many ways, Gardner's theory is an elegant generalization from claims other researchers have made about subject-matter learning. We have seen that children develop sophisticated informal knowledge in the domains of number (chapter 4), physical object (chapter 5), and language (chapters 6 and 7), starting in infancy. Their intelligences—the powers of their unschooled minds—are manifest long before they start school. These are also domains where prodigies do appear and, neuroscientists tell us, specific brain areas might support learning. A message that emerged repeatedly in the previous chapters was that formal school instruction, particularly in the early years, should build on children's informal knowledge. In other words, we might be able to develop better "schooled minds" if we appreciate the powers of children's unschooled minds. Gardner's theory goes farther. On his theory our unschooled minds are with us for life in two senses: first, many of an individual's early theories and conceptions are deeply entrenched; second, one's ensemble of intelligences is part of one's biological inheritance. Developing and tapping the powers of the unschooled mind is a challenge for education and training at every level, from the first formal instruction in arithmetic through job training or graduate school.

Gardner and numerous collaborators are attempting to apply this theory in the classroom. Project Spectrum (a collaboration among Gardner, Mara Krechevsky, and David Feldman) began as an effort to see if preschool children had distinct intelligence profiles. Gardner and his colleagues found that children as young as 4 years already show clear individual differences in the development and use of the seven intelligences. This encouraged the researchers to think about how they might improve learning environments for preschool and early-primary-grade children. They created a classroom environment that surrounded children with rich, engaging opportunities to use their multiple intelligences. The "naturalist's corner," for example, allows children to learn about life sciences and encourages the use of sensorimotor intelligence and logico-quantitative skills. The "storytelling corner" offers opportunities to use linguistic skills and to develop dramatic, imaginative talents. Over the course of a school year, most of the children in the study spontaneously use all these learning opportunities. Those that don't are encouraged to do so. During the year, then, the teachers can directly observe children's interests and talents and analyze them in terms of the seven intelligences. If teachers can observe the intelligences in action, there is no need for special tests and assessments. Nonetheless, the research team has devised special games and activities that yield more precise measures.

The result of the teachers' assessment of a child in this project is a brief essay in which the teachers describe the child's strengths and weaknesses within the theoretical framework of multiple intelligences and make recommendations for parents and teachers about how to help the child build on his strengths and address his weaknesses. Such informal assessment is a departure from the usual reliance on grades, comparisons, and rankings. "In my view," Gardner writes, "psychologists have traditionally been far too concerned with norming and ranking" (1991, p. 207). Informal assessments also have a place in our educational system.

Project Spectrum is not unique in providing rich early-childhood learning environments. What makes this project different is that it is grounded in a cognitive theory about intelligence and learning. Gardner's criterion that an intelligence must have a clear developmental trajectory is fundamental to the project and to the teachers' assessments. Spelke, Baillargeon, Case, Griffin, and Siegler describe developmental trajectories in a variety of domains in some detail. With this knowledge, early-childhood educators can better design learning environments and opportunities to nurture children's multiple intelligences. This knowledge also provides a theoretical context to guide informal assessment of how children's unschooled minds develop.

The Key School, an inner-city elementary school in Indianapolis, has developed an entire curriculum around the theory of multiple intelligences. Teaching practices and school activities attempt to stimulate each of the child's seven intelligences daily. As part of the curriculum, there are three 10-week *themes* each school year—e.g., "The Renaissance" and "Our Mexican Heritage." Every student does a major project on each theme. At the end of each theme period, the students display, describe, and explain their work to their schoolmates. The school and Gardner's research team videotape the presentations so that they have a video portfolio of each student's work.

Educators are looking with increased interest at using projects, exhibitions, and portfolios of students' work as assessment tools. Their interest springs from the realization that school projects can be reasonably authentic cognitive tasks—more authentic, at least, than most of the current assessment devices. Multiple-choice and true-false exams are not common in life outside school, but working on projects, alone or collaboratively, is. If students can develop into better writers by engaging in authentic writing tasks (chapter 7 above), maybe they can better develop other aspects of their intelligence by engaging in more authentic learning tasks.

Gardner and his collaborators are attempting to develop methods to evaluate students' portfolios—collections of more authentic learning tasks—in ways that are fair, practical, and helpful to both students and teachers. This is a challenge for all advocates of portfolios and exhibitions as reliable assessment tools. According to Gardner (1991, p. 246), "The portfolio may be considered as an evolving cognitive model of the student's development over the course of his life in the Key School." Looking at a portfolio assembled over a period of years, on this view, is like looking at a map of the student's learning trajectory.

To use portfolios as assessment tools, teachers need a way to read and interpret these maps of individual students' cognitive terrains. Teachers would like to know, or at least estimate, how well a student's mental terrain matches the one they are trying to impart. One way to make these estimates is to rely on what cognitive research tells them. Glaser's notion of a developmental psychology of performance changes can help teachers describe the learning trajectories they would like their students to follow. In assessing portfolios, teachers can ask "How close is the student's learning trajectory, as revealed by the portfolio, to the trajectory we envision as most desirable and appropriate?" The cognitivists' detailed descriptions of performances in different domains at different ages gives teachers a way to answer this question. The developmental psychology of performance changes can act as a standard for portfolio assessment. As Gardner writes (1991, p. 217), "one would expect beginning students to exhibit the performance of a novice and students with more experience to advance toward the level of journeyman or even master." So, although exhibitions and portfolios appear to be much different from BUGGY or DIAGNOSER, the effective use of all these assessment tools derives from the same underlying cognitive theory.

Using cognitive theory with its detailed descriptions of learning given in terms of knowledge representations and procedural skills, teachers can make theoretically grounded judgments about students' progress and identify where students might need additional help. Once teachers place a project from a student's portfolio within this developmental trajectory, they can consider other aspects of the student's progress, accomplishment, and participation. This is also part of the evaluation effort at the Key School. How well did the student plan the project? How well did the student execute the plan? Did the student become engaged in the project? What was the student's motivation? Did the student view the project as an authentic opportunity for creative expression? To what extent did the project involve cooperation with other students, teachers, or mentors? Answers to these questions give teachers additional diagnostic information to use in helping individual students learn in their own way, each at his own pace. When backed by a cognitive theory about how expertise develops, a videotape of a student's projects over the years becomes a powerful diagnostic and therapeutic tool.

Dynamic Assessment: Helping Weak Learners

Another aspect of intelligence that surfaced in chapter 3 was that weak students often need direct, in-depth, informed instruction before they can learn new problem-solving strategies and use them spontaneously in novel situations. More capable students might need only a general hint before they can learn the strategies and transfer them to novel problems. Some people, such as the research psychologist who learned physics, are skilled learners. If there are significant differences among students in their responses to instruction and their abilities to transfer what they learn to novel problems and situations, it would be useful to have a way to measure these differences. If teachers could assess these individual differences, they could structure their classrooms to give less instructional support to the capable learners, who don't need it, and more to the weak learners, who do. Ann Brown and Joe Campione, now in the Division of Education in Mathematics, Science, and Technology at the University of California at Berkeley, are trying to develop *dynamic testing methods* that eventually might help teachers make reliable predictions about students' abilities to learn and transfer learning in various subject domains (Campione and Brown 1990).

Dynamic assessment starts from a detailed task analysis of problem solving in a domain to find out what knowledge and what skills students need. On the basis of this analysis, Brown and Campione develop a series of hints a teacher could use to help students learn in the domain. The hints, which contain elements of the knowledge that underlies competence in the domains, are ordered on a list from very general to very specific. The content and the order of the hints model the steps and the thinking processes an expert might use to solve problems in the domain. Using the ordered list of hints as instructional scaffolding, a teacher helps a student learn by giving increasingly specific hints until the student can solve a problem or a series of problems.

Roberta Ferrara, a graduate student working under Brown and Campione, studied what dynamic assessment might reveal about learning elementary arithmetic (Ferrara 1987). She worked with 5-year-olds who were learning to solve elementary addition and subtraction problems. First, she tested the children on their knowledge of number words, counting principles, and advanced counting skills. (She also had their IQ and their standardized math test scores.) She then presented simple problems to the children (e.g. "3 + 2 = ?") using props such as Cookie Monster, his cookie jar, and some cookies. When a child had trouble with a problem, Ferrara would start giving hints from her standardized list. The first hint was: "That's a good try, but it's not quite right. Do you want to try again?" In the second hint, she would repeat part of the problem verbatim if the child asked or had not been paying attention. Subsequent hints included reminders about the quantities in the problem, a suggestion to do the current problem the same way the child had done previous ones, and finally a complete demonstration and explanation of how to use the props to solve the problem using the *count all* method. (Construct two sets, one for each addend; then combine them into one set and count all the objects in the big set.) When the children reached a predefined competence level—being able to solve six problems in a row with no help from the teacher—Ferrara took the number of hints a student needed to reach this level as a measure of the student's learning efficiency.

Next, to measure the ability to transfer, Ferrara repeated the exercise using the same hints but using a second set of problems, some of which were nearly identical to the original ones and some of which were sufficiently novel that the students would have to transfer what they had previously learned to new situations. The prior task analysis of problems in the domain allowed her to estimate how novel the transfer problems were relative to the original training problems. On the transfer test, problems ranged from *near* transfer (two-digit addition, but with new quantities and different props) to *far* transfer (three addends: 3 + 2 + 4 = ?) to *very far* transfer (missing-addend problems: 4 + ? = 6). Ferrara took the number of hints a child needed to reach a predetermined performance level on this second set of problems as a measure of the child's ability to transfer prior learning to new problems.

After the learning and transfer experiences, Ferrara gave the children a posttest of their arithmetic knowledge to find out how much they had learned during the two dynamic assessment sessions. She wanted to find out what factors or variables—original number knowledge, IQ, learning efficiency, transfer propensity—best predicted gains in students scores from pretest to posttest. She found that the dynamic measures of learning and transfer were much better than IQ scores and measures of background knowledge in predicting improvement. Background knowledge and IQ together could explain about 22 percent of the students' improvement from pretest to posttest. The dynamic measures, primarily the transfer measure, accounted for an additional 34 percent of the improvement. Ferrara's results support Campione and Brown's (1990) more general conclusion that "if the interest is in predicting the learning trajectory of different students, the best indicant in not their IQ or how much they know already, nor even how readily they acquire new procedures, but how well they understand and make flexible use of those procedures in the service of solving novel problems." Dynamic assessment measures such as these should make it possible to distinguish strong from weak learners and to restructure classrooms so as to provide appropriate support for both strong and weak students.

The new theory of learning assessment promises to provide teachers with diagnostic information they can use to help students learn. We should not overlook a second advantage: The new assessment tools also will give insights directly to a student on how well he or she is learning. The new assessment tools create links for the student between learning and testing. In many classrooms today, children study lessons and do problems and then are tested on what they have learned. Testing is separate from learning. Often, too, students receive their test scores with little explanation of what (if anything) their scores reveal about how to improve their performance and their understanding. Tools like DIAGNOSER and dynamic assessment (discussed in this chapter), along with BUGGY and GPTutor (described in earlier chapters), are based on experts' cognitive models. When using these tools, students see from the beginning the kinds of performances that should be their goals in learning. The students receive coaching on their performances and can begin to evaluate how they are progressing. The new theories of testing promise that one day students may be able to take control of their assessment as well as their learning. "Our inspiration," writes Robert Glaser (1986, p. 339), "is that learning assessments will not provide merely a score, a label, a grade level, or a percentile, but also *instructional scoring* that makes apparent to the student and to the teacher the requirements for increasing competence."

Motivation: Thriving versus Withering

Teachers and parents often wonder why some students succeed and others fail as they progress through school. This is particularly puzzling when success and failure seem unrelated to ability or past performance. Unexpected failure is most prominent during adolescence, when young people change along every dimension—biological, social, and intellectual (Carnegie Council 1989). Cognitive and social forces interact powerfully to shape adolescents' understanding of themselves and of their social and school environments. Some social and cognitive psychologists have looked at how these factors influence learning and, in particular, how they affect motivation. To psychologists, motivation is more than wanting to do well. Motivation involves psychological processes distinct from intelligence that influence students' school goals and learning strategies.

This research is starting to explain why some students thrive while others wither, why some students seek challenges while others avoid them, and why some students come to value learning while others are content to satisfy minimum requirements.

Carol Dweck, now at Columbia University, is at the center of this research. She describes her basic research interest as "how the mind works given feedback that occurs in social situations." With this as her starting point, she has worked at the intersection of social and cognitive psychology to develop a theory that links beliefs about intelligence, motivation, and school performance.

In the 1960s, scientists studying animal behavior found that experimental animals subjected to inescapable electric shock would learn that it was useless to try to avoid the shock. After learning this, the animals would make no effort to escape the painful stimulus, even when they easily could do so. The animals had learned to be helpless in the experimental situation; they had learned there was nothing they could do to avoid the shock. The scientists had to retrain the animals to restore their desire to escape.

Dweck wondered if learned helplessness might occur with humans in learning situations. Can children learn, or come to believe, that in some school situations there is nothing they can do to improve their performance? While a graduate student at Yale, Dweck started to explore this possibility. In a 1973 study, she had one adult experimenter give fifth-graders easy problems and a second adult give them impossible ones. The children had randomly interspersed sessions with both experimenters. After the initial training, one day the "failure experimenter" gave the children some simple problems that the children had solved easily for the "success experimenter." The surprising result was that when the failure experimenter gave simple problems, the children couldn't do them; many didn't even try. Apparently the children had learned to be helpless in the presence of the failure experimenter (Dweck and Reppucci 1973).

In the late 1970s, Dweck and C. I. Diener conducted a variation on the 1973 experiment (Diener and Dweck 1978, 1980). They began by using psychological tests to assess the children's academic goal orientation. Generally, children adopt either *performance* goals or *learning* goals. For children who adopt performance goals, school provides occasions to demonstrate their competence and be rewarded for it. Public praise and external rewards motivate these children. For children who adopt learning goals, school provides opportunities to increase their competence and improve their skills. Personal satisfaction and internal standards drive these children.

In the Diener-Dweck study, each student attempted to solve 12 problems. The first eight were sufficiently easy that all the children could do them, but the final four were too hard for any of the children to solve. Adopting a method from cognitive psychology, Diener and Dweck asked the children to "think and feel aloud" as they worked on the problems. They also asked the children to make predictions about their future performance, both before and after they started to fail.

On the eight easy problems, there were no differences between the performance-goal and the learning-goal students in what they thought and felt. Once the students started to fail on the impossible problems, however, two distinct patterns emerged. Performance-goal children became bored and anxious. Many tried to avoid doing the problems entirely. Some regressed to using problem-solving strategies more typical of preschool children. They became pessimistic about their future success, though seconds before they had been consistently successful. They became highly negative about their cognitive abilities.

The learning-goal children didn't even think they were failing. They saw the unsolved problems as challenges and opportunities to learn. Their think-aloud commentaries showed much self-instruction, self-monitoring, and metacognitive awareness. They remained exuberantly optimistic, and two-thirds gave positive predictions about their future performance. They relished the tasks, making comments like "I love a challenge" and "I was hoping this would be informative." Most of these children persisted in their initial problem-solving strategies, and over 25 percent began to use more sophisticated strategies.

A second interesting finding was that the two groups of children explained and interpreted their experiences in different ways. The performance-goal children attributed failure to lack of intelligence, a deficiency they could do nothing about. To their minds, they could no more increase their intelligence than they could change their eye color. If you can't do anything about it, they reasoned, why keep trying? For them, the smart short-term strategy was to avoid the task and avoid embarrassment. In contrast, the learning-goal children attributed what they saw as only a temporary setback to lack of effort. For them, the intelligent thing to do was to exert more mental energy. On their view of the world, they could work their way out of their current predicament. They could improve their intellectual performance with mental effort, just as they might increase their athletic performance through greater physical effort.

The experiment showed that the two groups of children had different goals and different beliefs about intelligence which resulted in different behaviors when confronted with the possibility of failure. These results and those from other experiments led Dweck to develop a motivational process theory that linked naive theories of intelligence, school goals, academic confidence, and patterns of school behavior.

The theory (figure 8.1) recognizes two widely held naive theories of intelligence, the *entity theory* and the *incremental theory*. Entity theorists believe that intelligence is a fixed, innate trait that we can do little to change; incrementalists believe that intelligence is an ability we can develop gradually. Entity theorists tend to have per-

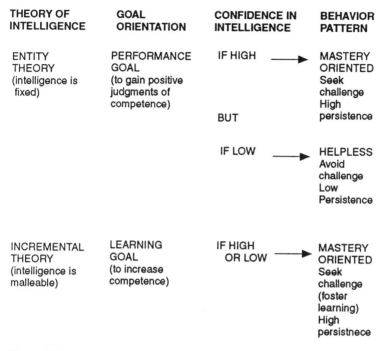

Figure 8.1
A process model of motivation. Beliefs about intelligence are associated with goal orientations, which in turn influence classroom behaviors. (From Feldman and Eliot 1990. Copyright 1990 President and Fellows of Harvard College.)

formance goals; they seek occasions to prove they have a lot of the intelligence entity. Incrementalists tend to embrace learning goals; they seek and value opportunities to develop and extend their intellectual skills. Both types of children can do well in school, as long as they remain successful and confident. But the entity theory and its associated performance goals is a riskier path. When academic adversities shake students' confidence, their resulting classroom behaviors are predictable from their naive beliefs about intelligence. When setbacks occur and challenges arise, entity theorists tend to become educationally helpless; incrementalists keep on trying.

To test this theory, Valanne Henderson and Carol Dweck (1990) used it to predict how some students would do in the seventh grade, their first year of junior high school. On the basis of extensive testing before the school year began, Henderson and Dweck divided the students into four groups: entity–high confidence, entity–low confidence, incremental–high confidence, and incremental–low confidence. They used the students' sixth-grade achievement scores to estimate their expected performance in seventh grade.

The results confirmed the theory's predictions. The incremental–high confidence group was the highest-performing group in seventh grade, followed closely by the incremental–low confidence group. Both entity-theory groups performed poorly. In short, the incrementalists flourished in the new, challenging environment, and the entity theorists withered, independent of previous school success. Thus, as Henderson and Dweck note, "the way students think about their intelligence may affect their ability and desire to master academic material" (1990, p. 319).

Motivation and Classroom Practices

Carol Ames, at the University of Illinois, is exploring the classroom implications of Dweck's motivational process theory. She finds that many classroom practices encourage students to become entity theorists and performers. Ames, and others, have observed that children entering school usually are optimistic about their abilities, have positive expectations for themselves, and tend to bounce back from failure. Most young children are incrementalists and learners, believing that "hard workers are smart and smart children work hard" (Ames 1990, p. 412).

As children progress through school, it seems, they begin to believe that, although trying harder might help, their innate intellectual ability sets boundaries on what they can achieve. Already in the primary grades, Ames notes, students become more interested in getting work done—performing and moving on to the next lesson—than in understanding a lesson's purpose and content. Being the first student in the class to get the right answer becomes important, because teachers often reward such performance but don't reward more deliberate problem solving. What students think about their intelligence depends on "their classroom experiences, essentially their perceptions of how the teacher structures the classroom" (Ames 1990, p. 414).

Many classroom practices appear to value performing over learning, thus negatively influencing students' ideas about intelligence and learning. Grouping students by ability is an obvious, public sign that performance, rather than diligence, is what counts. Giving the same daily assignments to all students, as some curricula require, ignores individual differences in learning rates. It discounts the time and effort some students might need and be willing to spend to master a topic, and it implicitly tells students that mastery and the effort it might require are not important enough to be given time in the curriculum.

Traditional testing and assessment practices can also promote the entity theory and performance goals. We often evaluate students publicly by comparing them directly, or indirectly via normed standardized tests, with their classmates. We compare students in terms of letter grades, percentages, percentiles, and grade equivalents. We reward students who perform well, but because many of our favorite tests yield scant diagnostic information we can do little to help students who test poorly. Students might rightly conclude that tests are trials that separate the scholarly sheep from the vocational goats. "Well," a student might think, "if the standardized tests say I don't have the right stuff for school, why try? Why stay in this situation?" Common school practices may be discouraging students from trying in school—and, in extreme cases, may be driving them out of school.

On Dweck's theory, much of our common-sense thinking about how to use positive reinforcement may be counterproductive. Sometimes, for example, teachers attempt to motivate low-performing, low-confidence children by giving them easy tasks. The children nearly always succeed, and the teachers praise them for it. This, the thinking goes, should make the low-confidence children feel like high-confidence children. What this strategy overlooks is that if these children are victims of learned helplessness, they see no connection between what they do and what they achieve. Not seeing this connection, they don't interpret the teacher's praise as a reward for what they have done; they don't interpret the praise as positive reenforcement. Furthermore, if children's problems start when they experience failure or challenge, as Dweck's experiments show, no series of triumphs on simple tasks can prepare them to deal with failure. Given what we know about motivation, we should scrap these practices.

Ames is in the midst of an experiment within the Champaign-Urbana public schools in which she and her colleagues are attempting to create classroom environments where incrementalism and learning goals can prevail. They are trying to create classrooms that emphasize the process of learning, reward effort, focus on children's individual progress, and encourage students to take an active part in learning and in classroom management. From the research literature, Ames and her colleagues identified classroom teaching strategies consistent with these goals, such as designing assignments for novelty and individual challenge, using mixed-skill rather than ability groups, giving students opportunities to revise their own work on specific assignments, evaluating students on how much they improve rather than on how well they perform relative to others, and assessing students' progress privately rather than publicly. The research team then had 73 elementary school teachers suggest ways to implement these strategies in their schools. The teachers, with support of the research team, designed a program they thought would work in their classrooms and assumed responsibility for making the strategies part of their daily classroom practice.

Ames reports positive results from the first year of the study. Other research had shown that there is a significant decline in student motivation over the course of the school year. The Champaign-Urbana team found the same trend in their traditional control classrooms. In the experimental classrooms, however, student motivation increased over the year. Children they had identified as at risk for academic failure responded to the new environment extremely well. These students showed increased willingness to use more effective learning strategies and to take on challenging tasks, and had a more positive attitude toward school than comparable children in traditional classrooms. The at-risk children became genuinely interested in learning; they started to take on and persist at difficult tasks.

Year 2 of the experiment, underway as of this writing, involves more than 100 teachers. Data on traditional achievement measures are not yet available. "We don't know about achievement yet," Ames says, "but we should not expect immediate effects on achievement anyway. Motivation affects achievement over the long term. As children become more willing to take risks and embrace challenges, their opportunities to learn will expand, and with that one would expect marked impacts on achievement in the long run." If classrooms meet students' motivational needs, we might see yet another Matthew Effect in education.

Motivation is one of the foremost problems in education; yet, as Ames (1990) points out, many teacher training programs do not adequately address it. If we want more students to thrive and fewer to wither, we should equip teachers with the knowledge and skills they need to promote learning over performing. Understanding how the mind works when given the feedback that occurs in social situations—Dweck's basic research interest—is emerging as an integral part of teaching's professional knowledge base.

Teacher Cognition: What Does Nancy Know?

We are only beginning to appreciate the specialized knowledge that skilled teachers possess. Cognitive scientists, who began to study teacher cognition in the late 1970s, have found that teaching is a formidable cognitive task. Understanding how teachers use their knowledge and skills to solve complex pedagogical problems is a first step toward the development of training programs that would prepare teachers to teach from a cognitive perspective.

Cognitive research has had some impact on teacher education, but, as with early attempts to apply cognitive research to writing instruction, the impact may be superficial. Lee Shulman, a pioneer in the field of teacher cognition, observes: "If we wandered into teacher training programs, we could find a number of people teaching teachers using cognitive language. But should you conclude that beyond the jargon the perspective is imbued through the program? We just don't know."

Outstanding teachers' performances rarely have appreciative audiences. Most teachers work in a classroom where they are the only adult, so other professionals do not see their work. Some students might recognize a great teaching performance, but few, if any, could say explicitly what made it great. As part of their work, Shulman and his colleagues at Stanford University are collecting and analyzing case studies of skilled teachers at work in the classroom.

Among Shulman's experts is Nancy, a 25-year veteran of teaching high school English. Shulman (1987, p. 2) describes one of Nancy's classroom performances this way: "She was like a symphony conductor, posing questions, probing for alternative views, drawing out the shy while tempering the boisterous. . . . Her combination of subject-matter understanding and pedagogical skill was quite dazzling." Nancy is energetic and active; she controls the pace, the structure, and the rhythm of what goes on in her classroom.

Interviews with Nancy revealed that she uses a theory of her own to guide her teaching. According to Nancy, one can read a book at four levels. Level 1 is understanding the literal meaning of the words. Level 2 is understanding the symbolic or figurative use of the words. At level 3, the reader constructs the author's larger message from the implications of the literal and the figurative language. Level 4 is application, where readers evaluate the meaning of the larger message for their own lives.

Nancy uses this theory to construct her lessons, but also teaches it explicitly to her students so they can use it to guide their reading. Her expertise is most evident in how she can apply the theory flexibly to all the books she teaches, to all her students, and to every classroom situation. Nancy's flexible style can accommodate levels of genre difficulty (an O. Henry short story versus *Finnegans Wake*), levels of ability (remedial versus advanced placement students), and how she feels on a given day. Once, when she was ill and couldn't talk, she had the class work in small groups and communicated with them by notes and whispers. She sat in the back of the room and interacted with the class only when students asked for her help. The lesson unfolded flawlessly. Pursuing his simile, Shulman notes that "she not only can conduct her orchestra from the podium, she can sit back and watch it play with virtuosity by itself."

Nancy's ability goes beyond managing students and knowing the material. Nancy knows how to manage ideas and their flow in the classroom. How does she do it? What does she know that enables her to give such masterful performances? Can we teach it to others? Studying teacher cognition can help us answer these questions. We can use the answers to improve teacher training and to extend the knowledge base of teaching as a learned profession. This is what drives Lee Shulman, who writes that "the hope that teaching like Nancy's can become typical instead of unusual motivates much of the effort in the newly proposed reforms of teaching."

The rhetoric of teaching reform assumes, correctly, that teaching is a profession, like law or medicine. By definition, a profession requires mastery of a specialized body of knowledge. We also assume that members of a profession are the keepers of that knowledge, are the authorities on how to apply that knowledge, and are the best judges of who should be admitted into their ranks. One problem with the effort to reform teaching is that we often underestimate the character and the extent of the profession's specialized knowledge base.

Popular discussions and some reform programs characterize teaching's knowledge base as consisting of basic literacy skills, subject-matter knowledge, and general domain-independent teaching skills. Basic skills and mastery of the subject matter are important to skilled teaching, and unfortunately some teachers are not as expert in their subjects as we might like. Subject-matter expertise is not by itself a sufficient basis for skilled teaching, however. Many subject-matter experts have been miserable failures in the classroom.

The role of general domain-independent skills in effective teaching is the legacy of *process-product* research on teaching, a line of research that was heavily influenced by behaviorism. Process-product research looked at rather superficial characteristics of teachers' classroom behavior (process) and tried to correlate behaviors with student outcomes (product). (For a discussion, see Brophy 1986.) The researchers would look, for example, at how long a teacher would waited after asking a question for the students to respond or at the frequency with which teachers gave positive or negative responses to the students. This research discovered some interesting relationships between these domain-independent teacher behaviors and students' scores on standardized tests, but it didn't give deeper insights into why the relationships exist or into the mental processes skilled teachers use to regulate their classroom behavior.

Shulman argues that portraying teaching expertise solely in terms of basic skills, subject-matter mastery, and repertoires of general classroom behaviors seriously underestimates and trivializes it. Such a portrayal would not capture what makes Nancy extraordinary. It would never reveal that Nancy has a theory about literature and how to teach it, nor would it reveal how that theory guides Nancy in her lesson planning and in her teaching. Part of Nancy's expertise resides in her ability to manage subject-specific ideas and to choose specific teaching methods almost instantaneously in highly fluid classroom situations. How does Nancy prepare to teach? How does she reflect on and evaluate her performance? What goes on in Nancy's head as she teaches? What kinds of on-the-spot problem solving contribute to her virtuoso performances?

The Missing Research Program

By the mid 1970s, educational researchers such as Shulman realized that teaching research was still firmly rooted in behaviorism while much of behavioral science had become cognitive. They saw how cognitive theories and methods might address deficiencies in process-product research and help expand the knowledge base that the earlier research program had started to establish for teaching. The challenge became to find out how teachers' knowledge and reasoning guides their classroom behavior.

Gaea Leinhardt, a researcher at the Learning Research and Development Center who took up this challenge, claims that teaching is a most interesting and complex form of human problem solving. Leinhardt observes that teaching requires command of subject knowledge, pedagogical skills, sensitivity to the student audience, and the ability to integrate these almost instantaneously while standing at the front of a classroom. Each of the teacher's actions can immediately create a new learning opportunity or a new learning obstacle for the students. This makes teaching different from other kinds of problem solving that are usually considered difficult. As Leinhardt writes, "the physician diagnosing a patient or the aircraft mechanic inspecting a part does not have an instantaneous change to multiple patients or airplanes as a consequence of each move" (1990, p. 58).

An initial focus of research on teacher cognition has been the relation between teachers' knowledge of subject matter and their knowledge about how to teach that subject matter. We expect teachers to be expert in their subject areas. However, being an expert teacher requires subject-matter knowledge *plus* the skills to convey that knowledge to others. Shulman calls these necessary additional skills *pedagogical content knowledge* and notes that it includes knowledge of the most effective examples, analogies, and explanations for key topics in a domain. It includes "the ways of representing and formulating the subject that make it comprehensible to others" (Shulman 1986, p. 9). It includes the teacher's awareness of how students usually misunderstand topics, principles, and skills in a subject domain. It includes the teacher's understanding of the cognitive bottlenecks students might encounter on the road to mastery and the teacher's practical knowledge about how to help students negotiate them. The teacher, although a subject-matter expert, still must be able to see the subject as novices do. To Shulman (1987, p. 8), pedagogical content knowledge is at the heart of teaching's professional knowledge base; it is the distinct body of knowledge needed for expert teaching.

Shulman once called our relative ignorance of pedagogical content knowledge "the missing research program." Since the early 1980s, however, research on teacher cognition has revealed the central role of pedagogical content knowledge in teaching expertise. In the mid 1980s, Gaea Leinhardt, James Greeno, and Donald Smith published some of the first studies on how topic knowledge and teaching skills interact in effective teaching (Leinhardt and Smith 1985; Leinhardt and Greeno 1986). Their work illustrates both the flavor and the importance of such research.

Leinhardt and her co-workers conducted a series of expert-novice studies on how math teachers taught fractions to fourth-graders—a notoriously difficult task, according to most teachers. The novices were student teachers in their final semester of pre-service classroom training; the experts were experienced teachers whose students consistently showed great improvement in math achievement. Rather than just watch the teachers and count behaviors, the researchers had the teachers talk about and explain their planning and thinking. Before a lesson, the research team asked each teacher about her plans for that lesson. They then observed and videotaped the teacher while she taught. After class, they showed the videotapes to the teacher and had her comment on what she was doing and thinking while she taught. They found that every classroom lesson contained an *agenda, lesson segments,* and *explanations,* and that expert-novice differences in pedagogical content knowledge were evident in all three of those features.

The agenda is the teacher's mental lesson plan; it is the teacher's mental representation of the goals of the lesson and the strategies for achieving them. The agenda goes beyond the written lesson plan in content and detail, as the researchers found out when they asked teachers about their plans.

Here are two lesson agendas, one from a novice and one from an expert, reported in Leinhardt 1990a.

Novice: Well, I think when they get back from lunch I'm going to water them down and let them use the restroom to calm them, and then we're going to do . . . a little activity with erasers, paper clips, string, and books. And we're going to talk about pendulums and clocks. We're going to make a pendulum and then they're going to chart the differences between the amounts of swings and the length of the string.

Expert: We're hopefully going to work on finding the fractions of a set. Given eight objects—eight separate objects to find . . . one half of them, one fourth of them, as opposed to what we were doing last week, which was finding a fraction of one object.

Although the novice's agenda is longer than the expert's, it is more superficial. The novice's agenda begins with physical (using the restroom and getting a drink) rather than intellectual activity. She then lists activities and objects; however, she doesn't state a lesson goal, doesn't say how the objects relate to the goal, and doesn't say how this lesson builds on previous ones. The expert, in contrast, states the topic and the goal (finding fractions of a set) immediately, and connects the goal with previous lessons.

Leinhardt also found that experts' and novices' agendas differ in their sensitivity to the students and to their possible responses to the teacher and the lesson. The novice, though she uses the word "we", simply lists a set of activities she plans to present to the students. There is no mention of what the students might think and no inkling of what might go wrong with the lesson. Although the expert's agenda isn't explicit about the students' possible responses, there is an implicit recognition that the lesson might not go as envisioned. The expert teacher begins her agenda with "hopefully." She is aware that there may be divergences between her agenda and what the students will accomplish.

Typically, expert teachers think of a lesson on two parallel tracks: what they will do to teach the lesson and what cognitive responses the students may have to the lesson. Leinhardt (1990a, p. 33) writes: "The presence or absence of this parallel planning is an important aspect of forming an agenda. It shows a linkage between the content being taught and the kinds of learning behaviors that are likely to lead to acquiring the knowledge." Thus, these differences in the agendas of experts and novices are differences in pedagogical content knowledge. Experts, unlike novices, are constantly sensitive to how the students might misunderstand and are aware of what the cognitive bottlenecks might be. Experts attempt to see the lesson as a student might.

Lesson segments are classroom events in which the teacher and the students assume specific roles. A typical lesson includes a segment in which a transition occurs from the previous activity to the new lesson, followed by a segment in which new material is presented and explained, then a segment of guided practice in which the teacher helps students do the new skill, and finally monitored practice in which the teacher observes and corrects the students as they work independently. The particulars of lesson segments vary from subject to subject and even from topic to topic within a subject.

A most striking difference between expert and novice teachers is evident in a comparison of their day-to-day use of lesson segments. Experts move smoothly from transition to presentation to practice and from total teacher control to independent student work. Expert teachers incorporate *routines*—automatic set pieces in which the teacher and the students know their parts—into their lesson segments. Routines include activities as simple as passing out papers, correcting homework in class, and doing work at the blackboard. Routines free both the teacher and the students from worrying about the details of classroom management, so that all can concentrate on the lesson goal. Expert teachers run their lessons using routines in order to keep surprises at a minimum. Shulman's likening Nancy to a symphony conductor is most apt. Expert teachers have mastered a set of routines that guide their class performances, much as mastery of a score guides the conductor. The routines, like a score, provide a structure within which the teacher can use his or her creative talents to tailor lessons to the needs of particular classes and situations. In teaching, as in conducting, mastery of the underlying structure provides a vehicle for creative, nuanced interpretation.

In contrast, as Leinhardt and Greeno found, "a novice might give a lengthy lecture one day, endlessly fill in a chart of number facts on the blackboard the next day, and give two quizzes sandwiching a presentation on the third day" (1986, p. 94). Novices don't use well-practiced routines, and this makes life harder for both the teacher and the students. Without routines, the teacher has to tell the students what to do continually, which causes confusion, wastes time, and diverts attention away from the lesson itself.

Expert-novice differences in lesson organization also reflect differences (at a general level) in pedagogical content knowledge. Experts implicitly know that the specifics of a topic presentation influence how the students will understand it. The topic representation should be the focus of the lesson, so that both the teacher and the students will be able to devote their limited cognitive resources to this representation. Experts, unlike novices, use their teaching skills and routines to reduce the cognitive noise surrounding a lesson, so the students can concentrate on the lesson goal. "Skilled teachers' mastery of routine makes creative cognition possible in their teaching," as Shulman says.

Explanation is the heart of a lesson. Expert teachers differ fundamentally from novices on this core aspect of lesson presentation

(Leinhardt 1989). In explanation, the teacher uses content knowledge plus pedagogical skills to help the students build a bridge from what they already know to what they should be learning. It is crucial to begin the explanation with things the students already know. In Leinhardt's study of fourth-grade math classes, 88 percent of the expert teachers used in their explanations ideas and examples that the students knew from previous lessons. None of the novices did. For example, one novice teacher tried to use the number line to explain the difference between 9 × 3 (nine steps, each three units long) and 3 × 9 (three steps, each nine units long). The children had never before used the number line this way, so the explanation was useless and confusing. Leinhardt comments: "Experts, in general, tend to use something familiar to teach something new, whereas novices often use something new to teach something new" (1989, p. 66). The expert has a grasp of the most effective examples, analogies, and explanations for various topics in the domain and chooses which ones to use on the basis of the students' prior understanding.

Novices often seem unaware of what is difficult about a topic or a procedure, and their explanations often fail for this reason. Leinhardt gives this example: In explaining how to reduce a fraction such as $\frac{28}{63}$ to its lowest terms, an expert teacher explained to her students that the word "reduce" meant they would have to divide, and that the hard part is choosing the best divisor. A novice didn't realize, or at least didn't explain, that the hard part is picking the divisor; she simply told the students what number to use. The novice failed to see the problem as the students did, and failed to appreciate what the cognitive bottleneck was for her students. Here, again, the expert showed superior pedagogical content knowledge.

Teaching and Knowledge Transforming

The above are just a few examples taken from one set of studies to show how investigators are beginning to fill in the missing research program. Our understanding of teaching's knowledge base and of the importance of pedagogical content knowledge will continue to expand. Efforts are underway to apply the results to both the training and the evaluation of teachers (Grover et al. 1989; Leinhardt 1990a,b). We are beginning to understand why some teachers are effective and to see that there is more to teaching than literacy skills, subject-matter competence, and domain-independent teaching skills. With these realizations, we should be able to take our assessments of teacher competence beyond subject-matter expertise and into the realm of pedagogical content knowledge. Teacher assessments should ask questions about students' misconceptions in (say) biology, physics, or multi-digit arithmetic and about the strategies and representations that would be most effective in correcting those misconceptions. Success on these tests would require that teachers understand student cognition and how to improve it. As Shulman says (1986, p. 10), such tests would "distinguish between a biology major and a biology teacher" and thus assess the abilities that are unique to the teaching professional.

Research on teacher cognition suggests many parallels between expert teaching and expert writing. Teaching, like writing, presents ill-structured problems for which there are not unique, best solutions. Expert teachers, like expert writers, define and refine their problem as they respond to an ever-changing task environment of 20 to 30 children, each unique in learning style, motivation, and prior subject-matter understanding. Expert teachers, like expert writers, solve their problems while always keeping their audience and its response in mind. Expert teachers do not present material exactly as they recall it from their memories. Lesson agendas, segments, and explanations show that expert teachers integrate content knowledge with audience knowledge, just as expert writers do. Whereas the writer uses rhetorical knowledge, the teacher calls on pedagogical content knowledge. Expert teachers have pedagogical schemas, skills, and routines just as expert writers have rhetorical schemas, skills, and routines. Expert teaching, like expert writing, results in the effective communication of a gist to an audience—a gist that allows students to build representations of domain knowledge.

The new research program is beginning to describe what Nancy knows, and we are beginning to understand what Nancy does in the classroom: Like all expert teachers, Nancy *transforms knowledge*. As Shulman says (1987, p. 20), "A proper understanding of the knowledge base of teaching, the sources of that knowledge, and the complexities of the pedagogical process will make the emergence of such teachers more likely."

9

Changing Our Representations: Thinking of Education in New Ways

Two railway stations are 50 miles apart. At 2 o'clock one Saturday afternoon the trains, one from each station, start toward each other. As the first train pulls out of its station, a bird springs into the air in front of it and flies ahead to the front of the second train. When the bird reaches the second train, it turns and flies back to the first train. The bird continues to fly between the trains until they meet. If the trains travel at a rate of 25 miles per hour and the bird flies at 100 miles per hour, how many miles will the bird have flown when the trains meet?

Michael Posner (1973, p. 150) used this problem to illustrate how important initial representations are when one is trying to solve problems. As he points out, if you represent the problem initially in terms of the *distance* the bird flies, you have to calculate the distance the bird covers on each round trip and the problem becomes difficult. If you represent it initially in terms of the *time* the bird spends flying, the problem is trivial. It takes the trains one hour to meet (initially 50 miles apart, they move at a closing speed of 25 + 25 = 50 mph). The bird flies at 100 mph; thus, the bird flies 100 miles.

In the previous chapters, we have often seen that how one first thinks about a problem can determine how difficult it is to solve. Sometimes, as with the nine-dot problem, a poor initial representation makes it impossible to solve a problem. With ill-structured problems, such as writing, the initial representation can influence not only how we solve the problem but also what we take to be a satisfactory answer. Educational reform is a complex, ill-structured problem that many of us are trying to help solve. How we think about it will determine the problem's difficulty and will influence what we take to be an adequate solution.

A Science of Learning in the Classroom

My argument has been that cognitive science can help us think about our educational problem. Cognitive science can help expand our educational problem space—it can help us see new possibilities and search for solutions in new ways.

Scientists look for simple, consistent schemas that can explain multiple phenomena. Cognitive scientists bring their simple, consistent schemas to the varied phenomena of our mental lives. On their theory, the human cognitive architecture manipulates symbolic representations to solve problems. Using the schemas of cognitive science, we can describe much of our conscious mental activity—doing math, planning trips, writing essays, teaching elementary school math—as problem solving. In activities as different as solving balance-scale problems and teaching in a classroom, we apply operators to transform representations into problem solutions that guide our actions.

Starting with Siegler's balance-scale studies, we have seen the power and the utility of applying these schemas to problems in learning and teaching. Children learn by constructing, elaborating, and modifying representations. Knowledge is constructed by learners, not transmitted by teachers. Learning is active, not passive. Applying the cognitivists' schemas, methods, and insights across a variety of domains and across all age groups results in Glaser's developmental psychology of performance changes—a new, cognitive theory of learning.

Based on this research, Siegler and others rightly counsel us to teach the appropriate representations. Among the representations we should teach are the facts that underlie domain expertise. But, as the research shows, teaching just the facts is not enough. If children are to learn the appropriate representations, which include both schemas and production rules, we also have to teach them general strategies (weak methods) and teach them to be aware of and to control their mental processing (metacognition).

Representations, strategies, and metacognitive skills are all elements of human intelligence. If we can successfully incorporate these elements into school instruction, we can help children learn the subject matter. More important, we can help them become intelligent novices. If school subjects are taught as high-order cognitive skills, more children will attain the higher NAEP proficiencies. We can teach children how to learn if we change our representations of intelligence and learning.

Teaching, too, is a form of problem solving, and one that requires unique knowledge and skills. The knowledge base for teaching goes beyond mastery of the subject matter; teachers also must know how to teach the subject matter. This realization should prompt a change in how we think about the teaching profession. We often hear the claim, from the lay public and from some educators, that teaching is an art and that even good teachers don't always know what they are doing. Teaching is indeed an art, and good teachers may not know what they are doing, but that doesn't mean we can't find out what they are doing.

Expert teachers, like experts in other domains, have implicit knowledge—knowledge they are no longer aware of because it is so highly practiced and automatic. Cognitive research can make the expert's implicit knowledge explicit. What Shulman called "the missing research program" is now making effective teaching practices explicit. If we can describe the expert practices explicitly, we can incorporate them into teacher training programs.

If we change our representations of intelligence, learning, and teaching, we can change the interactions between students and teachers in the classroom. This is where the restructuring of our schools must begin. We can have new learning environments based on cognitive principles, but many of us—superintendents, principals, political and business leaders, parents—may have to change our representations of what classrooms and schools should look like. An improved learning environment that applies what we know about learning and teaching may not be a classroom where a teacher lectures, where children sit quietly in rows working alone on the same assignment, and where students perform for teachers on multiple-choice tests or on knowledge-telling writing assignments. It may be a classroom in which children work in groups (as with CSILE), or at their own pace (as with GPTutor), or with the most able remedial reader leading the group (as in some of the reciprocal teaching experiments). The teacher may not be the focus of attention in these classrooms. Students may get different assignments, have opportunities to correct their work, and be graded on effort and personal advancement rather than on a single standard. We may have to get over the idea that good schools should be like the ones we attended.

Is this a realistic vision for education? Will interventions based on cognitive science work in ordinary classrooms? These are legitimate concerns. It is true that some of the most impressive demonstrations of an applied science of learning have occurred in situations where researchers are in the classroom and where hundreds of thousands of dollars in outside support are available. Some might argue that almost any intervention could be made to work under these circumstances. What would happen in ordinary classrooms that lack these resources?

There are at least three replies to such concerns. First, new interventions derived from basic research in any field will work better under controlled experimental conditions than in the real world. In this respect, educational research is no different from medical and agricultural research—research driven by the desire to find real-world applications. Second, whether or not a medical or an educational innovation will work in the real world can't be answered in the abstract. The only way to find out is to try it, first in the lab, then in the clinic, and finally in daily practice. Third, there are examples in the chapters above of new ideas and methods working in ordinary classrooms with no immediate support from a research team.

Reciprocal Teaching continues in Springfield, Illinois, and it has been adopted by other school systems around the United States. Palincsar and Brown have moved on to other educational problems. Although the evaluation is still in progress, Jasper appears to work in a wide variety of ordinary classrooms with minimal technical support and no direct involvement of the research team. And curriculum designers and teachers are applying other insights from cognitive research—the importance of automaticity for word recognition in reading, the importance of background knowledge for reading comprehension, and ideas about how to teach vocabulary more effectively—with no help from the research community.

Admittedly, some of the other examples are not yet that far along. Attempts to see how well Minstrell's physics curriculum and CSILE work in classrooms without the direct control and supervision of the innovators have just started. Other interventions—Case and Griffin's remedial arithmetic modules, ThinkerTools, and dynamic assessment, for example—are in earlier stages of research and development. The examples taken together, though, support the claim that these efforts should continue and that we should search for additional applications of cognitive science in the classroom.

It is a fact the designing, developing, and testing such applications may cost hundreds of thousands of dollars each. If we want to improve our schools, and if existing methods aren't working, we have little choice but to make this investment.

Representations of Research

To solve our educational problems, then, we also must change our representations of the importance and the role of educational research. Even among other scientists, educational research is often held in low esteem. Yet sound theory and solid research generate compelling applications. Research, both basic and applied, is as important to educational practice as it is to medical practice.

In contrast with medical research, which many people want to know about and whose outcomes many want immediate access to, there is little interest in educational research and little awareness that it contributes to instructional advances. The brief history and the legacy of the National Institute of Education serve as an example. This federal agency was started during the Nixon administration and gutted during the Reagan years. The NIE lacked a viable political constituency, partly because of the research community's inability to reach out to the political leadership on terms that politicians could understand and appreciate (Graham 1992). Although many perceive the NIE as a failure, it helped make a science of learning possible.

Patricia Graham, now president of the Spencer Foundation and a former director of the NIE, relates that during the 1970s it was hard to find any serious researchers or funding agencies interested in schools. The NIE began supporting the work of people such as Lauren Resnick and Lee Shulman—investigators who were interested in schools—in the late 1970s. We have seen where that research has led. The NIE supported much of the work discussed above on reading comprehension and thinking skills. This defunct agency, generally thought of as a failure, anticipated the policy and practice needs of the 1980s and the 1990s. We are now applying in our schools the research this agency funded 15 years ago. Unfortunately, there is now no comparable agency anticipating the educational needs of the early 21st century.

If we want to improve our schools, now and in the future, we need a research base. Research isn't free. Many of the methods described in this book are time consuming and labor intensive. As

Alan Schoenfeld noted, a cognitive scientist may well spend 100 hours analyzing a 1-hour videotape from a problem-solving session, and 2 or 3 years writing a computer simulation. Little of the research described here could have occurred without the support of federal agencies and private foundations. Yet support for educational research is shockingly small.

In 1988 the Department of Defense spent $39 billion on research and development, the National Institutes of Health $5.5 billion, the National Aeronautics and Space Administration $4.2 billion, the National Science Foundation $1.6 billion, and the Department of Agriculture $1 billion. In the same year, the Department of Education spent $130 *million*—about 0.6 percent of its budget—on research and development. In 1990 it spent $153 million, again 0.6 percent of its budget. In real, inflation-adjusted dollars, federal funding for educational research has decreased 80 percent over the last 15 years (Sheekey 1988). We wouldn't tolerate this in the case of medical or defense-related research, because we believe research in those areas contributes to our national and personal well-being. Apparently, we don't believe this about educational research.

There are over 7500 private foundations with assets over $1 million and annual giving of at least $100,000 in the United States. The annual expenditure of all private foundations for all purposes is approximately $8 billion. The Foundation Index, a computerized database that records foundation grants awarded since 1973, lists 158 grants to support cognitive science. Of these grants made over 20 years, only 23 supported cognitive research that addressed instructional issues in pre-collegiate education. The total value of these grants was $2.8 million. As of this writing, only four private foundations have programs that fund research on applications of cognitive science to school instruction.

Educational research is crucial. We need it to solve our problem. But we're not funding it. Lee Shulman describes one way in which our representations must change: "We have to work hard to detoxify the idea of supporting educational research."

Solving an Ill-Structured Problem

Our educational problem is, of course, different from the nine-dot, the bird-and-trains, or the balance-scale problem. Those problems have standard representations and definitive answers. We can learn rules or algorithms, such as Siegler's rule IV, to solve problems like those. The education problem, in contrast, is an ill-structured problem—there is no standard solution path, no algorithm, no single best answer. Solving the education problem is more like writing a convincing persuasive essay on a difficult topic.

Planning is important when one is trying to solve an ill-structured problem. We plan carefully; then we start to implement the plan. When we begin to see the results—in writing, when we see the words on the page—we often revise our plan. When we revise our plan, we also change our understanding of what a suitable solution might be. We become enmeshed in a recursive process, in which our plans influence our actions and our actions influence our plans. In such a process, we constantly redefine our problem and modify our goals.

We should think about education this way, too. If educational reform presents an ill-structured problem, we shouldn't be looking for *the* solution. There isn't one. There is nothing that we can take off the shelf to solve the problem, nor is there much hope of finding the ideal curriculum or pedagogical method. Rather than search for a nonexistent algorithm, we should focus on the process—education as process, rather than product. How can we organize ourselves so that we can continually find out more about learning and put that knowledge into practice? We need a system, a process, in which our understanding and our educational practice can constantly evolve.

Here, too, an analogy with writing is apt. In education we need the analogues of planning, translating, and revising. For education, basic and applied research are at the heart of the planning process. For the most part, such research originates in universities. Translation takes place in the classroom and depends on the practical expertise of classroom professionals. Revision entails comparing the latest translation with the current plan, and it usually results in refinement of the plan.

For education, revision—the interaction between research and practice—can occur only if there is close professional collaboration between researchers and classroom teachers. In this professional collaboration, teachers should be involved in ways that go beyond just translating theory into practice. In writing, to solve rhetorical problems, we have to combine topic knowledge with audience knowledge. Researchers know about (say) the cognitive capacities of children, but often lack the rich understanding of the audience that comes from daily classroom experience. Teachers have pedagogical content knowledge; researchers often do not. If we want to transform our research knowledge, we have to bring these two domains of expertise together. Thus, classroom teachers should be involved in the planning process, collaborating with researchers in designing and conducting instructional research.

We have seen several examples—Jasper and reciprocal teaching, to name two—of what can happen when such collaboration occurs. Part of our problem is that we don't have a system to foster and support such collaboration. We are barely supporting the research, let alone systematic collaborations between the research and teaching communities. Collaborations between researchers and schools occur on a small scale, usually confined to a single research project in a single school or classroom for a short period of time. Even these interactions often depend on the personal good will of teachers and researchers and the benign neglect of administrators. Jasper and reciprocal teaching were able to move beyond these limitations not because we had a system that encouraged interested teachers and committed researchers to scale up their projects, but because there happened to be a Joe Wyatt or a Kathryn Ransom around who had a larger vision—a serendipitous occurrence and hardly a system.

In thinking about educational reform, we should think about a system of research, teacher training, and practice in which the components are highly interactive and constantly evolving. We need such a system to support the process of solving our ill-structured educational problem. As we work on the problem, our understanding of it will change, our teaching practices will change, and our educational goals and expectations will change. Not having such a system has contributed to our current educational problem. Over the past 20 years our educational goals and expectations have changed, but our understanding and our practices haven't. It appears unlikely that we will attain our new goals unless we change our representations and implement new practices based on them.

Knowing Why

Knowing why is a theme that has appeared, with variations, throughout this book. Lauren Resnick said that cognitive research can tell us why instruction works. The new synthesis showed the importance of teaching children why general problem-solving and learning strategies work. Isabel Beck, her colleagues, and others have dedicated their careers to research that helps explain to teachers why children learn as they do. It would be useful to have diagnostic tests that tell us why some students can't master some aspects of math, science, reading, or writing. The value of educational research—cognitive research in particular—is that it can tell us why.

Successful school reform depends on knowing why. The National Academy of Education's report "Research and the Renewal of Education" states that current efforts to implement broad-based school reforms will fail without adequate research to guide the direction of change (James 1991). We need change because, as was succinctly stated by Diane Ravitch in chapter 1 above, what was good enough 20 years ago isn't good enough today. She is as succinct in stating what is needed to solve our problem: "To push for change without continuing to deepen our understanding of what we are doing will only intensify the problems we seek to solve. We need solid research to tell us which experiments work best and under what conditions. . . ." (NCATE 1992, p. 7)

If we are to have a successful national policy to improve our schools, we must all try to understand why. Just as we should all have a better understanding of physics and geometry, we should all have a better understanding of education, learning, and teaching. If we are to be a nation informed, rather than a nation at risk, we have to transform our informal, fragmented, local, and often inconsistent education schemas into more expert-like representations.

Suggested Reading

If you are new to the field and want to learn more about cognition and education, you might want to start with the following books written for a general audience. Howard Gardner's *The Mind's New Science: a History of the Cognitive Revolution* (Basic Books, 1985) provides a good introduction. In his most recent book, *The Unschooled Mind: How Children Think and Schools Should Teach* (Basic Books, 1991), Gardner describes how his theory of multiple intelligences can be applied in the classroom. Philip Johnson-Laird's *The Computer and the Mind: An Introduction to Cognitive Science* (Harvard University Press, 1988) explains how computational theory contributes to our understanding of human cognition. Morton Hunt's *The Universe Within: A New Science Explores the Human Mind* (Simon & Schuster, 1982) is an older, popular introduction to cognitive science. Herbert A. Simon's scientific autobiography, *Models of My Life* (Basic Books, 1991), presents the cognitive revolution as seen 30 years later by one of the revolutionaries.

There are several good books on problem solving and thinking skills. Two of the best are *The Complete Problem Solver*, by John R. Hayes (second edition: Erlbaum, 1989) and *The Teaching of Thinking*, by Raymond S. Nickerson, David N. Perkins, and Edward E. Smith (Erlbaum, 1985).

If you want to explore further, there are several readable textbooks. Two of them are John R. Anderson's *Cognitive Psychology and its Implications* (Freeman, 1985) and Arnold L. Glass and Keith J. Holyoak's *Cognition* (Random House, 1986).

For readers interested in cognitive development, Robert S. Siegler's *Children's Thinking* (Prentice-Hall, 1986) relates what cognitive methods have revealed about children's mental development. *Mechanisms of Cognitive Development*, edited by Robert J. Sternberg (Freeman, 1984), contains articles by a variety of authors on aspects of children's cognitive development. *Concepts, Kinds, and Cognitive Development*, by Frank J. Keil (MIT Press, 1989) is becoming a popular text for undergraduate courses on cognitive development.

Most of these books also contain excellent suggestions for further reading.

Readers interested in classroom applications would do best to scan the bibliography of the present volume for articles in the education journals, such as *Educational Researcher, Review of Educational Research, Mathematics Teacher, The Reading Teacher, Reading Research Quarterly,* and *College Composition and Communication.* Articles in these journals provide references to the basic research behind the applications, most of which is reported in the journals *Cognition, Cognitive Science, Cognitive Psychology,* and *Cognition and Instruction.*

The October 1986 *American Psychologist* (volume 41, number 10) was a special issue on psychological science and education. The review articles in that issue cover all the topics addressed in this book and more. They contain extensive references to basic and applied research and to published accounts of classroom applications.

Notes

Chapter 2

1. Here is one possible solution to the nine-dot problem:

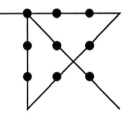

Chapter 4

1. Shen Lin, a mathematician, explained to me in about 30 seconds why casting out nines works. Why is it that when you take the *sum* of digits in a decimal number and divide by 9 the remainder is the same as when you *divide* the original number by 9? Casting out nines is an application of modular arithmetic. In modular arithmetic, a number is equal to its remainder after division by the modulus. For example, to find 11 modulo 3, divide 11 by 3, which equals 3 remainder 2. So, $11 \bmod 3 = 2$. Now notice that any multiple of 10 can be written as $(N \times 10)$. If we choose 9 as the modulus, then

$$(N \times 10) \bmod 9 = (N \bmod 9) \times (10 \bmod 9) = N/9 \times 1 = N/9.$$

In the decimal number system, we represent all numbers as multiples of 10. In the example,

$$237 = (2 \times 10^2) + (3 \times 10^1) + (7 \times 10^0).$$

Therefore, $237 \bmod 9 = (2 + 3 + 7) \bmod 9 = 3$. In other words, dividing a decimal number by 9 gives the same remainder as dividing the sum of it digits by 9. This is why casting out nines works. This is a general number-theoretic result. Indeed, in a base-N number system, casting out $N - 1$'s works.

2. Answers to the buggy subtraction problems follow.

   (a) This bug is called Smaller-from-Larger:

       731
     −452
       321

   (b) This bug is Borrow-from-Zero:

       307
     −168
       239

   (c) This bug is called Borrow-Across-Zero:

       504
     −199
       395

How the bugs work and how children invent them are explained in the section "Marrying Concepts to Procedures."

Chapter 5

1. Answers to the physics quiz:

   1. C
   2. (i) B; (ii) C
   3. 10 lb
   4. 1.0 sec

Chapter 6

1. Isabel Beck attributes this example to John Carroll.

Bibliography

Ames, C. A. 1990. Motivation: What teachers need to know. *Teachers College Record* 91: 409–421.

Anderson, J. R. 1985. *Cognitive Psychology and Its Implications,* second edition. Freeman.

Anderson, J. R., Boyle, C. F., and Yost, G. 1985. The geometry tutor. In Proceedings of the Ninth International Joint Conference on Artificial Intelligence.

Anderson, T. H. 1980. Study strategies and adjunct aids. In R. J. Spiro, B. C. Bruce, and W. F. Brewer, eds., *Theoretical Issues in Reading Comprehension.* Erlbaum.

Applebee, A. N. 1984. Writing and reasoning. *Review of Educational Research* 54(4): 577–596.

Applebee, A. N. 1986. Problems in process approaches: Toward a reconceptualization of process instruction. In D. Bartholmae and A. R. Petrosky, eds., *The Teaching of Writing.* University of Chicago Press.

Applebee, A. N., Langer, J. A., Mullis, I. V. S., and Jenkins, L. B. 1990. *The Writing Report Card, 1984–88: Findings from the Nation's Report Card.* Office of Educational Research and Improvement, US Department of Education.

Baddeley, A. 1992. Working memory. *Science* 255: 556–559.

Baillargeon, R. 1986. Representing the existence and the location of hidden objects: Object permanence in 6- and 8-month-old infants. *Cognition* 23: 21–41.

Beck, I. L. 1981. Reading problems and instructional practices. In T. S. Waller and G. E. MacKinnon, eds., *Reading Research: Advances in Theory and Practice,* volume 2. Academic Press.

Beck, I. L., and Carpenter, P. A. 1986. Cognitive approaches to understanding reading. *American Psychologist* 41(10): 1098–1105.

Beck, I. L., and McKeown, M. G. 1983. Learning words well—a program to enhance vocabulary and comprehension. *Reading Teacher* 36: 622–625.

Beck, I. L., McKeown, M., McCaslin, E., and Burkes, A. 1979. Instructional dimensions that may affect reading comprehension: Examples from two commercial reading programs. Publication 1979/20, Learning Research and Development Center, University of Pittsburgh.

Beck, I. L., McKeown, M. G., and Omanson, R. C. 1987. The effects and uses of diverse vocabulary instructional techniques. In M. G. McKeown and M. E. Curtis, eds., *The Nature of Vocabulary Acquisition.* Erlbaum.

Beck, I. L., McKeown, M. G, Sinatra, G. M., and Loxterman, J. A. 1991. Revising social studies text from a text-processing perspective: Evidence of improved comprehensibility. *Reading Research Quarterly* 26: 251–276.

Beck, I. L., Omanson, R. C., and McKeown, M. G. 1982. An instructional redesign of reading lessons: Effects on comprehension. *Reading Research Quarterly* 17: 462–481.

Beck, I. L., Perfetti, C. A., and McKeown, M. G. 1982. Effects of long-term vocabulary instruction on lexical access and reading comprehension. *Journal of Educational Psychology* 74(4): 506–521.

Bereiter, C., and Scardamalia, M. 1982. From conversation to composition: The role of instruction in a developmental process. In R. Glaser, ed., *Advances in Instructional Psychology,* volume 2. Erlbaum.

Bereiter, C., and Scardamalia, M. 1985. Cognitive coping strategies and the problem of "inert knowledge." In S. F. Chipman, J. W. Segal, and R. Glaser, eds., *Thinking and Learning Skills,* volume 2: *Research and Open Questions.* Erlbaum.

Bransford, J. D., Franks, J. J., Vye, N. J., and Sherwood, R. D. 1989. New approaches to instruction: Because wisdom can't be told. In S. Vosniadou and A. Ortony, eds., *Similarity and Analogical Reasoning.* Cambridge University Press.

Bransford, J. D., Goldman, S. R., Hasselbring, T., and Pellegrino, J. W. n.d. Invitations to Thinking II: Designs for Generative Learning. Proposal submitted to James S. McDonnell Foundation.

Bransford, J. D., Hasselbring, T., Barron, B., Kulewicz, S., Littlefield, J., and Goin, L. 1988. Uses of macro-contexts to facilitate mathematical thinking. In R. Charles and E. Silver, eds., *Teaching and Evaluating Mathematical Thinking.* National Council of Teachers of Mathematics.

Bransford, J. D., and Johnson, M. K. 1972. Contextual prerequisites for understanding: Some investigations of comprehension and recall. *Journal of Verbal Learning and Verbal Behavior* 11: 717–726.

Bransford, J. D., Sherwood, R., Vye, N., and Rieser, J. 1986. Teaching thinking and problem solving. *American Psychologist* 41(10): 1078–1089.

Bransford, J. D., and Stein, B. S. 1984. *The IDEAL problem solver.* Freeman.

Bransford, J. D., Stein, B. S., Arbitman-Smith, R., and Vye, N. J. 1985. Improving thinking and learning skills: An analysis of three approaches. In J. W. Segal, S. F. Chipman, and R. Glaser, eds., *Thinking and Learning Skills*, volume 1: *Relating Instruction to Research*. Erlbaum.

Bransford, J. D., Stein, B. S., Vye, N. J., Franks, J. J., Auble, P. M., Mezynski, K. J., and Perfetto, G. A. 1982. Differences in approaches to learning: An overview. *Journal of Experimental Psychology: General* 111: 390–398.

Brewer, W. F., and Treyens, J. C. 1981. Role of schemata in memory for places. *Cognitive Psychology* 13: 207–230.

Briars, D., and Siegler, R. 1984. A featural analysis of preschoolers' counting knowledge. *Developmental Psychology* 20: 607–618.

Britton, J., Burgess, T., Martin, N., McLeod, A., and Rosen, H. 1975. *The Development of Writing Abilities*. Macmillan.

Brophy, J. 1986. Teacher influences on student achievement. *American Psychologist* 41: 1069–1077.

Brown, A. L. 1985. Mental orthopedics, the training of cognitive skills: An interview with Alfred Binet. In S. F. Chipman, J. W. Segal, and R. Glaser, eds., *Thinking and Learning Skills*, volume 2: *Research and Open Questions*. Erlbaum.

Brown, A. L. 1989. Analogical learning and transfer: What develops? In S. Vosniadou and A. Ortony, eds., *Similarity and Analogical Reasoning*. Cambridge University Press.

Brown, A. L. 1990. Domain-specific principles affect learning and transfer in children. *Cognitive Science* 14: 107–133.

Brown, A. L., Bransford, J. D., Ferrara, R. A., and Campione, J. C. 1983. Learning, remembering, and understanding. In P. H. Mussen, ed., *Handbook of Child Psychology*, volume 3: *Cognitive Development*. Wiley.

Brown, A. L., Campione, J. C., and Barclay, C. R. 1979. Training self-checking routines for estimating test readiness: Generalization from list learning to prose recall. *Child Development* 50: 501–512.

Brown, A. L., Campione, J. C., and Day, J. D. 1981. Learning to learn: On training students to learn from texts. *Educational Researcher* 10: 14–21.

Brown, A. L., and DeLoache, J. S. 1978. Skills, plans, and self-regulation. In R. S. Siegler, ed., *Children's Thinking: What Develops?* Erlbaum.

Brown, A. L., and Palincsar, A. S. 1982. Inducing strategic learning from text by means of informed, self-control training. *Topics in Learning and Learning Disabilities* 2: 1–17.

Brown, A. L., and Palincsar, A. S. 1987. Reciprocal teaching of comprehension strategies: A natural history of one program for enhancing learning. In J. D. Day and J. G. Borkowski, eds., *Intelligence and Exceptionality: New Directions for Theory, Assessment, and Instructional Practices*. Ablex.

Brown, A. L., and Palincsar, A. S. 1989. Guided, cooperative learning and individual knowledge acquisition. In L. B. Resnick, ed., *Knowing, Learning, and Instruction: Essays in Honor of Robert Glaser.* Erlbaum.

Brown, J. S., and Burton, R. R. 1978. Diagnostic models for procedural bugs in basic mathematical skills. *Cognitive Science* 2: 155–192.

Burtis, P. J., Bereiter, C., Scardamalia, M., and Tetroe, J. 1983. The development of planning in writing. In B. M. Kroll and G. Wells, eds., *Explorations in the Development of Writing.* Wiley.

Campione, J. C., and Brown, A. L. 1990. Guided learning and transfer: Implications for approaches to assessment. In N. Frederiksen, R. Glaser, A. Lesgold, and M. Shafto, eds., *Diagnostic Monitoring of Skill and Knowledge Acquisition.* Erlbaum.

Carey, L. J., and Flower, L. 1989. Foundations for Creativity in the Writing Process: Rhetorical Representations of Ill-Defined Problems. Technical report 32, Center for the Study of Writing, University of California at Berkeley and Carnegie Mellon University.

Carey, L., Flower, L., Hayes, J. R., Schriver, K. A., and Haas, C. 1989. Differences in Writers' Initial Task Representations. Technical report 35, Center for the Study of Writing, University of California at Berkeley and Carnegie Mellon University.

Carey, S. 1985. *Conceptual Change in Childhood.* MIT Press.

Carnegie Council on Adolescent Development. 1989. Turning Points: Preparing American Youth for the 21st Century. Washington, DC.

Case, R. n.d. Rightstart: An Early Intervention Program to Improve Children's First Formal Learning of Arithmetic. (Interim report submitted to James S. McDonnell Foundation in October 1989.)

Case, R., and Griffin, S. 1990. Child cognitive development: The role of control conceptual structures in the development of scientific thought. In C. A. Hauert, ed., *Developmental Psychology: Cognitive, Perceptuo-Motor, and Neurophysiological Perspectives.* North-Holland.

Case, R., and Griffin, S. n.d. Rightstart: An Early Intervention Program for Insuring that Children's First Formal Learning of Arithmetic is Grounded in Their Intuitive Knowledge of Number. (Year 2 report submitted to James S. McDonnell Foundation, in November 1990.)

Chall, J. 1983. *Learning to Read: The Great Debate,* second edition. McGraw-Hill.

Chase, W. G., and Ericsson, K. A. 1981. Skilled memory. In J. R. Anderson, ed., *Cognitive Skills and Their Acquisition.* Erlbaum.

Chase, W. G., and Simon, H. A. 1973. Perception in chess. *Cognitive Psychology* 4: 55–81.

Chi, M. T. H., Glaser, R., and Rees, E. 1982. Expertise in problem solving. In R. Sternberg, ed., *Advances in the Psychology of Human Intelligence,* volume 1. Erlbaum.

Chipman, S. F. 1992. The higher-order cognitive skills: What they are and how they might be transmitted. In T. G. Sticht, B. A. McDonald, and M. J. Beeler, eds., *The Intergenerational Transfer of Cognitive Skills*. Ablex.

Chipman, S. F., Segal, J. W., and Glaser, R. 1985. *Thinking and Learning Skills*, volume 2: *Research and Open Questions*. Erlbaum.

Chomsky, N. 1956. Three models for the description of language. *IRE Transactions of Information Theory* 2–3: 113–124.

Clement, J. 1982. Students' preconceptions in introductory mechanics. *American Journal of Physics* 50: 66–71.

Cognition and Technology Group at Vanderbilt. 1991. The Jasper series: A generative approach to improving mathematical thinking. In *This Year in School Science*. American Association for the Advancement of Science.

Covington, M. V. 1985. Strategic thinking and the fear of failure. In J. W. Segal, S. F. Chipman, and R. Glaser, eds., *Thinking and Learning Skills*, volume 1: *Relating Instruction to Research*. Erlbaum.

Daneman, M., and Carpenter, P. A. 1980. Individual differences in working memory and reading. *Journal of Verbal Learning and Verbal Behavior* 19: 450–466.

De Groot, A. D. 1965. *Thought and Choice in Chess*. Mouton.

Diener, C. I., and Dweck, C. S. 1978. An analysis of learned helplessness: Continuous changes in performance, strategy, and achievement cognitions following failure. *Journal of Personality and Social Psychology* 36: 451–462.

Diener, C. I., and Dweck, C. S. 1980. An analysis of learned helplessness II: The processing of success. *Journal of Personality and Social Psychology* 39: 940–952.

diSessa, A. A. 1982. Unlearning Aristotelian Physics: A study of knowledge-based learning. *Cognitive Science* 6: 37–75.

Donaldson, L. 1989. A learning partnership: The social studies and collaborative planning. In *Planning to Write, Notes on Collaborative Planning*, ERIC document ED335682, January 1992.

Dossey, J. A., Mullis, I. V. S., Lindquist, M. M., and Chamber, D. L. 1988. *The Mathematics Report Card: Are We Measuring Up?* Educational Testing Service.

Doyle, D. P. 1989. Endangered Species: Children of Promise. *Business Week* white paper, October.

Dweck, C. S., and Reppucci, N. D. 1973. Learned helplessness and reinforcement responsibility in children. *Journal of Personality and Social Psychology* 25: 109–116.

Emig, J. 1971. The Composing Process of Twelfth Graders. Research report 13, National Council of Teachers of English.

Ernst, G. W., and Newell, A. 1969. *GPS: A Case Study in General Problem Solving*. Academic Press.

Feldman, S. S., and Eliot, G. R., eds. 1990. *At the Threshold: The Developing Adolescent*. Harvard University Press.

Ferrara, R. A. 1987. Learning Mathematics in the Zone of Proximal Development: The Importance of Flexible Use of Knowledge. Ph.D. Thesis, University of Illinois, Urbana-Champaign.

Feuerstein, R., Hoffman, M. B., Jensen, M. R., and Rand, Y. 1985. Instrumental enrichment, an intervention program for structural cognitive modifiability: Theory and practice. In J. W. Segal, S. F. Chipman, and R. Glaser, eds., *Thinking and Learning Skills,* volume 1: *Relating Instruction to Research*. Erlbaum.

Flavell, J. H. 1979. Metacognition and cognitive monitoring: A new area of cognitive-developmental inquiry. *American Psychologist* 34(10): 906–911.

Flavell, J. H., and Wellman, H. M. 1977. Metamemory. In R. V. Kail, Jr., and J. W. Hagen, eds., *Perspectives on the Development of Memory and Cognition*. Erlbaum.

Flower, L. 1989. Cognition, context, and theory building. *College Composition and Communication* 40(3): 282–311.

Flower, L. 1989b. Writers planning: Four snapshots from research. In *Planning to Write: Notes on Collaborative Planning,* ERIC document ED335682, January 1992.

Flower, L., and Hayes, J. R. 1980. The dynamics of composing: Making plans and juggling constraints. In L. W. Gregg and E. R. Steinberg, eds., *Cognitive Processes in Writing*. Erlbaum.

Flower, L., and Hayes, J. R. 1981. A cognitive process theory of writing. *College Composition and Communication* 32: 365–387.

Flower, L., and Higgins, L. 1990. Collaboration and the Construction of Meaning. Unpublished manuscript.

Flower, L., Norris, L., Wallace, D., and Burnett, R. 1992. *Making Thinking Visible: A Collaborative Look at Collaborative Planning*. National Council of Teachers of English.

Flower, L., Schriver, K. A., Carey, L., Haas, C., and Hayes, J. R. 1992. Planning in writing: The cognition of a constructive process. In S. Witte, N. Nakadate, and R. Cherry, eds., *A Rhetoric of Doing*. Southern Illinois University Press.

Freedman, S. W., Dyson, A. H., Flower, L., and Chafe, W. 1987. Research in Writing: Past, Present, and Future. Technical report 1, Center for the Study of Writing, University of California at Berkeley and Carnegie Mellon University.

Gardner, H. 1983. *Frames of Mind*. Basic Books.

Gardner, H. 1985. *The Mind's New Science*. Basic Books.

Gardner, H. 1991. *The Unschooled Mind: How Children Think and How Schools Should Teach*. Basic Books.

Glaser, R. 1986. The integration of instruction and testing. In E. Freeman, ed., *The Redesign of Testing in the 21st century: Proceedings of the 1985 ETS Invitational Conference.* Educational Testing Service.

Glaser, R. 1988. Cognitive science and education. *International Social Science Journal* 40(1): 21–44.

Glaser, R., Lesgold, A., and Lajoie, S. 1987. Toward a cognitive theory for the measurement of achievement. In R. R. Ronning, J. Glover, J. C. Conoley, and J. C. Witt, eds., *The Influence of Cognitive Psychology on Testing and Measurement.* Erlbaum.

Goldman, S. R., Vye, N. J., Williams, S., Rewey, K., Pellegrino, J. W., and the Cognition and Technology Group at Vanderbilt. 1991. Solution space analyses of the Jasper problems and students' attempts to solve them. Paper presented at the poster symposium "The Jasper Problem Solving Series: A Collaborative Experiment Involving Teachers, Corporate Partners, Cognitive Researchers, and Experts in Instruction, Video, and Computer Design," American Educational Research Association Meetings, Chicago.

Graham, P. A. 1992. *SOS: Sustain our Schools.* Hill and Wang.

Greeno, J. G., Riley, M. S., and Gelman, R. 1984. Conceptual competence and children's counting. *Cognitive Psychology* 16: 94–143.

Groen, G., and Resnick, L. B. 1977. Can preschool children invent addition algorithms? *Journal of Educational Psychology* 69: 645–652.

Grosslight, L., and Snir, J. 1989. Description of the New Weight and Density Software. Report on the development of software for the grant "Teaching for Conceptual Change in Middle School Science: The Role of Models and of Metaconceptual Understanding." Submitted to the James S. McDonnell Foundation Program in Cognitive Studies for Educational Practice.

Grover, B. W., Zaslavsky, O. P., and Leinhardt, G. 1989. An Approach to the Design and Development of a Scoring System for a New Teacher Assessment. Technical report CLIP-89-82, Learning Research and Development Center, University of Pittsburgh.

Hammack, D. C. 1990. *The US History Report Card: The Achievement of Fourth-, Eighth-, and Twelfth-Grade Students in 1988 and Trends from 1986 to 1988 in the Factual Knowledge of High School Juniors.* Educational Testing Service.

Handbook for Planning an Effective Writing Program: Kindergarten through Grade Twelve. 1983. California State Department of Education.

Hayes, J. R., and Flower, L. 1980. Identifying the organization of writing processes. In L. W. Gregg and E. R. Steinberg, eds., *Cognitive Processes in Writing.* Erlbaum.

Henderson, V. L., and Dweck, C. S. 1990. Motivation and achievement. In S. Feldman and G. Elliot, eds., *At the Threshold: Adolescent Development.* Harvard University Press.

Hiebert, J., and Wearne, D. 1985. A model of students' decimal computation procedures. *Cognition and Instruction* 2: 175–205.

Hillocks, G. 1984. What works in teaching composition: A meta-analysis of experimental treatment studies. *American Journal of Education* 93: 133–170.

Hirsch, E. D. 1987. *Cultural Literacy.* Vintage Books.

Hofstadter, D. R. 1980. *Gödel, Escher, Bach: An Eternal Golden Braid.* Vintage Books.

Horwitz, P. 1988. Interactive simulations and their implications for science teaching. In *The 1988 AETS Year Book.*

Hull, G. 1989. Research on writing: Building a cognitive and social understanding of composing. In L. B. Resnick and L. E. Klopfer, eds., *Toward the Thinking Curriculum.* Association for Supervision and Curriculum Development.

Hull, G., and Rose, M. 1989a. Rethinking remediation: Towards a social-cognitive understanding of problematic reading and writing. *Written Communication* 6(2): 139–154.

Hull, G., and Rose, M. 1989b. The Other Side of Excellence: Literacy, Underpreparation, and the Cognition of Composing. Final report to the James S. McDonnell Foundation's Program in Cognitive Studies for Educational Practice.

Hunt, E. 1993. *Thoughts on Thought: An Analysis of Formal Models of Cognition.* Erlbaum.

Inhelder, B., and Piaget, J. 1958. *The Growth of Logical Thinking from Childhood to Adolescence.* Basic Books.

James, T. 1991. *Research and the Renewal of Education.* National Academy of Education.

Johnson-Laird, P. N. 1983. *Mental Models.* Harvard University Press.

Just, M. A., and Carpenter, P. A. 1980. A theory of reading: From eye fixations to comprehension. *Psychological Review* 87: 329–354.

Just, M. A., and Carpenter, P. A. 1987. *The Psychology of Reading and Language Comprehension.* Allyn and Bacon.

Klahr, D., and Siegler, R. S. 1978. The representation of children's knowledge. In H. Reese and L. P. Lipsett, eds., *Advances in Child Development and Behavior,* volume 12. Academic Press.

Koedinger, K. R. 1991. On the design of novel notations and actions to facilitate thinking and learning. In *Proceedings of the International Conference on the Learning Sciences.* Association for the Advancement of Computing in Education.

Koedinger, K. R., and Anderson, J. R. 1990. Abstract planning and perceptual chunks: Elements of expertise in geometry. *Cognitive Science* 14: 511–550.

Koedinger, K. R., and Anderson, J. R. 1993. Reifying implicit planning in geometry: Guidelines for model-based intelligent tutoring system design. In S. P. Lajoie and S. J. Derry, eds., *Computers as Cognitive Tools.* Erlbaum.

Larkin, J. H. 1985. Understanding, problem representations, and skill in physics. In S. F. Chipman, J. W. Segal, and R. Glaser, eds., *Thinking and Learning Skills,* volume 2: *Research and Open Questions.* Erlbaum.

Larkin, J. H. 1989. What kind of knowledge transfers? In L. B. Resnick, ed., *Knowing, Learning, and Instruction: Essays in Honor of Robert Glaser.* Erlbaum.

Larkin, J. H., and Chabay, R. W. 1989. Research on teaching scientific thinking: Implications for computer-based instruction. In L. B. Resnick and L. E. Klopfer, eds., *Toward the Thinking Curriculum.* Association for Supervision and Curriculum Development.

Larkin, J. H., and Reif, F. 1979. Understanding and teaching problem-solving in physics. *European Journal of Science Education* 1: 191–203.

Learning Technology Center. 1990. Designing Invitations to Thinking. Final report to the James S. McDonnell Foundation.

Learning Technology Center. 1991. The 1990–1991 Jasper Implementation Project: The Assessment Program Summary Report. Vanderbilt University.

Leinhardt, G. 1989. Math lessons: A contrast of novice and expert competence. *Journal for Research in Mathematics Education* 20: 52–75.

Leinhardt, G. 1990a. On Teaching. To appear in R. Glaser, ed., *Advances in Instructional Psychology,* volume 4. Erlbaum.

Leinhardt, G. 1990b. Capturing craft knowledge in teaching. *Educational Researcher* March: 18–25.

Leinhardt, G., and Greeno, J. G. 1986. The cognitive skill of teaching. *Journal of Educational Psychology* 78: 75–95.

Leinhardt, G., and Smith, D. A. 1985. Expertise in mathematics instruction: Subject matter knowledge. *Journal of Educational Psychology* 77: 247–271.

Lesgold, A., Resnick, L. B., and Hammond, K. 1985. Learning to read: A longitudinal study of word skill development in two curricula. In G. E. MacKinnon and T. G. Waller, eds., *Reading Research: Advances in Theory and Practice,* volume 4. Academic Press.

Lindberg, M. 1980. Is knowledge base development a necessary and sufficient condition for memory development? *Journal of Experimental Child Psychology* 30: 401–410.

Mansfield, R. S., Busse, T. V., and Krepelka, E. J. 1978. The effectiveness of creativity training. *Review of Educational Research* 48(4): 517–536.

Markman, E. M. 1985. Comprehension monitoring: Developmental and educational issues. In S. F. Chipman, J. W. Segal, and R. Glaser, eds., *Thinking and Learning Skills,* volume 2: *Research and Open Questions.* Erlbaum.

Matz, M. 1982. Towards a process model for high school algebra errors. In D. Sleeman and J. S. Brown, eds., *Intelligent Tutoring Systems.* Academic Press.

McKeown, M. G., and Beck, I. L. 1990. The assessment and characterization of young learners' knowledge of a topic in history. *American Educational Research Journal* 27: 688–726.

Meichenbaum, D. 1985. Teaching thinking: A cognitive-behavioral perspective. In S. F. Chipman, J. W. Segal, and R. Glaser, eds., *Thinking and Learning Skills, volume 2: Research and Open Questions*. Erlbaum.

Merton, R. K. 1968. The Matthew Effect in science. *Science* 159: 56–63.

Miller, G. A. 1956. Human memory and the storage of information. *IRE Transactions of Information Theory* 2–3: 129–137.

Miller, G. A., and Gildea, P. M. 1987. How children learn words. *Scientific American* 257(3): 94–99.

Minsky, M., and Papert, S. 1974. *Artificial Intelligence*. Oregon State System of Higher Education.

Minstrell, J. 1984. Teaching for the development of understanding of ideas: Forces on moving objects. In *Observing Classrooms: Perspectives from Research and Practice*. Ohio State University.

Minstrell, J. 1989. Teaching science for understanding. In L. B. Resnick and L. E. Klopfer, eds., *Toward the Thinking Curriculum*. Association for Supervision and Curriculum Development.

Minstrell, J., and Stimpson, V. C. 1990. A teaching system for diagnosing student conceptions and prescribing relevant instruction. Paper prepared for AERA session "Classroom Perspectives on Conceptual Change Teaching," Boston.

Mullis, I. V. S., and Jenkins, L. B. 1988. *The Science Report Card: Elements of Risk and Recovery*. Educational Testing Service.

Mullis, I. V. S., and Jenkins, L. B. 1990. *The Reading Report Card, 1971–88: Trends from the Nation's Report Card*. Office of Educational Research and Improvement, US Department of Education.

National Commission on Excellence in Education. 1983. *A Nation at Risk: The Imperative for Educational Reform*. US Department of Education.

NCATE (National Council for Accreditation of Teacher Education). 1992. The case for renewal in education research. *Quality Teaching* Winter: 6–9.

Newell, A., and Simon, H. A. 1956. The logic theory machine: A complex information processing system. *IRE Transactions of Information Theory* 2–3: 61–79.

Newell, A., and Simon, H. A. 1972. *Human Problem Solving*. Prentice-Hall.

Nickerson, R. S., Perkins, D. N., and Smith, E. E. 1985. *The Teaching of Thinking*. Erlbaum.

Palincsar, A. S., and Brown, A. L. 1984. Reciprocal teaching of comprehension-fostering and comprehension-monitoring activities. *Cognition and Instruction* 1(2): 117–175.

Palincsar, A. S., and Brown, A. L. 1986. Interactive teaching to promote independent learning from text. *Reading Teacher* 39: 771–777.

Palincsar, A. S., Ransom, K., and Derber, S. 1988. Collaborative research and the development of reciprocal teaching. *Educational Leadership* 46: 37–40.

Paris, S. G., and Jacobs, J. E. 1984. The benefits of informed instruction for children's reading awareness and comprehension skills. *Child Development* 55: 2083–2093.

Paris, S. G., Newman, R. S., and McVey, K. A. 1982. Learning the functional significance of mnemonic actions: A microgenetic study of strategy acquisition. *Journal of Experimental Child Psychology* 34: 490–509.

Perkins, D. N., and Salomon, G. 1989. Are cognitive skills context-bound? *Educational Researcher* 18: 16–25.

Posner, M. 1973. *Cognition: An Introduction*. Scott, Foresman.

Ravitch, D., and Finn, C. E., Jr. 1987. *What Do Our 17-year-olds Know? A Report on the First National Assessment of History and Literature*. Harper and Row.

Rayner, K., and Pollatsek, A. 1981. Eye movement control during reading: Evidence for direct control. *Quarterly Journal of Experimental Psychology* 33A: 351–373.

Rayner, K., and Pollatsek, A. 1989. *The Psychology of Reading*. Prentice-Hall.

Rayner, K., Inhoff, A. W., Morrison, R. E., Slowiaczek, M. L., and Bertera, J. H. 1981. Masking of foveal and parafoveal vision during eye fixations in reading. *Journal of Experimental Psychology: Human Perception and Performance* 7: 167–179.

Reif, F. 1986. Scientific approaches to science education. *Physics Today* 39: 48–54.

Resnick, L. B. 1980. The role of invention in the development of mathematical competence. In R. H. Kluwe and H. Spada, eds., *Developmental Models of Thinking*. Academic Press.

Resnick, L. B. 1982. Syntax and semantics in learning to subtract. In T. P. Carpenter, J. M. Moser, and T. A. Romberg, eds., *Addition and Substraction: A Cognitive Perspective*. Erlbaum.

Resnick, L. B. 1983. A developmental theory of number understanding. In H. P. Ginsburg, ed., *The Development of Mathematical Thinking*. Academic Press.

Resnick, L. B. 1984. Cognitive science as educational research: Why we need it now. In *Improving Education: Perspectives on Educational Research*. National Academy of Education.

Resnick, L. B. 1986. Education and Learning to Think: A Special Report Prepared for the Commission on Behavioral and Social Sciences and Education. National Research Council.

Savell, J. M., Wohig, P. T., and Rachford, D. L. 1986. Empirical status of Feuerstein's "Instrumental Enrichment" (FIE) technique as a method of teaching thinking skills. *Review of Educational Research* 56(4): 381–409.

Scardamalia, M., and Bereiter, C. 1986. Writing. In R. F. Dillon and R. J. Sternberg, eds., *Cognition and Instruction*. Academic Press.

Scardamalia, M., and Bereiter, C. 1987. Knowledge telling and knowledge transforming in written composition. In S. Rosenberg, ed., *Advances in Applied Psycholinguistics,* volume 2: *Reading, Writing, and Language Learning.* Cambridge University Press.

Scardamalia, M., Bereiter, C., and Steinbach, R. 1984. Teachability of reflective processes in written composition. *Cognitive Science* 8: 173–190.

Scardamalia, M., and Paris, P. 1985. The function of explicit discourse knowledge in the development of text representations and composing strategies. *Cognition and Instruction* 2(1): 1–39.

Schoenfeld, A. H. 1987. Cognitive science and mathematics education: An overview. In A. H. Schoenfeld, ed., *Cognitive Science and Mathematics Education.* Erlbaum.

Schofield, J., and Verban, D. 1988. Barriers and Incentives to Computer Usage in Teaching. Technical report 1, Learning Research and Development Center, University of Pittsburgh.

Segal, J. W., Chipman, S. F., and Glaser, R. 1985. *Thinking and Learning Skills,* volume 1: *Relating Instruction to Research.* Erlbaum.

Sheekey, A. D. 1988. Federal Support of Educational R & D. Office of Research, Education Information Resources Division, Office of the Assistant Secretary for Educational Research and Improvement, US Department of Education.

Shulman, L. S. 1986. Those who understand: Knowledge growth in teaching. *Educational Researcher* 15: 4–14.

Shulman, L. S. 1987. Knowledge and teaching: Foundations of the new reform. *Harvard Educational Review* 57: 1–22.

Siegler, R. S. 1976. Three aspects of cognitive development. *Cognitive Psychology* 8: 481–520.

Siegler, R. S. 1985. Encoding and the development of problem solving. In S. F. Chipman, J. W. Segal, and R. Glaser, eds., *Thinking and Learning Skills,* volume 2: *Research and Open Questions.* Erlbaum.

Siegler, R. S. 1988. Individual differences in strategy choices: Good students, not-so-good students, and perfectionists. *Child Development* 59: 833–851.

Siegler, R. S. 1991. In young children's counting, procedures precede principles. *Educational Psychology Review* 3: 127–135.

Siegler, R. S., and Klahr, D. 1982. When do children learn? The relationship between existing knowledge and the acquisition of new knowledge. In R. Glaser, ed., *Advances in Instructional Psychology,* volume 2. Erlbaum.

Silver, E. A. 1986. Using conceptual and procedural knowledge: A focus on relationships. In J. Hiebert, ed., *Conceptual and Procedural Knowledge: The Case of Mathematics.* Erlbaum.

Simon, D. P., and Simon, H. A. 1978. Individual differences in solving physics problems. In R. S. Siegler, ed., *Children's Thinking: What Develops?* Erlbaum.

Simon, H. A., and Chase, W. G. 1973. Skill in chess. *American Scientist* 61: 394–403.

Singley, M. K., and Anderson, J. R. 1985. The transfer of text-editing skill. *International Journal of Man-Machine Studies* 22: 403–423.

Smith, C. 1990. Presentation at the McDonnell Foundation program meeting "Cognitive Studies for Educational Practice." Carnegie Mellon University.

Smith, C., Carey, S., and Wiser, M. 1985. On differentiation: A case study of the development of the concepts of size, weight, and density. *Cognition* 21: 177–237.

Spelke, E. S. 1990. Principles of object perception. *Cognitive Science* 14: 29–56.

Starkey, P., Spelke, E. S., and Gelman R. 1983. Detection of intermodal numerical correspondences by human infants. *Science* 222: 179–181.

Starkey, P., Spelke, E. S., and Gelman, R. 1990. Numerical abstraction by human infants. *Cognition* 36: 97–127.

Stein, B. S., Bransford, J. D., Franks, J. J., Vye, N. J., and Perfetto, G. A. 1982. Differences in judgments of learning difficulty. *Journal of Experimental Psychology (General)* 111: 406–413.

Thorndike, E. L., and Woodworth, R. S. 1901. The influence of improvement in one mental function upon the efficacy of other functions. *Psychological Review* 8: 247–261.

Van Haneghan, J., Barron, L., Young, M., Williams, S., Vye, N., and Bransford, J. 1991. The Jasper Series: An Experiment with New Ways to Enhance Mathematical Thinking. Learning Technology Center, Vanderbilt University.

Van Lehn, K. 1983. On the representation of procedures in repair theory. In H. P. Ginsburg, ed., *The Development of Mathematical Thinking.* Academic Press.

Wertheimer, R. 1990. The geometry proof tutor: An "intelligent" computer-based tutor in the classroom. *Mathematics Teacher* 33: 308–317.

White, B. Y. 1988. ThinkerTools: Causal Models, Conceptual Change, and Science Education. Report 6873, Bolt, Beranek, & Newman Laboratories, Cambridge, Mass.

White, B. Y. In press. Intermediate causal models: The missing links for successful science education? To appear in R. Glaser, ed., *Advances in Instructional Psychology,* volume 4. Erlbaum.

White, B. Y., and Horwitz, P. 1987. ThinkerTools: Enabling Children to Understand Physical Laws. Report 6470, Bolt, Beranek, & Newman Laboratories, Cambridge, Mass.

White, B. Y., and Horwitz, P. 1988. Computer microworlds and conceptual change: A new approach to science education. In P. Ramsden, ed., *Improving Learning: New Perspectives.* Kogan Page.

Wise, A. E. 1989. Calling for "National Institutes of Education". *Education Week,* October 18: 36.

Yussen, S. R., and Levy, V. M. 1975. Developmental changes in predicting one's own span of short-term memory. *Journal of Experimental Child Psychology* 19: 502–508.

Index